SEBASTIAN JUNGER grew [illegible]
worked as a tree-feller, wa[illegible]
adventurer. *The Perfect St*[illegible]
three years on the bestseller lists and its film adaptation was a huge box-office success. Junger is a contributing editor to *Vanity Fair*, and winner of the National Magazine Award for reporting. He has also written for magazines including *Harper's*, the *New York Times Magazine* and *National Geographic Adventure*.

Visit www.AuthorTracker.co.uk for exclusive information on your favourite HarperCollins authors.

From the reviews of *The Perfect Storm*:

'If one knows anything at all about the sea, one feels the enormous strengths of the hurricane winds and the incredibly towering mass of the hundred-foot waves'

PATRICK O'BRIAN

'Sebastian Junger's compassionate, intelligent voice instructs us effortlessly on the sea life of the swordfisherman, the physics of a sinking steel ship, and the details of death by drowning. It is a terrifying read' DAVA SOBEL

'Junger moves seamlessly between the wrenching human dramas and the awesome details of the storm. *The Perfect Storm* is terrifying, sad, exhilarating, humbling and unforgettable' *Daily Mail*

'Junger has found a language to match the stature of the sea at its worst, and to capture its mysteries . . . it's a chilling account that registers 12 on the Beaufort Scale'

Sunday Times

'A magnificent sea yarn . . . but a true story and all the more compelling for that' *Observer*

'Cuts every facet of raw material to flashing brilliance . . . It amounts to a Homeric epic in its control of overwhelming natural forces and the grim demands they make of human life and effort' *Scotland on Sunday*

'The closest you will come to drowning at sea without actually having to do so' *The Times*

'Sometimes a story comes along that's almost too good to be believable. *The Perfect Storm* may read like a novel but it isn't one. It's chillingly true . . . more fabulous than fiction, it will become a classic for a jaded modern world'

Independent

'Masterly, an essay in fear . . . He writes like a poet who has been to meteorology school'

RUTH RENDELL, *Daily Telegraph*

'Reading *The Perfect Storm* is like trawling back through every watery dream, and nightmare, you have ever had. It confirms your wildest hopes of quiet heroism as well as your greatest fears' *Independent*

'Puts the reader in the eye of the storm and into the hearts and minds of all those whose lives were lost or hearts seared by the disaster . . . the result is total authenticity and perhaps the best writing since *Moby Dick* on the awesome power, terror and grandeur of the sea and on the character of the people who confront it' *Lloyds List*

'A *tour de force* of descriptive writing . . . simultaneously thrilling and sobering' *Financial Times*

By the same author

Fire
A Death in Belmont

SEBASTIAN JUNGER

The Perfect Storm

A True Story of Men Against the Sea

HARPER PERENNIAL
London, New York, Toronto and Sydney

This edition produced for The Book People Ltd,
Hall Wood Avenue, Haydock, St Helens, WA11 9UL

Harper Perennial
An imprint of HarperCollins*Publishers*
77–85 Fulham Palace Road
Hammersmith
London W6 8JB

www.harperperennial.co.uk

This *Stranger Than* . . . edition published by Harper Perennial 2007

1

First published in Great Britain by Fourth Estate in 1997

A catalogue record for this book is
available from the British Library

ISBN-13 978 0 00 779018 0

Printed and bound in Great Britain by Clays Ltd, St Ives plc

This book is dedicated

to my father, who

first introduced me

to the sea.

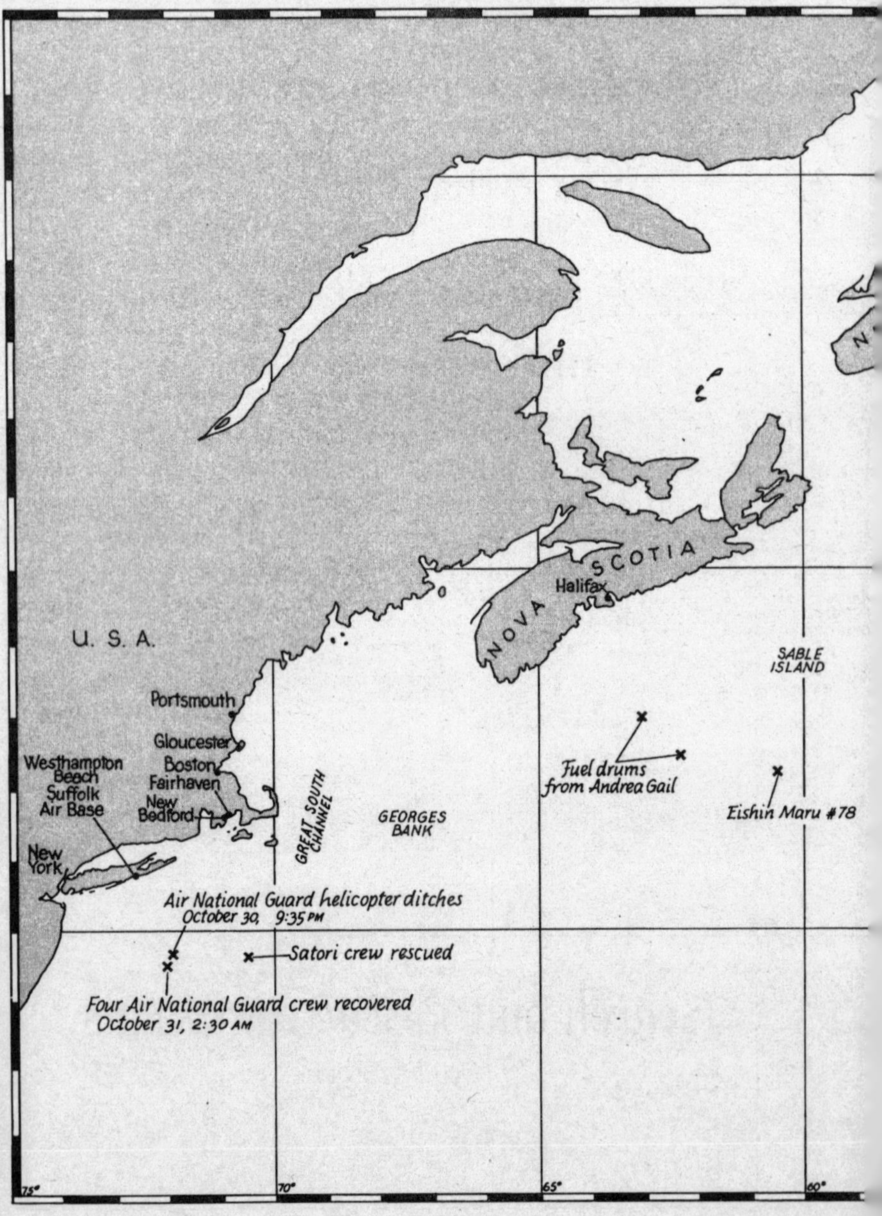

U. S. A.
NOVA SCOTIA
Halifax
SABLE ISLAND
Portsmouth
Gloucester
Boston
Fairhaven
New Bedford
Westhampton Beach Suffolk Air Base
New York
GREAT SOUTH CHANNEL
GEORGES BANK
Fuel drums from Andrea Gail
Eishin Maru #78
Air National Guard helicopter ditches October 30, 9:35 PM
Satori crew rescued
Four Air National Guard crew recovered October 31, 2:30 AM
75°
70°
65°
60°

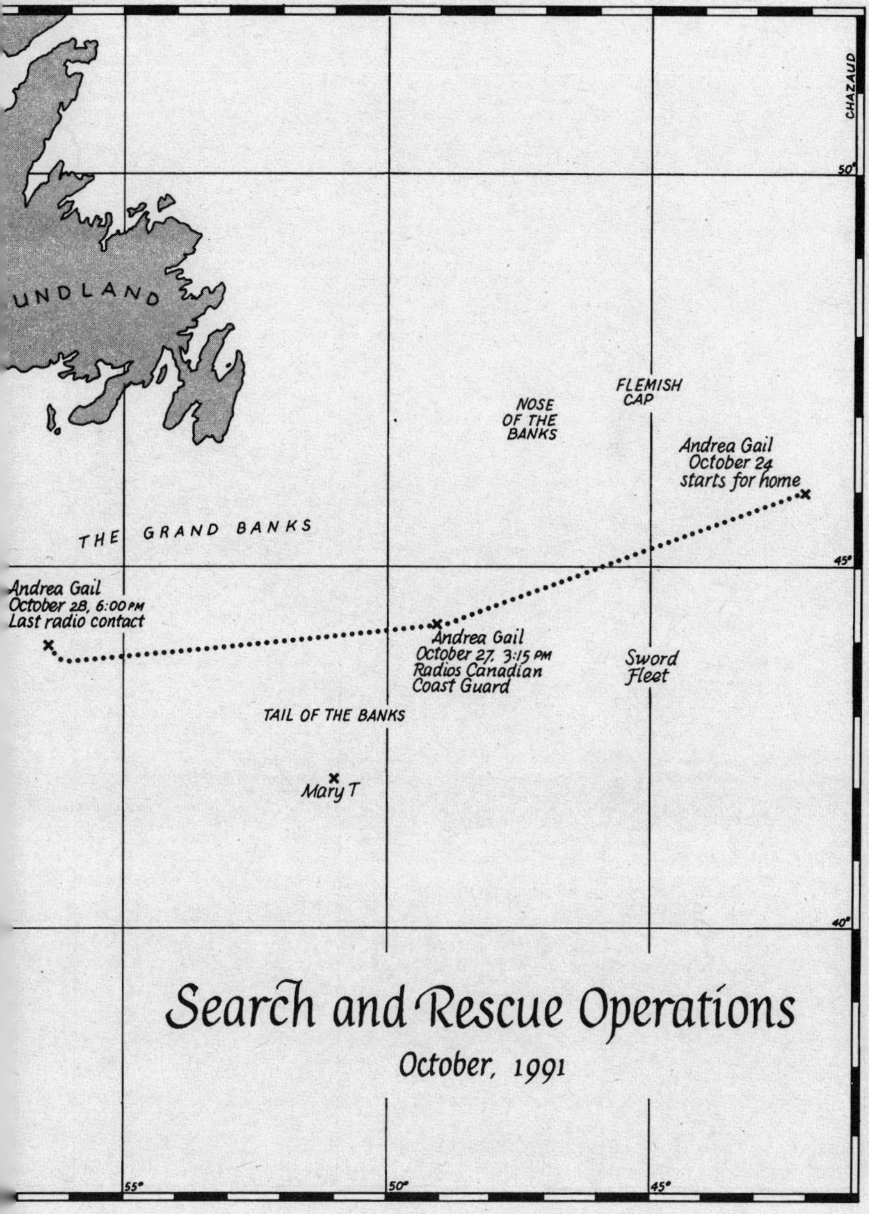

Search and Rescue Operations

October, 1991

CONTENTS

FOREWORD

RECREATING the last days of six men who disappeared at sea presented some obvious problems for me. On the one hand, I wanted to write a completely factual book that would stand on its own as a piece of journalism. On the other hand, I didn't want the narrative to asphyxiate under a mass of technical detail and conjecture. I toyed with the idea of fictionalizing minor parts of the story—conversations, personal thoughts, day-to-day routines—to make it more readable, but that risked diminishing the value of whatever facts I *was* able to determine. In the end I wound up sticking strictly to the facts, but in as wide-ranging a way as possible. If I didn't know exactly what happened aboard the doomed boat, for example, I would interview people who had been through similar situations, and survived. Their experiences, I felt, would provide a fairly good description of what the six men on the *Andrea Gail* had gone through, and said, and perhaps even felt.

As a result, there are varying kinds of information in the book. Anything in direct quotes was recorded by me in a formal interview, either in person or on the telephone, and was altered as little as possible for grammar and clarity. All dialogue is based on the recollection of people who are still alive, and appears in dialogue form without quotation marks. *No* dialogue was made up. Radio conversations are also based on people's recollections, and appear in italics in the text. Quotes from published material are in italics, and have occasionally been condensed to better fit the text. Technical discussions of meteorology, wave motion, ship stability, etc., are based on my own library research and are generally not referenced, but I feel compelled to recommend William Van Dorn's *The Oceanography of Seamanship* as a comprehensive and immensely readable text on ships and the sea.

In short, I've written as complete an account as possible of something that can never be fully known. It is exactly that unknowable element, however, that has made it an interesting book to write and, I hope, to read. I had some misgivings about calling it *The Perfect Storm,* but in the end I decided that the intent was sufficiently clear. I use *perfect* in the meteorological sense: a storm that could not possibly have been worse. I certainly mean no disrespect to the men who died at sea or the people who still grieve them.

My own experience in the storm was limited to standing on Gloucester's Back Shore watching thirty-foot swells advance on Cape Ann, but that was all it took. The next day I read in the paper that a Gloucester boat was feared lost at sea, and I clipped the article and stuck it in a drawer. Without even knowing it, I had begun to write *The Perfect Storm.*

THE PERFECT STORM

GEORGES BANK, 1896

ONE mid-winter day off the coast of Massachusetts, the crew of a mackerel schooner spotted a bottle with a note in it. The schooner was on Georges Bank, one of the most dangerous fishing grounds in the world, and a bottle with a note in it was a dire sign indeed. A deckhand scooped it out of the water, the sea grass was stripped away, and the captain uncorked the bottle and turned to his assembled crew: "On Georges Bank with our cable gone our rudder gone and leaking. Two men have been swept away and all hands have been given up as our cable is gone and our rudder is gone. The one that picks this up let it be known. God have mercy on us."

The note was from the *Falcon*, a boat that had set sail from Gloucester the year before. She hadn't been heard from since. A boat that parts her cable off Georges careens helplessly along until she fetches up in some shallow water and gets pounded to pieces by the surf. One of the *Falcon*'s crew must have wedged himself against a bunk in the fo'c'sle and written furiously beneath the heaving light of a storm lantern. This was the end, and everyone on the boat would have known it. How do men act on a sinking ship? Do they hold each other? Do they pass around the whisky? Do they cry?

This man wrote; he put down on a scrap of paper the last moments of twenty men in this world. Then he corked the bottle and threw it overboard. There's not a chance in hell, he must have thought. And then he went below again. He breathed in deep. He tried to calm himself. He readied himself for the first shock of sea.

GLOUCESTER, MASS., 1991

It's no fish ye're buying, it's men's lives.

—*SIR WALTER SCOTT*
The Antiquary, *Chapter 11*

A SOFT fall rain slips down through the trees and the smell of ocean is so strong that it can almost be licked off the air.  Trucks rumble along Rogers Street and men in t-shirts stained with fishblood shout to each other from the decks of boats. Beneath them the ocean swells up against the black pilings and sucks back down to the barnacles. Beer cans and old pieces of styrofoam rise and fall and pools of spilled diesel fuel undulate like huge iridescent jellyfish. The boats rock and creak against their ropes and seagulls complain and hunker down and complain some more. Across Rogers Street and around the back of the Crow's Nest Inn, through the door and up the cement stairs, down the carpeted hallway and into one of the doors on the left, stretched out on a double bed in room #27 with a sheet pulled over him, Bobby Shatford lies asleep.

He's got one black eye. There are beer cans and food wrappers scattered around the room and a duffel bag on the floor with t-shirts and flannel shirts and blue jeans spilling out.

Lying asleep next to him is his girlfriend, Christina Cotter. She's an attractive woman in her early forties with rust-blond hair and a strong, narrow face. There's a T.V. in the room and a low chest of drawers with a mirror on top of it and a chair of the sort they have in high-school cafeterias. The plastic cushion cover has cigarette burns in it. The window looks out on Rogers Street where trucks ease themselves into fish-plant bays.

It's still raining. Across the street is Rose Marine, where fishing boats fuel up, and across a small leg of water is the State Fish Pier, where they unload their catch. The State Pier is essentially a huge parking lot on pilings, and on the far side, across another leg of water, is a boatyard and a small park where mothers bring their children to play. Looking over the park on the corner of Haskell Street is an elegant brick house built by the famous Boston architect, Charles Bulfinch. It originally stood on the corner of Washington and Summer Streets in Boston, but in 1850 it was jacked up, rolled onto a barge, and transported to Gloucester. That is where Bobby's mother, Ethel, raised four sons and two daughters. For the past fourteen years she has been a day-time bartender at the Crow's Nest. Ethel's grandfather was a fisherman and both her daughters dated fishermen and all four of the sons fished at one point or another. Most of them still do.

The Crow's Nest windows face east into the coming day over a street used at dawn by reefer trucks. Guests don't tend to sleep late. Around eight o'clock in the morning, Bobby Shatford struggles awake. He has flax-brown hair, hollow cheeks, and a sinewy build that has seen a lot of work. In a few hours he's due on a swordfishing boat named the *Andrea Gail,* which is headed on a one-month trip to the Grand Banks. He could return with five thousand dollars in his pocket or he could not return at all. Outside, the rain drips on. Chris groans, opens her eyes, and squints up at him. One of Bobby's eyes is the color of an overripe plum.

Did I do that?

Yeah.

Jesus.

She considers his eye for a moment. How did I reach that high?

They smoke a cigarette and then pull on their clothes and grope their way downstairs. A metal fire door opens onto a back alley, they push it open and walk around to the Rogers Street entrance. The Crow's Nest is a block-long faux-Tudor construction across from the J. B. Wright Fish Company and Rose Marine. The plate-glass window in front is said to be the biggest barroom window in town. That's quite a distinction in a town where barroom windows are made small so that patrons don't get thrown through them. There's an old pool table, a pay phone by the door, and a horseshoe-shaped bar. Budweiser costs a dollar seventy-five, but as often as not there's a fisherman just in from a trip who's buying for the whole house. Money flows through a fisherman like water through a fishing net; one regular ran up a $4,000 tab in a week.

Bobby and Chris walk in and look around. Ethel's behind the bar, and a couple of the town's earlier risers are already gripping bottles of beer. A shipmate of Bobby's named Bugsy Moran is seated at the bar, a little dazed. Rough night, huh? Bobby says. Bugsy grunts. His real name is Michael. He's got wild long hair and a crazy reputation and everyone in town loves him. Chris invites him to join them for breakfast and Bugsy slides off his stool and follows them out the door into the light rain. They climb into Chris's 20-year-old Volvo and drive down to the White Hen Pantry and shuffle in, eyes bloodshot, heads throbbing. They buy sandwiches and cheap sunglasses and then they make their way out into the unrelenting greyness of the day. Chris drives them back to the Nest and they pick up 30-year-old Dale Murphy, another crew member from the *Andrea Gail,* and head out of town.

Dale's nickname is Murph, he's a big grizzly bear of a guy

from Bradenton Beach, Florida. He has shaggy black hair, a thin beard, and angled, almost Mongolian eyes; he gets a lot of looks around town. He has a three-year-old baby, also named Dale, whom he openly adores. His ex-wife, Debra, was three-time Southwestern Florida Women's boxing champion and by all rights, young Dale is going to be a bruiser. Murph wants to get him some toys before he leaves, and Chris takes the three men to the shopping center out by Good Harbor Beach. They go into the Ames and Bobby and Bugsy get extra thermals and sweats for the trip and Murph walks down the aisles, filling a cart with Tonka trucks and firemen's helmets and ray guns. When he can't fit any more in he pays for it, and they all pile into the car and drive back to the Nest. Murph gets out and the other three decide to drive around the corner to the Green Tavern for another drink.

The Green Tavern looks like a smaller version of the Nest, all brick and false timber. Across the street is a bar called Bill's; the three bars form the Bermuda Triangle of downtown Gloucester. Chris and Bugsy and Bobby walk in and seat themselves at the bar and order a round of beers. The television's going and they watch it idly and talk about the trip and the last night of craziness at the Nest. Their hangovers are starting to soften. They drink another round and maybe half an hour goes by and finally Bobby's sister Mary Anne walks in. She's a tall blonde who inspires crushes in the teenaged sons of some of her friends, but there's a certain no-nonsense air about her that has always kept Bobby on his toes. Oh shit, here she comes, he whispers.

He hides his beer behind his arm and pulls the sunglasses down over his black eye. Mary Anne walks up. What do you think I am, stupid? she asks. Bobby pulls the beer out from hiding. She looks at his eye. Nice one, she says.

I was in a riff downtown.

Right.

Someone buys her a wine cooler and she takes a couple of

sips. I just came to make sure you were getting on the boat, she says. You shouldn't be drinking so early in the day.

Bobby's a big, rugged kid. He was sickly as a child—he had a twin who died a few weeks after birth—but as he got older he got stronger and stronger. He used to play tackle football in pick-up games where broken bones were a weekly occurrence. In his jeans and hooded sweatshirt he looks like such a typical fisherman that a photographer once took a picture of him for a postcard of the waterfront; but still, Mary Anne's his older sister, and he's in no position to contradict her.

Chris loves you, he says suddenly. I do, too.

Mary Anne isn't sure how to react. She's been angry at Chris lately—because of the drinking, because of the black eye—but Bobby's candor has thrown her off. He's never said anything like that to her before. She stays long enough to finish her wine cooler and then heads out the door.

THE first time Chris Cotter saw the Crow's Nest she swore she'd never go in; it just looked too far down some road in life she didn't want to be on. She happened to be friends with Mary Anne Shatford, however, and one day Mary Anne dragged her through the heavy wooden door and introduced her around. It was a fine place: people bought drinks for each other like they said hello and Ethel cooked up a big pot of fish chowder from time to time, and before Chris knew it she was a regular. One night she noticed a tall young man looking at her and she waited for him to come over, but he never did. He had a taut, angular face, square shoulders, and a shy cast to his eyes that made her think of Bob Dylan. The eyes alone were enough. He kept looking at her but wouldn't come over, and finally he started heading for the door.

Where are *you* goin'? she said, blocking his way.

To the Mariner.

The Irish Mariner was next door and in Chris's mind it

was *really* down the road to hell. I'm not crossin' over, thought Chris, I'm in the Nest and that's enough, the Mariner's the bottom of the bucket. And so Bobby Shatford walked out of her life for a month or so. She didn't see him again until New Year's Eve.

"I'm in the Nest," she says, "and he's across the bar and the place is packed and insane and it's gettin' near the twelve o'clock thing and finally Bobby and I talk and go over to another party. I hung with Bobby, and I did, I brought him home and we did our thing, our drunken thing and I remember waking up the next morning and looking at him and thinking, Oh my God this is a nice man what have I done? I told him, You gotta get out of here before my kids wake up, and after that he started callin' me."

Chris was divorced and had three children and Bobby was separated and had two. He was bartending and fishing to pay off a child-support debt and splitting his time between Haskell Street and his room above the Nest. (There are a dozen or so rooms available, and they're very cheap if you know the right person. Like your mother, the bartender.) Soon Chris and Bobby were spending every minute together; it was as if they'd known each other their whole lives. One evening while drinking mudslides at the Mariner—Chris had crossed over—Bobby got down on his knees and asked her to marry him. Of *course* I will! she screamed, and then, as far as they were concerned, a life together was only a matter of time.

Time—and money. Bobby's wife had sued him for non-payment of child support, and it went to court late in the spring of 1991. Bobby's choice was to make a payment or go to jail right then and there, so Ethel came up with the money, and afterward they all went to a bar to recover. Bobby proposed to Chris again, in front of Ethel this time, and when they were alone he said that he had a site on the *Andrea Gail* if he wanted it. The *Andrea Gail* was a well-known sword boat captained by an old friend of the family's,

Billy Tyne. Tyne had essentially been handed the job by the previous skipper, Charlie Reed, who was getting out of swordfishing because the money was starting to dwindle. (Reed had sent three children to private college on the money he made on the *Andrea Gail.*) Those days were over, but she was still one of the most lucrative boats in the harbor. Bobby was lucky to get a site on her.

Swordfishing's a lot of money, it'll pay off everything I owe, he told Chris.

That's good, how long do you go out for?

Thirty days.

Thirty days? Are you crazy?

"We were in love and we were jealous and I just couldn't imagine it," says Chris. "I couldn't even imagine half a day."

SWORD boats are also called longliners because their mainline is up to forty miles long. It's baited at intervals and paid out and hauled back every day for ten or twenty days. The boats follow the swordfish population like seagulls after a day trawler, up to the Grand Banks in the summer and down to the Caribbean in the winter, eight or nine trips a year. They're big boats that make big money and they're rarely in port more than a week at a time to gear-up and make repairs. Some boats go as far away as the coast of Chile to catch their fish, and fishermen think nothing of grabbing a plane to Miami or San Juan to secure a site on a boat. They're away for two or three months and then they come home, see their families, and head back out again. They're the high rollers of the fishing world and a lot of them end up exactly where they started. "They suffer from a lack of dreams," as one local said.

Bobby Shatford, however, did happen to have some dreams. He wanted to settle down, get his money problems behind him, and marry Chris Cotter. According to Bobby Shatford, the woman he was separated from was from a very wealthy family, and he didn't understand why he should owe so much money, but obviously the courts didn't see it that way. He wasn't going to be free until everything was paid off, which would be seven or eight trips on the *Andrea Gail*—a good year of fishing. So in early August, 1991, Bobby left on the first swordfishing trip of his life. When they left the dock his eyes swept the parking lot, but Chris had already gone. It was bad luck, they'd decided, to watch your lover steam out to sea.

Chris had no way of knowing when Bobby was due in, so after several weeks she started spending a lot of time down at Rose's wharf, where the *Andrea Gail* takes out, waiting for her to come into view. There are houses in Gloucester where grooves have been worn into the floorboards by women pacing past an upstairs window, looking out to sea. Chris didn't wear down any floorboards, but day after day she filled up the ash tray in her car. In late August a particularly bad hurricane swept up the coast—Hurricane Bob—and Chris went over to Ethel's and did nothing but watch the Weather Channel and wait for the phone to ring. The storm flattened entire groves of locust trees on Cape Cod, but there was no bad news from the fishing fleet so, uneasily, Chris went back to her lookout at Rose's.

Finally, one night in early September, the phone rang in Chris's apartment. It was Billy Tyne's new girlfriend, calling from Florida. They're coming in tomorrow night, she said. I'm flying into Boston, could you pick me up?

"I was a wreck, I was out of my mind," says Chris. "I picked Billy's girlfriend up at Logan and the boat came in while I was gone. We pulled up across the street from the Nest and we could see the *Andrea Gail* tied up by Rose's and so I flew across the street and the door opens and it was Bobby. He went, 'Aaagh,' and he picked me up in the air and I had my legs wrapped around his waist and we must've been there twenty minutes like that, I wouldn't get off him, I couldn't, it had been thirty days and there was no way in hell."

The collected company in the bar watched the reunion through the window. Chris asked Bobby if he'd found a card that she'd hidden in his seabag before he left. He had, he said. He read it every night.

Yeah, right, said Chris.

Bobby put her down in front of the door and recited the letter word for word. The guys were bustin' my balls so bad I had to hide it in a magazine, he said. Bobby pulled Chris into the Nest and bought her a drink and they clinked bottles for his safe homecoming. Billy was there with his girlfriend hanging off him and Alfred was on the payphone to his girlfriend in Maine and Bugsy was getting down to business at the bar. The night had achieved a nearly vertical takeoff, everyone was drinking and screaming because they were home safe and with people they loved. Bobby Shatford was now crew on one of the best sword boats on the East Coast.

THEY'D been at sea a month and taken fifteen tons of swordfish. Prices fluctuate so wildly, though, that a sword boat crew often has no idea how well they've done until after the fish have been sold. And even then there's room for error: boat owners have been known to negotiate a lower price with the buyer and then recover part of their loss in secret. That way they don't share the entire profit with their crew. Be that as it may, the *Andrea Gail* sold her catch to O'Hara Seafoods for $136,812, plus another $4,770 for a small amount of tuna. Bob Brown, the owner, first took out for fuel, fishing tackle, bait, a new mainline, wharfage, ice, and a hundred other odds and ends that added up to over $35,000. That was deducted from the gross, and Brown took home half of what was left: roughly $53,000. The collected crew expenses—food, gloves, shore help—were paid on credit and then deducted from the other $53,000, and the remainder was divided up among the crew: Almost $20,000 to Captain Billy Tyne, $6,453 to Pierre and Murphy, $5,495 to Moran, and $4,537 each to Shatford and Kosco. The shares were calculated by seniority and if Shatford and Kosco didn't like it, they were free to find another boat.

The week on shore started hard. That first night, before the fish had even been looked at, Brown cut each crew member a check for two hundred dollars, and by dawn it was all pretty much spent. Bobby crawled into bed with Chris around one or two in the morning and crawled out again four hours later to help take out the catch. His younger brother Brian—built like a lumberjack and filled with one desire, to fish like his brothers—showed up to help, along with another brother, Rusty. Bob Brown was there, and even some of the women showed up. The fish were hoisted out of the hold, swung up onto the dock, and then wheeled into the chill recesses of Rose's. Next they hauled twenty tons of ice out of the hold, scrubbed the decks, and stowed the gear away. It was an eight- or nine-hour day. At the end of the afternoon Brown showed up with checks for half the money they were owed—the rest would be paid after the dealer had actually sold the fish—and the crew went across the street to a bar called Pratty's. The partying, if possible, reached heights not attained the night before. "Most of them are single kids with no better thing to do than spend a lot of dough," says Charlie Reed, former captain of the boat. "They're high-rollers for a couple of days. Then they go back out to sea."

High-rollers or not, the crew is still supposed to show up at the dock every morning for work. Inevitably, something has broken on the trip—a line gets wound around the drive shaft and must be dove on, the antennas get snapped off, the radios go dead. Depending on the problem, it can take anywhere from an afternoon to several days to fix. Then the engine has to be overhauled: change the belts and filters, check the oil, fill the hydraulics, clean the injectors, clean the plugs, test the generators. Finally, there's the endless task of maintaining the deck gear. Blocks have to be greased, ropes have to be spliced, chains and cables have to be replaced, rust spots have to be ground down and painted. One ill-kept piece of gear can kill a man. Charlie Reed saw a hoisting block fall on someone and shear his arm right off; another crew member had forgotten to tighten a shackle.

The crew isn't exactly military in their sense of duty, though. Several times that week Bobby woke up at the Nest, looked out the window, and then crawled back into bed. One can hardly blame him: from now on his life would unfold in brutally short bursts between long stretches at sea, and all he'd have to tide him over would be photos taped to a wall and maybe a letter in a seabag. And if it was hard on the men, it was even harder on the women. "It was like I had one life and when he came back I had another," says Jodi Tyne, who divorced Billy over it. "I did it for a long time and I just got tired of it, it was never gonna change, he was never gonna quit fishin', though he said he wanted to. If he had to pick between me and the boat he picked the boat."

Billy was an exception in that he really, truly loved to fish. Charlie Reed was the same way; it was one reason the two men got along so well. "It's wide open—I got all the solitude in the world," says Reed. "Nobody pressurin' me about nothin'. And I see things other people don't get to see—whales breaching right beside me, porpoises followin' the boat. I've caught shit they don't even have in books—really weird shit, monstrous-looking things. And when I walk down the street in town, everyone's respectful to me: 'Hi, Cap, how ya doin' Cap.' It's nice to sit down and have a 70-year-old man say, 'Hi, Cap.' It's a beautiful thing."

Perhaps you'd have to be a skipper to really fall in love with the life. (A $20,000 paycheck must help.) Most deckhands have precious little affection for the business, though; for them, fishing is a brutal, dead-end job that they try to get clear of as fast as possible. At memorial services in Gloucester people are always saying things like, "Fishing was his life," or "He died doing what he loved," but by and large those sentiments are to comfort the living. By and large, young men from Gloucester find themselves at sea because they're broke and need money fast.

The only compensation for such mind-numbing work, it

would seem, is equally mind-numbing indulgence. A swordfisherman off a month at sea is a small typhoon of cash. He cannot get rid of the stuff fast enough. He buys lottery tickets fifty at a time and passes them around the bar. If anything hits he buys fifty more plus drinks for the house. Ten minutes later he'll tip the bartender twenty dollars and set the house up again; slower drinkers may have two or three bottles lined up in front of them. When too many bottles are lined up in front of someone, plastic tokens are put down instead, so that the beer doesn't get warm. (It's said that when someone passes out at the Irish Mariner, arguments break out over who gets his tokens.) A fisherman off a trip gives the impression that he'd hardly bother to bend down and pick up a twenty-dollar bill that happened to flutter to the floor. The money is pushed around the bartop like dirty playing cards, and by closing time a week's worth of pay may well have been spent. For some, acting like the money means nothing is the only compensation for what it actually must mean.

"The last night, oh my God, the drunkenness was just unreal," says Chris. "The bar was jam-packed and Bugsy was in a real bad mood cause he hadn't gotten laid, he was really losin' his mind about it. That's important when you only have six days, you know. They were drinkin' more and more and it was time to go and they didn't get enough time on land and didn't get enough money. The last morning we woke up over the Nest 'cause we were really ruined and Bobby had this big black eye, we'd gotten physically violent a little bit, which was the alcohol, believe me. Now I think about it and I can't believe I sent him off to sea like that. I can't believe I sent him off to sea with a black eye."

In the year 1850, Herman Melville wrote his masterpiece, *Moby Dick,* based on his own experience aboard a South Seas whaling ship. It starts with the narrator, Ishmael, stumbling through a snowstorm in New Bedford, Massachusetts, looking for a place to spend the night. He doesn't have much money and passes up one place, called the Crossed Harpoons, because it looks "too expensive and jolly." The next place he finds is called the Swordfish Inn, but it, too, radiates too much warmth and good cheer. Finally he comes to the Spouter Inn. "As the light looked so dim," he writes, "and the dilapidated little wooden house itself looked as if it might have been carted here from the ruins of some burnt district, and as the swinging sign had a poverty-stricken sort of creak to it, I thought that here was the very spot for cheap lodging and the best of pea coffee."

His instincts were sound, of course: he was given hot food and a bed to share with a South Seas cannibal called Queequeg. Queequeg became his adopted brother and eventually saved his life. Since the beginning of fishing, there have been places that have taken in the Ishmaels of the world—and the Murphs, and the Bugsys, and the Bobbys. Without them, conceivably, fishing wouldn't even be possible. One night a swordfisherman came into the Crow's Nest reeling drunk after a month at sea. Bills were literally falling out of his pocket. Greg, the owner of the bar, took the money—a full paycheck—and locked it up in the safe. The next morning the fisherman came down looking a little chagrined. Jesus what a night last night, he said. And I can't *believe* how much money I spent . . .

That a fisherman is capable of believing he spent a couple thousand dollars in one night says a lot about fishermen. And that a bartender put the money away for safe-keeping says a lot about how fishermen choose their bars. They find places that are second homes because a lot of them don't have real homes. The older guys do, of course—they have families, mortgages, the rest of it—but there aren't many older guys on the longline boats. There are mainly guys like Murph and Bobby and Bugsy who go through their youth with a roll of tens and twenties in their pockets. "It's a young man's game, a single man's game," as Ethel Shatford says.

As a result, the Crow's Nest has a touch of the orphanage to it. It takes people in, gives them a place, loans them a family. Some may have just come off a trip to the Grand Banks, others may be weathering a private North Atlantic of their own: divorce, drug addiction, or just a tough couple of years. One night at the bar a thin old man who had lost his niece to AIDS wrapped his arms around Ethel and just held onto her for five or ten minutes. At the other end of the spectrum is a violent little alcoholic named Wally who's a walking testimony to the effects of child abuse. He has multiple restraining orders against him and occasionally slides into realms of such transcendent obscenity that Ethel has to yell out to him to shut the hell up. She has a soft spot for him, though, because she knows what he went through as a child, and one year she wrapped up a present and gave it to him Christmas morning. (She's in the habit of doing that for anyone stuck upstairs over the holidays.) All day long Wally avoided opening it, and finally Ethel told him she was going to get offended if he didn't unwrap the damn thing. Looking a little uneasy, he slowly pulled the paper off—it was a scarf or something—and suddenly the most violent man in Gloucester was crying in front of her.

Ethel, he said, shaking his head, no one's ever given me a present before.

Ethel Shatford was born in Gloucester and has lived out her whole life half a mile from the Crow's Nest Inn. There are people in town, she says, who have never driven the forty-five minutes to Boston, and there are others who have never even been over the bridge. To put this into perspective, the bridge spans a piece of water so narrow that fishing boats have trouble negotiating it. In a lot of ways the bridge might as well not even be there; a good many people in town see the Grand Banks more often than, say, the next town down the coast.

The bridge was built in 1948, when Ethel was twelve. Gloucester schooners were still sailing to the Grand Banks to dory-fish for cod. That spring Ethel remembers the older boys being excused from school to fight the brush fires that were raging across Cape Ann; the fires burned through a wild area called Dogtown Common, an expanse of swamp and glacial moraine that was once home to the local crazy and forgotten. The bridge was the northern terminus of Boston's Route 128 beltway, and it basically brought the twentieth century to downtown Gloucester. Urban renewal paved over the waterfront in the 1970s, and soon there was a thriving drug trade and one of the highest heroin overdose rates in the country. In 1984, a Gloucester swordfishing boat named the *Valhalla* was busted for running guns to the Irish Republican Army; the guns had been bought with drug money from the Irish Mafia in Boston.

By the end of the 1980s the Georges Bank ecosystem had started to collapse, and the town was forced to raise revenue by joining a federal resettlement program. They provided cheap housing for people from other, even poorer, towns in Massachusetts, and in return received money from the government. The more people they took in, the higher the unemployment rate rose, stressing the fishing industry even further. By 1991, fish stocks were so depleted that the unthinkable was being discussed: Close Georges Bank to all fishing, indefinitely. For 150 years, Georges, off Cape Cod, had been the breadbasket of New England fishing; now it was virtually barren. Charlie Reed, who dropped out of school in tenth grade to work on a boat, saw the end coming: "None of my children have anything to do with fishing," he says. "They'd ask me to take them out on the boat, and I'd say, 'I'm not takin' you nowhere. You just might like it—brutal as it is, you just might like it.'"

Ethel has worked in the Crow's Nest since 1980. She gets there at 8:30 Tuesday morning, works until 4:30 and then often sits and has a few rum-and-cokes. She does that four days a week and occasionally works on weekends. From time to time one of the regulars brings in a fish and she cooks up some chowder in the back room. She passes it out in plastic bowls and whatever's left simmers away in a ceramic crockpot for the rest of the day. Patrons go over, sniff it, and dip in from time to time.

Clearly, this is a place a fisherman could get used to. The curtained windows up front have the immense advantage of allowing people to see out but not be seen. The entire bar can watch who's about to appear in their collective reality, and then the back door offers an alternative to having to deal with it. "It's saved many a guy from wives, girlfriends, whatever," says Ethel. Drunks reveal themselves as well: Their silhouettes careen past the window and Ethel watches them pause at the door to steady themselves and draw a deep breath. Then they fling the big brown door open and head straight for the corner of the bar.

People stay upstairs anywhere from hours to years, and sometimes it's hard to know at the outset which it's going to be. Rates are $27.40 a night for fishermen, truckers, and friends, and $32.90 for everyone else. There's also a weekly rate for long-term guests. One man stayed so long—five years—that he had his room painted and carpeted. He also hung a pair of chandeliers from the ceiling. Fishermen who don't have bank accounts cash paychecks at the Crow's Nest (it helps if they owe the bar money), and fishermen who don't have mailing addresses can have things sent right to the bar. This puts them at a distinct advantage over the I.R.S., a lawyer, or an ex-wife. The bartender, of course, takes messages, screens calls, and might even lie. The pay phone at the door has the same number as the house phone, and when it rings, customers signal to Ethel whether they're in or not.

By and large it's a bar of people who know each other; people who aren't known are invited over for a drink. It's hard to buy your own beer at the Crow's Nest, and it's hard to leave after just one; if you're there at all, you're there until closing. There are few fights at the Nest because everyone knows each other so well, but other waterfront bars—

Pratty's, Mitch's, the Irish Mariner—are known to disassemble themselves on a regular basis. Ethel worked at one place where the owner started so many brawls that she refused to serve him in his own place; the fact that he was a state trooper didn't help matters much. John, another bartender at the Nest, recalls a wedding where the bride and groom got into an argument and the groom stormed off, dutifully followed by all the men in the party. Of course they went to the nearest bar and eventually one of them pitched a sarcastic comment to a quiet, stocky guy sitting off by himself. The man got up, took his hat off and walked down the bar, knocking out the entire male half of the wedding party, one by one.

The closest it's ever come to that at the Nest was one night when there was an ugly cluster of rednecks at one end of the room and a handful of black truckers at the other. The truckers were regulars at the Nest, but the rednecks were from out of town, as were a hopped-up bunch of swordfishermen who were talking loudly around the pool table. The focus of attention of this edgy mix was a black kid and a white kid who were playing pool and arguing, apparently over a drug deal. As the tension in the room climbed, one of the truckers called John over and said, Hey, don't worry, both those kids are trash and we'll back you up no matter what.

John thanked him and went back to washing glasses. The swordfishermen had just gotten off a trip and were reeling drunk, the rednecks were making barely-muted comments about the clientele, and John was just waiting for the cork to pop. Finally one of the rednecks called him over and jutted his chin across the bar at the black truckers.

Too bad you gotta serve 'em but I guess it's the law, he said.

John considered this for a moment and then said, Yeah, and not only that, they're all friends of mine.

He walked across to the pool table and threw the kids out and then he turned to the swordfishermen and told them that if they wanted trouble, they would certainly find plenty.

John's friends were particularly large examples of humankind and the swordfishermen signalled that they understood. The rednecks finally left, and by the end of the night it was back to the same old place it had always been.

"It's a pretty good crowd," says Ethel. "Sometimes you get the wild scallopers in but mostly it's just friends. One of the best times I ever had here was when this Irishman walked in and ordered fifty beers. It was a dead Sunday afternoon and I just looked at him. He said that his friends would be along in a minute, and sure enough, an entire Irish soccer team came in. They'd been staying in Rockport, which is a dry town, and so they just started walking. They walked all the way down Route 127, five miles, and this was the first place they came to. They were drinking beer so fast we were selling it right out of the cases. They were doing three-part harmonies on the tabletops."

Early fishing in Gloucester was the roughest sort of business, and one of the deadliest. As early as the 1650s, three-man crews were venturing up the coast for a week at a time in small open boats that had stones for ballast and unstayed masts. In a big wind the masts sometimes blew down. The men wore canvas hats coated with tar, leather aprons, and cowhide boots known as "redjacks." The eating was spare: for a week-long trip one Gloucester skipper recorded that he shipped four pounds of flour, five pounds of pork fat, seven pounds of sea biscuit, and "a little New England rum." The meals, such as they were, were eaten in the weather because there was no below-deck where the crews could take shelter. They had to take whatever God threw at them.

The first Gloucester fishing vessels worthy of the name were the thirty-foot chebaccos. They boasted two masts stepped well forward, a sharp stern, and cabins fore and aft. The bow rode the seas well, and the high stern kept out a following sea. Into the fo'c'sle were squeezed a couple of bunks and a brick fireplace where they smoked trashfish. That was for the crew to eat while at sea, cod being too valuable to waste on them. Each spring the chebaccos were scraped and caulked and tarred and sent out to the fishing grounds. Once there, the boats were anchored, and the men hand-lined over the side from the low midship rail. Each man had his spot, called a "berth," which was chosen by lottery and held throughout the trip. They fished two lines at twenty-five to sixty fathoms (150-360 feet) with a ten-pound lead weight, which they hauled up dozens of times a day. The shoulder muscles that resulted from a lifetime of such work made fishermen easily recognizable on the street. They were called "hand-liners" and people got out of their way.

The captain fished his own lines, like everyone else, and pay was reckoned by how much fish each man caught. The tongues were cut out of the fish and kept in separate buckets; at the end of the day the skipper entered the numbers in a log book and dumped the tongues overboard. It took a couple of months for the ships to fill their holds—the fish was either dried or, later, kept on ice—and then they'd head back to port. Some captains, on a run of fish, couldn't help themselves from loading their ship down until her decks were almost underwater. This was called deep-loading, and such a ship was in extreme peril if the weather turned ugly. The trip home took a couple of weeks, and the fish would compress under its own weight and squeeze all the excess fluid out of the flesh. The crew pumped the water over the sides, and deep-loaded Grand Bankers would gradually emerge from the sea as they sailed for port.

By the 1760s Gloucester had seventy-five fishing schooners in the water, about one-sixth of the New England fleet. Cod was so important to the economy that in 1784 a wooden effigy—the "Sacred Cod"—was hung in the Massachusetts State House by a wealthy statesman named John Rowe. Revenue from the New England codfishery alone was worth over a million dollars a year at the time of the Revolution, and John

Adams refused to sign the Treaty of Paris until the British granted American fishing rights to the Grand Banks. The final agreement held that American schooners could fish in Canada's territorial waters unhindered and come ashore on deserted parts of Nova Scotia and Labrador to salt-dry their catch.

Cod was divided into three categories. The best, known as "dun fish," was caught in the spring and shipped to Portugal and Spain, where it fetched the highest prices. (Lisbon restaurants still offer *baccalao*, dried codfish.) The next grade of fish was sold domestically, and the worst grade—"refuse fish"—was used to feed slaves in the West Indian canefields. Gloucester merchants left for the Caribbean with holdsfull of salt cod and returned with rum, molasses, and cane sugar; when this lucrative trade was impeded by the British during the War of 1812, local captains simply left port on moonless nights and sailed smaller boats. Georges Bank opened up in the 1830s, the first railway spur reached Gloucester in 1848, and the first ice companies were established that same year. By the 1880s—the heyday of the fishing schooner—Gloucester had a fleet of four or five hundred sail in her harbor. It was said you could walk clear across to Rocky Neck without getting your feet wet.

Cod was a blessing but could not, alone, have accounted for such riches. In 1816, a Cape Ann fisherman named Abraham Lurvey invented the mackerel jig by attaching a steel hook to a drop-shaped piece of cast lead. Not only did the lead act as a sinker, but, jiggled up and down, it became irresistible to mackerel. After two centuries of watching these elusive fish swim past in schools so dense they discolored the sea, New England fishermen suddenly had a way to catch them. Gloucester captains ignored a federal bounty on cod and sailed for Sable Island with men in the cross-trees looking for the tell-tale darkening of mackerel in the water. "School-O!" they would shout, the ship would come around into the wind, and ground-up baitfish—"chum"—would be thrown out into the water. The riper the chum was, the better it attracted the fish; rotting chum on the breeze meant a mackerel schooner was somewhere upwind.

Jigging for mackerel worked well, but it was inevitable that the Yankee mind would come up with something more efficient. In 1855 the purse seine was invented, a 1,300-foot net of tarred twine with lead weights at the bottom and cork floats at the top. It was stowed in a dory that was towed behind the schooner, and when the fish were sighted, the dory quickly encircled them and cinched the net up tight. It was hauled aboard and the fish were split, gutted, beheaded, and thrown into barrels with salt. Sometimes the school escaped before the net was tightened and the crew drew up what was called a "water haul"; other times the net was so full that they could hardly winch it aboard.

Purse-seining passed for a glamorous occupation at the time, and it wasn't long before codfishermen came up with their own version of it. It was called tub trawling and if it was more efficient at killing fish, it was also more efficient at killing men. No longer did groundfishermen work from the relative safety of a schooner; now they were setting out from the mother ship in sixteen-foot wooden dories. Each dory carried half a dozen 300-foot trawl lines that were coiled in tubs and hung with baited hooks. The crews rowed out in the morning, paid out their trawls, and then hauled them back every few hours. There were 1,800 hooks to a dory, ten dories to a schooner, and several hundred ships in the fleet. Groundfish had several million chances a day to die.

Pulling a third of a mile's worth of trawl off the ocean floor was back-breaking work, though, and unspeakably dangerous in bad weather. In November of 1880, two fishermen named Lee and Devine rowed out from the schooner *Deep Water* in their dory. November was a hell of a time to be on the Grand Banks in any kind of vessel, and in a dory it was sheer insanity. They took a wave broadside while hauling their trawl and both men were thrown into the water. Devine managed to clamber back into the boat, but Lee, weighed down by boots and winter clothing, started to sink. He was several fathoms under when his hand touched the trawl line that led back up to the surface. He started to pull.

Almost immediately his right hand sunk into a hook. He jerked it away, leaving part of his finger on the barbed steel like a piece of herringbait, and kept pulling upwards towards the light. He finally broke the surface and heaved himself back into the dory. It was almost awash and Devine, who was bailing like mad, could do nothing to help him. Lee passed out from the pain and when he came to, he grabbed a bucket and started bailing as well. They had to empty the boat before they were hit by another freak wave. Twenty minutes later they were out of danger and Devine asked Lee if he needed to go back to the schooner. Lee shook his head and said that they should finish hauling the trawls. For the next hour he pulled gear out of the water with his mangled hand. That was dory-fishing in its heyday.

There are worse deaths than the one Lee almost suffered, though. Warm Gulf Stream water meets the Labrador Current over the Grand Banks, and the result is a wall of fog that can sweep in with no warning at all. Dory crews hauling their gear have been caught by the fog and simply never seen again. In 1883, a fisherman named Howard Blackburn—still a hero in town, Gloucester's answer to Paul Bunyan—was separated from his ship and endured three days at sea during a January gale. His dory-mate died of exposure, and Blackburn had to freeze his own hands around the oar handles to continue rowing for Newfoundland. In the end he lost all his fingers to frostbite. He made land on a deserted part of the coast and staggered around for several days before finally being rescued.

Every year brought a story of survival nearly as horrific as Blackburn's. A year earlier, two men had been picked up by a South American trader after eight days adrift. They wound up in Pernambuco, Brazil, and it took them two months to get back to Gloucester. From time to time dory crews were even blown across the Atlantic, drifting helplessly with the trade winds and surviving on raw fish and dew. These men had no way to notify their families when they finally made shore; they simply shipped home and came walking back up Rogers Street several months later like men returning from the dead.

For the families back home, dory-fishing gave rise to a new kind of hell. No longer was there just the grief of losing men at sea; now there was the agony of not knowing, as well. Missing dory crews could turn up at any time, and so there was never a point at which the families knew for sure they could grieve and get on with their lives. "We saw a father go morning and evening to the hill-top which overlooked the ocean," recorded the *Provincetown Advocate* after a terrible gale in 1841. "And there seating himself, would watch for hours, scanning the distant horizon . . . for some speck on which to build a hope."

And they prayed. They walked up Prospect Street to the top of a steep rise called Portagee Hill and stood beneath the twin bell towers of Our Lady of Good Voyage church. The bell towers are one of the highest points in Gloucester and can be seen for miles by incoming ships. Between the towers is a sculpture of the Virgin Mary, who gazes down with love and concern at a bundle in her arms. This is the Virgin who has been charged with the safety of the local fishermen. The bundle in her arms is not the infant Jesus; it's a Gloucester schooner.

After Mary Anne leaves the Green Tavern, Chris and Bobby finish up their drinks and then tell Bugsy that they're going out for a while. They step out of the barroom darkness into the soft grey light of Gloucester in the rain and walk across the street to Bill's. Bobby orders a couple of Budweisers while Chris fishes a dime out of her pocket and calls her friend Thea from a pay-phone. She and Thea used to be neighbors in a housing project, and Chris thinks she might be able to borrow Thea's apartment for a while to give Bobby a proper goodbye. She wants to be alone with him for a while, and she wants to help Bugsy out if she can. It's possible Thea might be interested in him—he's leaving in a few hours for the Grand Banks, but you never know.

Thea says come by any time, and Chris hangs up and goes back to the bar. Bobby's hangover has alchemized into a huge empty hunger, and they finish off their beers and leave a buck on the bartop and head back outside. They drive across town to a lunch place called Sammy J's and order two more beers and fishcakes and beans. Fishcakes are Bobby's favorite food and he probably won't see them again until he's back on shore. The last thing fishermen want to eat at sea is more fish. They eat fast and pick up Bugsy and then drive over to Ethel's. Chris has had a falling out with Ethel's boyfriend, and Chris is going to move out everything she has stored there. It's still raining a little, everything seems dark and oppressive, and they carry boxes of her belongings down one flight of stairs and pack it into the Volvo. They fill the car with lamps and clothes and house plants and then squeeze themselves in and drive across town to the projects on Arthur Street.

Thea doesn't go for Bugsy, as it turns out, she's already got a boyfriend. The four of them sit around talking and drinking beer for a while, and then the men have a terrible realization: They've forgotten the hotdogs. Murph, who is charged with buying food for the trip, won't get hotdogs on his own, so if they want any they'll have to get them on their own. They drive to Cape Ann Market and Bobby and Bugsy run into the store and come back a few minutes later with fifty dollars' worth of hotdogs. It's midafternoon now; it's getting close. Chris drives them back down Rogers Street, past Walgreen's and Americold and Gorton's, and turns down into the gravel lot behind Rose's Marine. Bobby and Bugsy get out with their hotdogs and jump from the pier to the deck of the *Andrea Gail.*

Watching the men move around the boat Chris thinks: this winter Bobby'll be down in Bradenton, next summer he'll be back up here but gone a month at a time, and that's just how it is; Bobby's a swordfisherman and owes a lot of money. At least they have a plan, though. Bobby signed a statement directing Bob Brown to give his settlement check from the last trip to Chris, and she's going to use the money—almost $3,000—to pay off some of his debts and get an apartment in Lanesville, on the north shore of Cape Ann. Maybe living out there, they'll spend a little less time at the Nest. And she's got two jobs lined up, one at the Old Farm Inn in Rockport, and another taking care of the retarded son of a friend. They'll get by. Bobby might be away a lot, but they'll get by.

Suddenly there are shouts coming from the boat: Bugsy and Bobby are standing toe to toe on the wharf in the rain, wrenching a jug of bleach back and forth. Fists are coming up and the bleach is going first one way, then another, and at any moment it looks like one of them's going to roundhouse the other. It doesn't happen; Bobby finally turns away, spitting swears, and goes back to work. Out of the corner of her eye Chris sees another fisherman named Sully angling across the gravel lot toward her car. He walks up and leans in the window.

I just got a site on the boat, he says, I'm replacin' some guy who backed out. He looks over at Bobby and Bugsy. Can you believe this shit? Thirty days together and it's startin' already?

THE *Andrea Gail,* in the language, is a raked-stem, hard-chined western-rig swordfisherman. That means her bow has a lot of angle to it, she has a nearly-square cross-section, and her pilothouse is up front rather than in the stern, atop an elevated deck called the whaleback. She's 72 feet long, has a hull of continuously-welded steel plate, and was built in Panama City, Florida, in 1978. She has a 365-horsepower, turbo-charged diesel engine, which is capable of speeds up to twelve knots. There are seven type-one life preservers on board, six Imperial survival suits, a 406-megahertz Emergency Position Indicating Radio Beacon (EPIRB), a 121.5-megahertz EPIRB, and a Givens auto-inflating life raft. There are forty miles of 700-pound test monofilament line on her, thousands of hooks, and room for five tons of baitfish. An ice machine that can make three tons of ice a day sits on her whaleback deck, and state-of-the-art electronics fill her pilothouse: radar, loran, single-sideband, VHF, weather track satellite receiver. There's a washer/dryer on board, and the galley has fake wood veneer and a four-burner stove.

The *Andrea Gail* is one of the biggest moneymakers in Gloucester harbor, and Billy Tyne and Bugsy Moran have driven all the way from Florida to grab sites onboard. The only other sword boat in the harbor that might be able to outfish her is the *Hannah Boden,* skippered by a Colby College graduate named Linda Greenlaw. Not only is Greenlaw one of the only women in the business, she's one of the best captains, period, on the entire East Coast. Year after year, trip after trip, she makes more money than almost anyone else. Both the *Andrea Gail* and the *Hannah Boden* are owned by Bob Brown, and they can take so much fish from the ocean that Ethel's son Ricky has been known to call in from Hawaii to find out if either one is in port. When the *Hannah Boden* unloads her catch in Gloucester, swordfish prices plummet halfway across the world.

So far, though, Billy's second trip on the *Andrea Gail* is off to a bad start. The boys have been drinking hard all week and everyone's in a foul mood. No one wants to go back out. For the past several days almost every attempt to work on the boat has degenerated either into a fight or an occasion to walk across the street to the bar. Now it's September 20th, late in the season to be heading out, and Tyne can barely round up a full crew. Alfred Pierre—an immense, kind Jamaican from New York City—is holed up with his girlfriend in one of the upstairs rooms at the Nest. One minute he says he's going, the next minute he's not—it's been like that all day long. Bobby's somewhere across town with a black eye and a hangover. Bugsy's in an ugly mood because he hasn't met a woman. Murph is complaining about money and misses his kid, and—the last straw—a new crew member walked off this morning without any explanation at all.

The guy's name was Adam Randall, and he was supposed to replace Doug Kosco, who'd crewed on the previous trip. Randall had driven up from East Bridgewater, Massachusetts, with his father-in-law that morning to take the job; he pulled into the dirt parking lot behind Rose's and got out to look the boat over. Randall was a lithe, intensely handsome 30-year-old man with a shag of blond rock-star hair and cold blue eyes. He was a welder, an engineer, a scuba diver, and had fished his whole life. He knew an unsafe boat when he saw one—he called them "slabs"—and the *Andrea Gail* was anything but. She looked like she could take an aircraft carrier broadside. Moreover, he knew most of her crew, and his girlfriend had practically told him not to bother coming home if he didn't take the job. He hadn't worked in three months. He walked back across the lot, told his father-in-law that he had a funny feeling, and the two of them drove off together to a bar.

People often get premonitions when they do jobs that could get them killed, and in commercial fishing—still one of the most dangerous pursuits in the country—people get premonitions all the time. The trick is knowing when to listen to them. In 1871, a cook named James Nelson shipped aboard the schooner *Sachem* for a fishing trip to Georges Bank. One night he was awakened by a recurring dream and ran aft to tell the captain. For God's sake get clear of the Banks, he begged, I've had my dream again. I've been shipwrecked twice after this dream.

The captain was an old salt named Wenzell. He asked what the dream was. I see women, dressed in white, standing in the rain, Nelson replied.

There was hardly a breath of wind and Wenzell was not impressed. He told Nelson to go back to bed. A while later a little breeze sprang up. Within an hour it was blowing hard and the *Sachem* was hove-to under close-reefed foresail. The hull started to open up and the crew manned the pumps. They couldn't keep up with the leak, and Wenzell desperately signalled to a nearby Gloucester schooner, the *Pescador.* The *Pescador* put dories over the side and managed to save the *Sachem's* crew. Within half an hour the *Sachem* rolled over, settled bow-down into the sea, and sank.

Even today, instincts are heeded and fears are listened to. Randall walked off and suddenly Tyne had another site to fill. He called around and finally got 28-year-old David Sullivan. Sully, as he's known, was mildly famous in town for having saved his entire crew one frigid January night. His boat, the *Harmony,* was tied to another boat when she began to take on water out at sea. Her crew started screaming for help but couldn't wake up the men on the other boat, so Sully jumped overboard and pulled himself across on a rope, legs dragging through the icy North Atlantic. Sullivan, in other words, was a good man to have on board.

Tyne said he'd be over to pick him up in half an hour. Sully packed a bag and made a few phone calls to tell people he'd be away for a while. Suddenly his plans for that evening were off; his life was on hold for the next month. Billy showed up around two o'clock and they drove back to Rose's just in time to see Bobby and Bugsy going at it. Wonderful, Sully thought. He stopped to say hello to Chris and then Billy sent him off to the Cape Ann Market to get the food for the trip. Murph went with him. Bulging in Sully's pocket was four thousand dollars cash.

One of the things about commercial fishing is that everything seems to be extreme. Fishermen don't work in any normal sense of the word, they're at sea for a month and then home celebrating for a week straight. They don't earn the same kind of money most other people do, they come home either busted or with a quarter million dollar's worth of fish in their hold. And when they buy food for the month, it's not something any normal person would recognize as shopping; it's a retail catastrophe of Biblical proportions.

Murph and Sully drive to the Cape Ann Market out on Route 127 and begin stalking up and down the aisles throwing food into their carts by the armful. They grab fifty loaves of bread, enough to fill two carts. They take a hundred pounds of potatoes, thirty pounds of onions, twenty-five gallons of milk, eighty-dollar racks of steak. Every time they fill a cart they push it to the back of the store and get another one. The herd of carts starts to grow—ten, fifteen, twenty carts—and people stare nervously and get out of the way. Murph and Sully grab anything they want and lots of it: ice cream sandwiches, Hostess cupcakes, bacon and eggs, creamy peanut butter, porterhouse steaks, chocolate-coated cereal, spaghetti, lasagna, frozen pizza. They get top-of-the-line food and the only thing they don't get is fish. Finally they get thirty cartons of cigarettes—enough to fill a whole cart—and round their carts up like so many stainless steel cattle. The store opens two cash registers especially for them, and it takes half an hour to ring them through. The total nearly cleans Sully out; he pays while Murph backs the truck up to a loading dock, and they heave the food on and then drive it down to Rose's wharf. Bag by bag, they carry four thousand dollars' worth of groceries down into the fish hold of the *Andrea Gail*.

The *Andrea Gail* has a small refrigerator in the galley and twenty tons of ice in the hold. The ice keeps the baitfish and groceries from spoiling on the way out and the swordfish from spoiling on the way home. (In a pinch it can even be used to keep a dead crew member fresh: once a desperately-alcoholic old fisherman died on the *Hannah Boden,* and Linda Greenlaw had to put him down the hole because the Coast Guard refused to fly him out.) Commercial fishing simply wouldn't be possible without ice. Without diesel engines, maybe; without loran, weather faxes, or hydraulic winches; but not without ice. There is simply no other way to get fresh fish to market. In the old days, Grand Banks fishermen used to run to Newfoundland to salt-dry their catch before heading home, but the coming of the railroads in the 1840s changed all that. Suddenly food could be moved faster than it would spoil, and ice companies sprang up practically overnight to accommodate the new market. They cut ice from ponds in the winter, packed it in sawdust and then sold it to schooners in the summer months. Properly-packed ice lasted so long—and was so valuable—that traders could ship it to India and still make a profit.

The market for fresh fish changed fishing forever. No longer could schooner captains return home at their leisure with a hold full of salt cod; now it was all one big race. Several full schooners pulling into port at once could saturate the market and ruin the efforts of anyone following. In the 1890s, one schooner had to dump 200 tons of halibut into Gloucester harbor because she'd been beaten into port by six other vessels. Overloaded schooners built like racing sloops dashed home through fall gales with every inch of canvas showing and their decks practically awash. Bad weather sank these elegant craft by the dozen, but a lot of people made a lot of money. And in cities like Boston and New York, people were suddenly eating fresh Atlantic cod.

Little has changed. Fishing boats still make the same mad dashes for shore they were making 150 years ago, and the smaller boats—the ones that don't have ice machines—are still buying it in bulk from Cape Pond Ice, located in a low brick building between Felicia Oil and Parisi Seafoods. In the old days, Cape Pond used to hire men to carve up a local pond with huge ice-saws, but now the ice is made in row upon row of 350-pound blocks, called "cans." The cans look like huge versions of the trays in people's refrigerators. They're extracted from freezers in the floor, skidded onto elevators, hoisted to the third floor, and dragged down a runway by men wielding huge steel hooks; the men work in a building-sized refrigerator and wear shirts that say, "Cape Pond Ice—The Coolest Guys Around." The ice blocks are shoved down a chute into a steel cutting drum, where they jump and rattle in terrible spasms until all 350 pounds have been eaten down to little chips and sprayed through a hose into the hold of a commercial boat outside.

Cape Pond is one of hundreds of businesses jammed into the Gloucester waterfront. Boats come into port, offload their catch, and then spend the next week making repairs and gearing up for the next trip. A good-sized wave can bury a sword boat underwater for a few seconds—"It just gets real dark in here," is how Linda Greenlaw describes the experience—and undoing the effects of a drubbing like that can take days, even weeks. (One boat came into port *twisted.*) Most boats are repaired at Gloucester Marine Railways, a haul-out place that's been in business since 1856. It consists of a massive wooden frame that rides steel rollers along two lengths of railroad track up out of the water. Six-hundred-ton boats are blocked up, lashed down, and hauled ashore by a double-shot of one-inch chain worked off a series of huge steel reduction gears. The gears were machined a hundred years ago and haven't been touched since. There are three railways in all, one in the Inner Harbor and two out on Rocky Neck. The harbor railway is the least robust of the three and terminates in a greasy little basement, which sports a pair of strangely Moorish-looking brick arches. The other two railways are surrounded by the famous galleries and piano bars of Rocky Neck. Tourists blithely wander past machinery that could rip their summer homes right off their foundations.

The *Andrea Gail* had been touched up at the Railways, but most of her major work was done in St. Augustine, Florida, in 1987. Almost three feet were added to her stern to accommodate two 1,900-gallon fuel tanks; the whaleback deck was extended aft nine feet; and a steel bulwark on the port side was raised and extended eighteen feet. In addition, 28 fuel-oil drums, seven water drums, and the ice machine were stored on the whaleback.

In all, perhaps about ten tons of steel, fuel, and machinery were added to the whaleback. The weight had been added high up, eight feet or so above the deck and perhaps twice that high above the waterline. The boat's center of gravity had been changed just a little. The *Andrea Gail* would now sit more deeply in the water, recover from rolls a bit more slowly.

On the other hand, she could now put to sea for six weeks at a time. That, after all, was the point; and no man on the boat would have disagreed.

GOD'S COUNTRY

Going to sea is going to prison,
with a chance at drowning besides.
—*SAMUEL JOHNSON*

BY midafternoon the *Andrea Gail* is ready: The food and bait have been stowed away, the fuel and water tanks have been topped off, spare drums of both have been lashed onto the whaleback, the gear's in good order, and the engine's running well. All there remains to do is leave. Bobby climbs off the boat without saying anything to Bugsy—they're still morose after their fight—and walks across the parking lot to Chris's Volvo. They drive back across town to Thea's and trot up her front steps in a soft warm rain. Thea hears their feet on the stoop and invites them in and takes her cue from a quick glance from Chris. I've got some errands to do, I'll be back in a few hours, she says. Make yourselves at home.

Chris and Bobby tug each other into the dark bedroom and lie down on the bed. Outside, the rain taps on. Chris and Bobby can't see the ocean but they can smell it, a dank taste of salt and seaweed that permeates the entire peninsula and lays claim to it as part of the sea. On rainy days there's no getting away from it, wherever you go you breathe in that smell, and this is one of those days. Chris and Bobby lie together on

Thea's bed, talking and smoking and trying to forget the fact that this is his last day, and after an hour the phone rings and Bobby jumps up to answer it. It's Sully on the line, calling from the Crow's Nest. It's five o'clock, Sully says. Time to go.

The mood is dark and grim when they get down to the Nest. Alfred Pierre is still locked in an upstairs room with his girlfriend and won't come out. Billy Tyne's just returned from a two-hour phone conversation with his ex-wife, Jodi. Murph's there with a pile of toys on the pool table, packing them into a cardboard box. Ethel's in the back room crying: Bobby's money problems, the black eye, the month offshore. The Grand Banks in October is no joke and everybody knows it. There won't be half a dozen boats out there from the whole East Coast fleet.

Alfred Pierre finally comes down and sidles into the bar. He's a big, shy man who's not well known around town, although people seem to like him. His girlfriend has come down from Maine to see him off and she's not handling it well, her eyes are red and she's holding him as if she might physically keep him from getting on the boat. Murph finishes strapping his package up with tape and asks Chris to run him across town on an errand. He wants to pick up some movies. Sully is talking to Bugsy in a corner, and everyone's congratulating Ethel's eldest son, Rusty, for his upcoming marriage next week. Most of the people in the room will be a thousand miles into the North Atlantic by then.

Chris and Murph return ten minutes later with a cardboard box spilling with videos. There's a VCR on the *Andrea Gail*, and someone off another boat offered Murph the movies. Alfred has a beer bottle clenched in one big hand and is still muttering about not wanting to go. Sully's saying the same thing; he's in a yellow slicker over by the pool table telling Bugsy how he's got a bad feeling about this trip. It's the money, he says; if I didn't need the money I wouldn't go near this thing.

Okay you guys, Billy says. One last drink. Everyone downs one last drink. Okay, one more, someone says. Everyone has one more. Bobby's drinking tequila. He's standing by Chris looking down at the floor and she's holding his hand and neither of them are saying much. Sully comes over and asks if they're going to be okay. Chris says, Sure, we'll be fine and then she says: Actually, I'm not sure. Actually, no, I don't think so.

Six men are leaving for a month and it feels as if things are shearing off into a new and empty direction from which they may never return. Ethel, trying to maintain her composure, goes around the room hugging all the men. The only person she doesn't hug is Alfred because she doesn't know him well enough. Bobby asks his mother if they can take the color T.V. above the bar. If it's okay with Billy, she says.

Billy looks up. Ethel, he says, they can take the T.V., but if they watch it instead of doin' their work it's goin' straight overboard.

That's fine, Billy, that's fine, Ethel says.

Billy's girlfriend sees Bobby's shiner under the brim of his Budweiser cap and glances over at Chris. She's of the old school where ladies don't slug their men.

You northern gals, she says.

I didn't mean it, says Chris. It was a mistake.

It's now way too late for anyone to back out. Not in the literal sense—any one of them could still take off running out the door—but people don't work like that. More or less, they do what others expect them to. If one of the crew backed out now he'd sit around for a month and then either go to a welcome-home party or a memorial service. Either would be horrible in its own way. Half the crew have misgivings about this trip, but they're going anyhow; they've crossed some invisible line, and now even the most desperate premonitions won't save them. Tyne, Pierre, Sullivan, Moran, Murphy, and Shatford are going to the Grand Banks on the *Andrea Gail.*

Okay, Billy says. Let's go.

Everyone files out the big wooden door. The rain has stopped and there are even a few scraps of clear sky off to the west. Pale, late-summer blue. Chris and Bobby get into her Volvo and Alfred and his girlfriend get into their car and everyone else walks. They cross Rogers Street through the impatient stream of Friday afternoon traffic and then angle down through the gate in the chain-link fence. There are fuel tanks on iron scaffolds behind Rose's, and small boats up with tarps over them, and a battered sign that says "Carter's Boat Yard." One of the fuel tanks has a pair of humpback whales painted on it. Chris drives past the little group, tires crunching on the gravel, and comes to a stop in front of the *Andrea Gail.* The boat is tied up to a small piece of wharf behind Old Port Seafoods, next to the fire boat and a dockside fuel pump. Bobby looks over at her.

I don't want to do this, he says. I really don't.

Chris is holding onto him in the front seat of her Volvo, with everything she owns in the back. Well don't go then, she says. Well fuck it. Don't go.

I got to go. The money; I got to.

Billy Tyne walks over and leans in the window. You gonna be all right? he asks. Chris nods her head. Bobby is really starting to fight the tears and he looks away so that Billy doesn't see. Okay, Billy says to Chris. We'll see you when we get back. He walks across the dock and jumps down onto the deck of the boat. Then Sully comes over. He's known Bobby most of his life—without Bobby he probably wouldn't even have taken the trip—and he's worried about him now. Worried that somehow Bobby isn't going to make it, that the trip's a huge mistake. Are you two okay? he says. Are you sure?

Yeah, we're okay, says Chris. We just need a minute.

Sully smiles and slaps the car roof and walks away. Bugsy and Murph don't have anyone to linger over and so they waste no time getting on the boat; now it's just the two couples in their cars. Alfred detaches himself from his girlfriend in the front seat and gets out and walks across the dock. His girlfriend looks around, crying, and spots Chris in the Volvo. She draws two fingers down her cheeks—"Yes, I'm sad, too"—and then just sits there, tears running down her cheeks. There's nothing more to wait for now, nothing more to say. Bobby's trying to keep it together because of the other five guys on the boat, but Chris is not trying to keep it together.

Well, I gotta go now, he says.

Yep.

And Christina, you know, I'll always love you.

She smiles at him through her tears. Yeah, I know, she says.

Bobby kisses her and gets out of the car, still holding hands. He closes the door and gives her a final smile and then starts walking across the gravel. As Chris remembers it he doesn't look back, not once, and he keeps his face hidden the entire way.

Almost as soon as the New World was discovered, Europeans were fishing it. Twelve years after Columbus, a Frenchman named Jean Denys crossed the Atlantic, worked the Grand Banks off Newfoundland, and returned home with a hold full of cod. Within a few years there were so many Portuguese boats on the Banks that their king felt compelled to impose an import tax in order to protect the fishermen at home. Codfish ran so thick off Newfoundland, it was said, that they slowed ships down in the water.

Codfish weren't quite that plentiful, but they were certainly worth crossing the Atlantic for. And they were easily transported: Crews salted them aboard ship, dried them when they got home, and then sold them by the hundreds of thousands. The alternative was to go over with two crews, one to fish and another to preserve the catch on shore. The fish were split down the middle and then laid on racks, called flakes, to cure all summer in the Newfoundland air. Either way, the result was a rugged slab of protein that could be treated as indelicately as shoe leather and then soaked back to a palatable form. Soon European ships were shuttling back and forth across the North Atlantic in a hugely lucrative—if perilous—trade.

For the first fifty years the European powers were content to fish off Newfoundland and leave the coastlines alone. They were jagged, gloomy places that seemed to offer little more than a chance to impale one's ship. Then, in 1598, a French marquis named Troïlus de Mesgouez pulled sixty convicts from French prisons and deposited them on a barren strip of sand called Sable Island, south of Nova Scotia. Left to shift for themselves, the men hunted wild cattle, constructed huts from shipwrecked vessels, rendered fish oil, and gradually killed one another off. By 1603, there were only eleven left alive, and these unfortunates were dragged back to France and presented to King Henri IV. They were clothed in animal skins and had beards halfway down their chests. Not only did the king pardon them their crimes, he gave them a bounty to make up for their suffering.

It was around this time that Cape Ann was first sighted by Europeans. In 1605, the great French explorer Samuel de Champlain was working his way south from Casco Bay, Maine, when he rounded the rock ledges of Thatcher's, Milk, and Salt islands and cast anchor off a sandy beach. The natives drew for him a map of the coastline to the south, and Champlain went on to explore the rest of New England before returning to Cape Ann the following year. This time he was clawing his way up the coast in some ugly fall weather when he sought shelter in a natural harbor he'd missed on his previous trip. He was greeted by a party of Wampanoag Indians, some of whom wore the scraps of Portuguese clothing they had traded for a hundred years before, and they made a great show of hospitality before launching a surprise attack from the woods of Rocky Neck. The Frenchmen easily fended them off and on the last day of September, 1606, with the Indians waving goodbye from the shore and the oaks and maples rusting into their fall colors, Champlain set sail again. Because of the sheltered coves and thick shellfish beds he called the place "Beauport"—The Good Harbor. Seventeen years later a group of Englishmen sailed into Beauport, eyed the local abundance of cod and cast their anchor. The year was 1623.

The ship was financed by the Dorchester Company, a group of London investors that wanted to start tapping the riches of the New World. Their idea was to establish a settlement on Cape Ann and use it to support a fleet of boats that would fish all spring and summer and return to Europe in the fall. The shore crew was charged with building a habitable colony and drying the catch as it came in. Unfortunately, luck was against the Dorchester men from the start. The first summer they caught a tremendous amount of fish, but the bottom dropped out of the cod market, and they didn't even make expenses. The next year prices returned to normal, but they caught almost no fish at all; and the third year violent gales damaged the boats and drove them back to England. The company was forced to liquidate their assets and bring their men home.

A few of the settlers refused to leave, though. They combined forces with a band of outcasts from the tyrannical Plymouth colony and formed the nucleus of a new colony at Gloucester. New England was an unforgiving land in those days, where only the desperate and the devout seemed to survive, and Gloucester wound up with more than its share of the former. Its most notorious citizen was the Reverend John Lyford, whose deeds were so un-Christian—he criticized the Church and groped a local servant girl—as to be deemed unprintable by a local historian; another was a "shipwrecked adventurer" named Fells who fled Plymouth to escape public whipping. His crime was that he'd had "unsanctioned relations" with a young woman.

Gloucester was a perfect place for loose cannons like

Lyford and Fells. It was poor, remote, and the Puritan fathers didn't particularly care what went on up there. After a brief period of desertion, the town was re-settled in 1631, and almost immediately the inhabitants took to fishing. They had little choice, Cape Ann being one big rock, but in some ways that was a blessing. Farmers are easy to control because they're tied to their land, but fishermen are not so easy to control. A twenty-year-old off a three-month trip to the Banks has precious little reason to heed the bourgeois mores of the town. Gloucester developed a reputation for tolerance, if not outright debauchery, that drew people from all over the Bay Colony. The town began to thrive.

Other communities also had a healthy streak of godlessness in them, but it was generaly relegated to the outskirts of town. (Wellfleet, for example, reserved an island across the harbor for its young men. In due time a brothel, a tavern, and a whale lookout were built there—just about everything a young fisherman needed.) Gloucester had no such buffer, though; everything happened right on the waterfront. Young women avoided certain streets, town constables were on the lookout for errant fishermen, and orchard-owners rigged guns up to trip-wires to protect their apple trees. Some Gloucester fishermen, apparently, didn't even respect the Sabbath: "Cape Cod captains went wild-eyed in an agony of inner conflict," recorded a Cape Cod historian named Josef Berger, "as they read the Scriptures to their crews while some godless Gloucester craft lay in plain sight . . . hauling up a full share of mackerel or cod."

If the fishermen lived hard, it was no doubt because they died hard as well. In the industry's heyday, Gloucester was losing a couple of hundred men every year to the sea, four percent of the town's population. Since 1650, an estimated ten thousand Gloucestermen have died at sea, far more Gloucestermen than died in all the country's wars. Sometimes a storm would hit the Grand Banks and half a dozen ships would go down, a hundred men lost overnight. On more than one occasion, Newfoundlanders woke up to find their beaches strewn with bodies.

The Grand Banks are so dangerous because they happen to sit on one of the worst storm tracks in the world. Low pressure systems form over the Great Lakes or Cape Hatteras and follow the jet stream out to sea, crossing right over the fishing grounds in the process. In the old days, there wasn't much the boats could do but put out extra anchor cable and try to ride it out. As dangerous as the Grand Banks were, though, Georges Bank—only 180 miles east of Cape Cod—was even worse. There was something so ominous about Georges that fishing captains refused to go near it for three hundred years. Currents ran in strange vortexes on Georges, and the tide was said to run off so fast that ocean bottom was left exposed for gulls to feed on. Men talked of strange dreams and visions they had there, and the uneasy feeling that dire forces were assembling themselves.

Unfortunately, Georges was also home to one of the greatest concentrations of marine life in the world, and it was only a matter of time before someone tried to fish it. In 1827, a Gloucester skipper named John Fletcher Wonson hove-to off Georges, threw out a fishing line, and pulled up a halibut. The ease with which the fish had been caught stuck in his mind, and three years later he went back to Georges expressly to fish. Nothing particularly awful happened, and soon ships were going back and forth to Georges without a second thought. It was only a one-day trip from Gloucester, and the superstitions about the place started to fade. That was when Georges turned deadly.

Because the fishing grounds were so small and close to shore, dozens of schooners might be anchored within sight of each other on a fair day. If a storm came on gradually, the fleet had time to weigh anchor and disperse into deeper water; but a sudden storm could pile ship upon ship until they all went down in a mass of tangled spars and rigging. Men would be stationed at the bow of each boat to cut their anchor cables if another boat were bearing down on them, but that was usually a death sentence in itself. The chances of sailing clear of the shoal water were horribly small.

One of the worst of these catastrophes happened in 1862, when a winter gale bore down on seventy schooners that were working a closely-packed school of cod. Without warning the sky turned black and the snow began to drive down almost horizontally. One fisherman described what ensued:

> My shipmates showed no sign of fear; they were now all on deck and the skipper was keeping a sharp lookout. Somewhere about nine o'clock, the skipper sang out, 'There's a vessel adrift right ahead of us! Stand by with your hatchet, but don't cut until you hear the word!' All eyes were bent now on the drifting craft. On she came, directly at us. A moment more and the signal to cut must be given. With the swiftness of a gull, she passed by, so near that I could have leaped aboard. The hopeless, terror-stricken faces of the crew we saw but a moment, as the doomed craft sped on her course. She struck one of the fleet a short distance astern, and we saw the waters close over both vessels almost instantly.

A FEW modern swordfishing boats still fish Georges Bank, but most make the long trip to the Grand. They're out for longer but come back with more fish—the old trade-off. It takes a week to reach the Grand Banks on a modern sword boat. You drive east-northeast around the clock until you're twelve hundred miles out of Gloucester and four hundred miles out of Newfoundland. From there it's easier to get to the Azores than back to the Crow's Nest Inn. Like Georges, the Grand Banks are shallow enough to allow sunlight to penetrate all the way to the bottom. An infusion of cold water called the Labrador Current crosses the shoals and creates the perfect environment for plankton; small fish collect to feed on the plankton, and big fish collect to feed on the small fish. Soon the whole food chain's there, right up to the seventy-foot sword boats.

The trips in and out are basically the parts of the month that swordfishermen sleep. In port they're too busy cramming as much life as they can into five or six days, and on the fishing grounds they're too busy working. They work twenty hours a day for two or three weeks straight and then fall into their bunks for the long steam back. The trips entail more than just eating and sleeping, though. Fishing gear, like deck gear, takes a terrific amount of abuse and must be repaired constantly. The crew doesn't want to waste a day's fishing because their gear's messed up, so they tend to it on the way out: they sharpen hooks, tie gangions, tie ball drops, set up the leader cart, check the radio buoys. At the Hague Line—where they enter Canadian waters—they must stow the gear in accordance with international law, and are briefly without anything to do. They sleep, talk, watch T.V., and read; there are high school dropouts who go through half a dozen books on the Grand Banks.

Around eight or nine at night the crew squeeze into the galley and shovel down whatever the cook has put together. (Murph is the cook on the *Andrea Gail*; he's paid extra and stands watch while the other men eat.) At dinner the crew talk about what men everywhere talk about—women, lack of women, kids, sports, horseracing, money, lack of money, work. They talk a lot about work; they talk about it the way men in prison talk about time. Work is what's keeping them from going home, and they all want to go home. The more fish they catch, the sooner the trip's over, which is a simple equation that turns them all into amateur marine biologists. After dinner someone takes his turn at the dishes, and Billy goes back up to the wheelhouse so Murph can eat. No one likes washing dishes, so guys sometimes trade the duty for a pack of cigarettes. The longer the trip, the cheaper labor gets, until a $50,000-a-year fisherman is washing dishes for a single smoke. Dinner, at the end of such a trip, might be a bowl of croutons with salad dressing.

Everyone on the crew stands watch twice a day. The shifts

are two hours long and involve little more than watching the radar and occasionally punching numbers into the autopilot. If the gear is out, the night watches might have to jog back onto the mainline to keep from drifting too far away. The *Andrea Gail* has a padded chair in her wheelhouse, but it's set back from the helm so that no one can fall asleep on watch. The radar and loran are bolted to the ceiling, along with the VHF and single sideband, and the video plotter and autopilot are on the control panel to the left. There are nine Lexan windows and a pistol-grip spotlight that protrudes from the ceiling. The wheel is the size of a bicycle tire and positioned at the very center of the helm, about waist high. There's no reason to touch the wheel unless the boat has been taken off autopilot, and there's almost no reason to take the boat off autopilot. From time to time the helmsman checks the engine room, but otherwise he just stares out at sea. Strangely, the sea doesn't get tedious to look at—wave trains converge and crisscross in patterns that have never happened before and will never happen again. It can take hours to tear one's eyes away.

Billy Tyne's been out to the Grand Banks dozens of times before, and he's also fished off the Carolinas, Florida, and deep into the Caribbean. He grew up on Gloucester Avenue, near where Route 128 crosses the Annisquam River, and married a teenaged girl who lived a few blocks away. Billy was exceptional for downtown Gloucester in that he didn't fish and his family was relatively well-off. He ran a Mexican import business for a while, worked for a vault manufacturer, sold waterbeds. His older brother was killed at age twenty-one by a landmine in Vietnam, and perhaps Billy drew the conclusion that life was not something to be pissed away in a bar. He enrolled in school, set his sights on being a psychologist, and started counselling drug-addicted teenagers. He was searching for something, trying out different lives, but nothing seemed to fit. He dropped out of school and started working again, but by then he had a wife and two daughters to support. His wife, Jodi, had been urging him to give fishing a try because she had a cousin whose husband made a lot of money at it. You never know, she told him, you just might like it.

"It was all over after that," says Jodi. "The men don't know anything else once they do it; they love it and it takes over and that's the bottom line. People get possessed with church or God and fishing's just another thing they're possessed with. It's something inside of them that nobody can take away and if they're not doin' it they're not gonna be happy."

It helped, of course, that Billy was good at it. He had an uncanny ability to find fish, a deep sense of where they were. "It was weird—it was like he had radar," says Jodi. "He was one of the few guys who could go out and catch fish all the time. Everyone always wanted to fish with him 'cause he always made money." Tyne's very first trip was on the *Andrea Gail*, and after that he switched over to the *Linnea C.*, owned by a man named Warren Cannon. Tyne and Cannon became close friends and, for eight years, Cannon taught him everything he knew. After his long apprenticeship Tyne decided to go out on his own, and he began to take out the *Haddit*—"that fuckin' Clorox bottle," as Charlie Reed called it. (It was a fiberglass boat.) By this time Tyne was fully hooked; the strains of being at sea had split up his marriage, but he still wouldn't give it up. He moved to Florida to be closer to his ex-wife and daughters, and fished harder than ever.

Every summer Tyne's two daughters, Erica and Billie Jo, went up to Gloucester to visit their grandparents, and Tyne would stop over between trips to see them. He also kept in touch with Charlie Reed, and when Reed stepped down from the *Andrea Gail*, Billy's name came up. Brown offered him a site as skipper of the boat and one-third of the crew share. It was a good deal; a man like Tyne could clear a hundred thousand a year that way. He accepted. In the mean time, Reed got a job on a ninety-foot steel dragger called the *Corey Pride*. He'd make less money, but he'd spend more time at home. "I just couldn't get into the gypsy life anymore," Reed says. "Movin' around, not comin' home three months at a time—I got by, but it was hell on my wife. And I thought I'd made enough to keep all my kids in school. I hadn't, but I thought I had."

THE *Andrea Gail* rides out to the fishing grounds on the back of a high pressure system that comes bulging out of Canada. The winds are out of the northwest and the skies are a deep sharp blue. These are the prevailing winds for the area; they are the reason people say "Down East" when they refer to northeast Maine. Schooners that hauled eastward downwind could be in St. John's or Halifax within twenty-four hours. A 365-horsepower diesel engine makes the effect less pronounced, but heading out is still a shorter trip than heading in. By September 26 or 27, Billy Tyne's around 42 north and 49 west, about 300 miles off the tip of Newfoundland, in a part of the Grand Banks known as the "Tail." Canadian National Waters, which extend two hundred miles offshore, exclude foreign boats from most of the Banks, but two small sections protrude to the northeast and southeast: the Nose and the Tail. Sword boats patrol an arc hinging on a spot around 50 degrees west and 44 degrees north. Inside that arc are the broad, fertile submarine plains of the Grand Banks, off-limits to all but Canadian boats and licensed foreign boats. Outside that arc are thousands of legal swordfish that might conceivably be fooled by a mackerel hung on a big steel hook.

Swordfish are not gentle animals. They swim through schools of fish slashing wildly with their swords, trying to eviscerate as many as possible; then they feast. Swordfish have attacked boats, pulled fishermen to their deaths, slashed fishermen on deck. The scientific name for swordfish is *Xiphias gladius;* the first word means "sword" in Greek and the second word means "sword" in Latin. "The scientist who named it was evidently impressed by the fact that it had a sword," as one guidebook says.

The sword, which is a bony extension of the upper jaw, is deadly sharp on the sides and can grow to a length of four or five feet. Backed up by five hundred pounds of sleek, muscular fish, the weapon can do quite a bit of damage. Swordfish have been known to drive their swords right through the hulls of boats. Usually this doesn't happen unless the fish has been hooked or harpooned, but in the nineteenth century a swordfish attacked a clipper ship for no apparent reason. The ship was so badly damaged that the owner applied to his insurer for compensation, and the whole affair wound up in court.

Grand Banks swordfish spawn in the Caribbean and then edge northward during the summer months, heading for the cold, protein-rich waters off Newfoundland. During the daylight hours the fish work their way down the water column to depths of 3,000 feet, chasing squid, hake, cod, butterfish, bluefish, mackerel, menhaden, and bonito, and at night they follow their prey back up to the surface. Their young hatch with scales and teeth, but no sword, and have been described as "wistful-looking." Although all manner of fish feed on larval swordfish, only mako, sperm whale, and killer whale attack them when they're fully grown. Mature swordfish are considered to be one of the most dangerous game fish in the world and have been known to fight non-stop for three or four hours. They have sunk small boats in their struggles. Sport fishermen need live bait on heavy steel hooks that are secured to 500-pound test steel wire or chain to catch swordfish; they also need a "numbing club" on board to beat the fish senseless. Commercial fishermen, who are in the business of avoiding the thrill of fishing, use different methods entirely. They hang a thousand baited hooks on forty miles of monofilament and then crawl into bed to get some sleep.

Bob Brown doesn't know when Billy makes his first set because Billy hates talking to him on the radio. He's been known to leave messages with Linda Greenlaw in order not to talk to Bob Brown; he's been known to fake static on the single sideband. But it's reasonable to assume that on the night of September 27th, Tyne's making his first set of the trip. The boat's outriggers are boomed out and two steel plates, known as "birds," hang by chain down into the water to provide stability. The ocean has already settled into the galloping darkness of mid-autumn, and the wind has swung around to the southeast. The surface of the ocean is cross-hatched with changing weather.

Baiting has all the glamour of a factory shift and considerably more of the danger. The line is spooled on a big Lindegren drum that sits under the shelter of the whaleback on the port side of the boat. It crosses diagonally over the deck, passes through an overhead block, and then bends straight back toward the stern. A steel ring guides it over the rail and into the water. That's where the baiters stand. There's a bait table on top of the stern rail—basically a wooden well with squid and mackerel in it—and a leader cart on either side. The leader carts are small drums spooled with hundreds of lengths of seven-fathom line, called gangions. Each gangion has a #10 hook at one end and a stainless steel snap on the other.

The baiter reaches behind him and takes a gangion from his back-up man, who's peeling them off the leader cart one at a time. The baiter impales a squid or mackerel onto the hook, snaps the gangion onto the mainline, and throws the whole thing over the side. The hook is easily big enough to pass through a man's hand, and if it catches some part of the baiter's body or clothing, he goes over the side with it. For this reason, baiters have complete control over the hook; no one handles the gangion while they're on it. There's also a knife holstered to the baiting table. A baiter might, conceivably, grab it fast enough to sever the line before going over.

Since swordfish feed at night, each hook is also fixed with a Cylume lightstick that illuminates the bait. Cylumes are cigar-sized plastic tubes with phosphorescent chemicals inside them that activate when the tube is snapped in half. They cost a dollar apiece, and a sword boat might go through five thousand in a trip. The hooks and lightsticks are spaced about thirty feet apart, but the exact interval is determined by the speed of the boat. If the captain wants to fish the hooks closer together, he slows down; if he wants to spread them apart, he speeds up. The typical speed for setting-out on the Grand Banks is six or seven knots. At that speed it takes about four hours to set out thirty miles of line.

Every three hooks the baiter snaps on a ball drop, which floats on the surface and keeps the longline from sinking to the bottom. A typical arrangement is to hang your line at five fathoms and dangle your hooks to twelve—that's about 70 feet down. Depending on currents and the temperature breaks, that's where swordfish like to feed. Every four miles, instead of a ball drop, the baiter clips on a highflyer. The highflyer is a float and aluminum pole with a radar-reflecting square on top. It bobs along on the surface of the ocean and shows up very clearly on the radar screen. Finally, every eight miles, a radio transmitter is attached. It has a big whip antenna that broadcasts a low-frequency signal back to the boat. This allows the captain to track the gear down if it parts off mid-string.

A fully-baited longline represents a significant amount of money, and captains have been known to risk the lives of their crew to get them back. Forty miles of monofilament line goes for $1,800. Each of the radio beacon buoys costs $1,800, and there are six of them on a longline. The polyballs cost six dollars apiece and are set every three hooks for one thousand hooks. The hooks are a dollar, the lightsticks are a dollar, the squid is a dollar, and the gangions are two dollars. Every night, in other words, a sword boat drops $20,000 worth of gear into the North Atlantic. One of the biggest disputes on a sword boat is whether to set out or not. Crews have hauled in a full gale because their captain misjudged the weather.

The baiting usually gets finished up late in the evening,

and the *Andrea Gail* crew hangs their rain gear in the tool room and tramps into the kitchen. They eat dinner quickly, and when they're done, Billy climbs up the companionway to take over the helm from Murph. He checks his loran bearings, which fix him on the chart, and the video plotter, which fixes him in relation to the mainline. The radar is always on and has a range of fifteen miles or so; the highflyers on the mainline register as small squares on the screen. The VHF is tuned to channel 16, and the single sideband is tuned to 2182 megahertz. They are both emergency channels, and if two boats need to communicate, they contact each other and switch to a separate working channel.

At 11 PM the National Oceanic and Atmospheric Administration (NOAA) broadcasts a weather forecast, and the captains generally check in with each other afterward to discuss its finer points. By then most of the crew has already turned in—they're into a stretch of twenty 20-hour work days, and sleep becomes as coveted as cigarettes. The bunks are bolted against the tapered sides of the bow, and the men fall asleep listening to the diesel engine and the smack of waves against the hull. Underwater, the prop whine and the cavitation of hundreds of thousands of air bubbles radiate outward into the ocean. The sound wraps around the foreshores of Newfoundland, refracts off the temperature discontinuity of the Gulf Stream, and dissipates into the crushing black depths beyond the continental shelf. Low frequency vibrations propagate almost forever underwater, and the throb of the *Andrea Gail's* machinery must reach just about every life form on the Banks.

DAWN at sea, a grey void emerging out of a vaster black one. "The earth was without form and darkness was upon the face of the deep." Whoever wrote that knew the sea—knew the pale emergence of the world every morning, a world that contained absolutely nothing, not one thing.

A long blast on the airhorn.

The men stagger out of their bunks and pour themselves coffee under the fluorescent lights of the galley, squinting through swollen lids and bad moods. They can just start to make out shapes on deck when they go out. It's cold and raw, and under their slickers they have sweat shirts and flannel shirts and thermal tops. Dawn's not for another hour, but they start work as soon as they can see anything. At 43 degrees north, a week after the equinox, that's 5:30 in the morning.

The boat is at the start of the mainline, about one hundred miles outside Canada's territorial limit. You generally set into the Gulf Stream and haul into the Gulf Stream, so the previous afternoon they'd set the gear while steaming west into the warm four-knot current. Then they'd turned around and headed east again, back to the start of the mainline. That gives the entire string the same amount of time in the water, and also keeps the boat from losing too much ground to the eastward currents. Billy has hunted down the beginning of the mainline with the radio beacon signals and now sits, bow toward America, ready to haul.

Haulback is less dangerous than setting-out because the hooks are coming in-board rather than going out-board, but the mainline still gets pulled at considerable velocity out of the water. The hooks can whiplash over the rail and snag people in all kinds of horrible ways; one crewman took a hook in the face that entered under his cheekbone and came out his eye socket. To make matters worse, the boat is rarely a stable platform, and rarely dry. Keeping one's feet while eighteen inches of deck slop pour out the scuppers can require the balance of an ironworker in a sleet storm.

Nevertheless, you're hauling up your lottery ticket, and even the most jaded deckhand wants to know what he's hit. The line has been unhooked from the stern guide-ring and now comes onboard through a cut-out in the starboard rail and into the overhead block. The captain steers the boat from an auxiliary helm on deck and runs up to the wheelhouse from time to time to check the radar for other boats in their path. The man at the line is called the hauler, and it's his job to unclip the gangions and hand them back to the coiler, who pulls the bait off and wraps them around the leader cart. Being a hauler is a high-stress job; one hauler described having to pry his fingers off the hydraulic lever at the end of the day because he was so tense. Haulers are paid extra for the trip and are chosen because they can unclip a gangion every few seconds for four hours straight.

A hooked swordfish puts a tell-tale heaviness in the line, and when the hauler feels that, he eases off on the hydraulic lever to keep the hook from tearing out. As soon as the fish is within reach, two men swing gaff hooks into his side and drag him on board. If the fish is alive, one of the gaffers might harpoon him and haul him up on a stouter line to make sure he doesn't get away. Then the fish just lays there eyes bulging, mouth working open and shut. If it's a good haul there are sometimes three or four half-dead swordfish sloshing back and forth in the deck wash, bumping into the men as they work. A puncture wound by a swordfish bill means a severe and nearly instantaneous infection. As the fish are brought on board their heads and tails are sawn off, and they're gutted and put on ice in the hold.

Mako shark eat pretty much what swordfish do, so occasionally longliners haul mako up as well. They're dangerous, though: A mako once bit Murph so badly that he had to be helicoptered back to shore. (Touching even a severed mako head can trigger it to bite.) The rule for mako is that they're not considered safe until they're on ice in the hold. For that reason some boats don't allow live mako on board; if one is caught, the gaffer pins him against the hull while another crew member blows his head open with a shotgun. Then he's hauled on board and gutted. "We fish too far out to take any chances," says a former crew member of the *Hannah Boden*. "You're out of helicopter range, and help is two days' drive to the west'ard. If you're still alive when we get there, we'll take you to a Newfoundland hospital. And then your troubles have just begun."

A longliner might pull up ten or twenty swordfish on a good day, one ton of meat. The most Bob Brown has ever heard of anyone catching was five tons a day for seven days—70,000 pounds of fish. That was on the *Hannah Boden* in the mid-eighties. The lowest crew member made ten thousand dollars. That's why people fish; that's why they spend ten months a year inside seventy feet of steel plate.

For every trip like that, though, there's a dozen busts. Fish are not distributed equally throughout the water column; they congregate in certain areas. You have to know where those areas are. You generally set westward into the current. With a thermocline scope you get temperature readings at different depths; with a Doppler you get the velocity and direction of subsurface currents at three different levels. You want to set in "fast water" because the gear covers more area. You might anchor one end of the gear in cold water, which moves more slowly, because then you know where to find it. You want to hang the bait between layers of warm and cold water because the food chain tends to collect there. Squid feed on cold-water plankton, and swordfish dart out of pockets of warm Gulf Stream water to feed on the squid. Warm-water eddies that spin off the Gulf Stream into the North Atlantic are particularly good places to fish; captains track them down with daily surface temperature maps from NOAA weather satellites. Finally, you want to avoid the dark of the moon when you plan your trips. No one knows why, but for several days before and after, the fish refuse to feed.

Sword boat captains are required by law to keep records of every position fished, every set made, every fish caught. Not only does this help determine whether the boat is adhering to federal regulations, but it allows marine biologists to assess the health of the swordfish stock. Migratory patterns, demographic shifts, mortality rates—it can all be inferred from catch logs. In addition, observers for the National Marine

Fisheries Service occasionally accompany boats offshore to get a better understanding of the industry they're charged with regulating. On August 18, 1982, the principal planner for the Massachusetts Coastal Zone Management Program, Joseph Pelczarski, left on such a trip. He steamed out of New Bedford aboard the *Tiffany Vance,* a California longliner that was going to try gillnetting off Georges Bank. (The gillnet was new to the East Coast and Pelczarski wanted to see how it worked.) Spotter planes, as it turned out, reported almost no swordfish on Georges, but infrared satellite imagery revealed an enormous warm water eddy at the Tail of the Banks. Alex Bueno, the ship's captain, decided to try longlining up north, and Pelczarski went with him. Pelczarski's account had almost no impact on gillnet regulations—they made just one set and caught just one fish—but it gave government biologists and statisticians one of their few glimpses of life on a longliner:

> The F/V *Tiffany Vance* arrived in Shelburne, Nova Scotia at first light on August 21. We left that afternoon at 5:30 P.M. with fuel and supplies and were escorted out of the harbor by dolphins riding the bow wake. Two Spanish fishing vessels (a crewman on the *Tiffany Vance* was from Spain) were sighted heading west. Numerous container vessels were seen heading towards Canada. We arrived on the Tail of the Banks on August 25. The water temperature was constantly monitored for "edges" where cold and warm water meet. On August 26, the captain found good water as well as an open area among the other swordfish longliners, and we were to set that evening. The set-out took an hour and a half and five hundred hooks were used.
>
> Haulback began at 5:10 A.M. with the pulling on board of the highflyer and radio beacon. Yankee hooks and traps were coiled and boxed as they came on board and monofilament hooks were wound on reels. The captain steering and throttling the boat fishes the longline for "weight." The first fish was a swordfish. With its bill breaking the water surface and then rolling on its back, dead, it was hauled to the vessel on the longline.

Gaffed, it is pulled aboard, its sword sawed off and the fish is cleaned. The crew checks the stomach contents and feels the internal body temperature for clues as to what type of water the fish has been in. Most of the swordfish were feeding on squid.

The next two days of fishing took place in the same general area south of the Tail of the Banks. On the second day we caught eleven swordfish, four blue sharks, one mako shark, one sea turtle (released alive) and one skate. We kept the mako in addition to the swordfish. The third day during set-out we had a gear conflict. Despite efforts by captains to establish berths and to contact all area boats on gear positions, we crossed a longline. Our vessel's stabilizers, which hang from outriggers about 18 feet below the surface, caught on a longline. The port stabilizer held fast but the starboard stabilizer, which is composed of lead and steel, left the water and slammed into the bait box just inches from a seaman.

To escape gear conflicts and the increased traffic, we moved northeast over the Newfoundland seamounts. The next fishing day, August 30-31, was fairly routine. The captain set out a lesser number of hooks (300) because the water wasn't quite right (flat water). Despite this we caught nine swordfish. During haulback we lost the gear for an hour due to the mainline parting. After haulback the captain, in order to find better waters, steamed all night and into the northeast approximately 170 miles towards the Flemish Cap. Whales were seen in the distance. On September 4 we set out 400 hooks and the catch consisted of twelve swordfish, one mako shark, three lancetfish, three skates, one blue shark and a leatherback turtle, which was released alive.

On the night of September 5, the captain rendezvoused with the swordfish vessel *Andrea Gail* so I could get home. The vessels tied stern-to-stern and transferred my gear on a second line. Then the vessels untied and the *Andrea Gail* aligned her starboard side to the stern of the *Tiffany Vance*, and I swam the 30 yards to the *Andrea Gail*. They pulled me on board, and two days later we landed at the port of Burin, Newfoundland. The owner of the *Andrea Gail*, Robert Brown, who flew to Newfoundland to replace malfunctioning generators, flew us home to Beverly Airport on September 9, 1982. The *Tiffany Vance* arrived in New Bedford on October 18—sixty-three days at sea with 25,000 pounds of swordfish.

Swordfish fishermen, in particular the Grand Banks fishermen, are at sea for extended periods of time without communication with the mainland. An opportunity to study short-term culture shock is available among these fishermen, and should be undertaken.

Through the end of September and the first week in October the crew of the *Andrea Gail* set out their gear, steam back, haul it up, and set it out again. The days are hot and the men are in t-shirts on deck, their skin curing to a salt-streaked brown in the afternoon sun. In the evening they put on jackets and sweatshirts and work the bait table with their hoods pulled up. The light angles and reddens and finally sinks into darkness with the decklights ruining the stars and the sharp cold air digging at memories of the New England fall. Around ten o'clock the men finish up and pitch into their bunks for a few hours sleep.

To a fisherman, the Grand Banks are as distinct and recognizable as, say, the Arizona deserts or the swamps of Georgia. They have their own particular water, light, wildlife, "feel." No bluewater fisherman could ever wake up on the Grand Banks and think he was off Georges, say, or Long Island. Cliffs of fog move in and smother the boats for weeks at a time. Winter cold fronts come howling down off the Canadian Shield and make the water smoke. The sea is so rich with plankton that it turns a dull green-grey and swallows light rather than reflects it. Petrels and shearwaters circle the boats hundreds of miles from land. Great skuas swoop over the waters, rasping *hah-hah-hah* at their empty world. Prehistoric-looking creatures called beaked whales spook the crews of fog-bound boats. Killer whales range up and down the longlines eating—strangely enough—only the pectoral fins of blue sharks.

Billy's fishing about two hundred miles east of the Tail,

near a set of shallows known as the Newfoundland Seamounts. On the horizon he can occasionally make out the white pilothouse of a boat called the *Mary T,* captained by a Florida man named Albert Johnston. Johnston and Billy fish end for end for about a week, setting their gear southwestward in two great parallel lines. The lines stitch back and forth across slight temperature breaks to anchor the gear in the slower-moving cold water. From time to time they see each other during the haul-back, but mostly they're just snowy images on each other's radar screens. Sword boats on the high seas don't socialize much. One would think they would—my God, all that emptiness—but generally they'd rather socialize in a barroom or in bed with their wives. (A waterfront joke: What's the second thing a fisherman does when he gets home? Puts down his bags.) Captains have been known to pull one steel bird out of the water on the trip home just because it slows them down by half a knot. Over the course of a week that means twelve more hours until they get home.

Four or five days into October, Johnston hauls his last set and tells the rest of the fleet he's heading in. He says he'll radio the weather conditions back as he goes. The boat rolls along atop an old decayed swell, and the crew catch up on their sleep and take turns at the helm. A new moon rises behind them on October 7th, and they follow its pale suggestion all through the day until late that afternoon. The sunset is a bloody rust-red on a sharp autumn horizon, and the night comes in fast with a northwest wind and a sky rivetted with stars. There's no sound but the smack of water on steel and the heavy gargle of the diesel engine. The *Mary T* makes port in Fairhaven, Massachusetts, on October 12th, after more than a month at sea.

Fairhaven is a smaller version of New Bedford, which sits half a mile away across the Acushnet River. Both cities are tough, bankrupt little places that never managed to diversify during the century-long decline of the New England fishing industry. If Gloucester is the delinquent kid who's had a few scrapes with the law, New Bedford is the truly mean older brother who's going to kill someone one day. One New Bedford bar was the scene of an infamous gang rape; another was known to employ a Doberman pinscher as a bouncer. A lot of heroin passes through New Bedford, and a lot of swordfishermen get in trouble there. One of Johnston's crew drew a $13,000 check in New Bedford and returned a week later without any shoes.

Johnston ties up at Union Wharf alongside McLean's Seafood and North Atlantic Diesel. McLean's is a battered two-story building with cement floors for draining fishblood and a rabbit-warren of offices upstairs where deals are cut. Dark, wild-haired young men stomp around in rubber boots and shout to each other in Portuguese as they heave fish around the room. With long knives they "loin" the fish—carve the meat off the bones—and then seal it in vacuum bags and load it onto trucks. A good worker can loin a full-sized fish in two minutes. McLean's moves two million pounds of swordfish a year, and a million pounds of tuna. They fly it overseas, ship it around the country, and sell it to the corner store.

Johnston's boat takes most of a day to unload, the next day he settles the accounts and starts fitting the boat out again. Food, diesel, water, ice, repairs, the usual. The faster the turnaround, the better—not only will his crew be more likely to survive New Bedford's charms, but it's getting late in the season to head out to the Grand Banks. The longer you wait, the worse the storms are. "You get in that kind of weather and if anything goes wrong—if a hatch busts off or one of the outriggers gets tangled up—you can really be in trouble," says Johnston. "Some of the guys get to where they feel invincible, but they don't realize that there's a real fine line between what they've seen and what it can get to. I know a guy who lost a 900-foot boat out there. It broke in half and sank with thirty men."

Sure enough, Johnston's still fitting-out when the first ugly weather blows through. It's a double-low that grinds off the coast and cranks the wind around to the southwest. The storm intensifies as it plows out to sea and catches Billy one morning while he's hauling back. The wind is thirty knots and the waves are washing over the deck, but they can't stop working until the gear is in. Late in the morning, they get slammed.

It's a rogue wave: steep, cresting, and maybe thirty feet high. It avalanches over the decks and buries the *Andrea Gail* under tons of water. One moment they're at the hauling station tending the line, the next they're way over on their side. Heavily, endlessly, the *Andrea Gail* rights herself, and Billy brings her around into the weather and checks for damages. The batteries have come out of their boxes down in the engine room, but that's about it. That evening Billy radios Charlie Johnson of the *Seneca* to tell him what happened. Charlie's in Bay Bulls, Newfoundland, getting a crankshaft fixed, and Billy calls him every evening to keep him updated on the fleet. *Jesus, we took a hell of a wave,* Billy says. *We went way over on our side. I didn't think we'd make it back up.*

They discuss the weather and the fishing for a few minutes and then sign off. The story of the wave doesn't sound good to Charlie Johnson—the *Andrea Gail*'s known as a tough little boat and shouldn't go over that easily. Not with a bird in the water and twenty thousand pounds of fish in the hold. "I didn't want to say anything, but it didn't seem right," Johnson says. "You're in God's country out there. You can't make any mistakes."

The *Andrea Gail* fishes east of the Tail for another week and does very poorly, the trip's shaping up to be a total bust. A boat can't stay indefinitely out at sea—supplies run low, the crew gets crazy, the fish get old. They've got to find some fish fast. Around mid-month they pull their gear and steam northeast all night to a set of shallows known as the Flemish Cap. The rest of the fleet is way off to the south and west:

Tommy Barrie on the *Allison,* Charlie Johnson on the *Seneca,* Larry Horn on the *Miss Millie,* Mike Hebert on the *Mr. Simon,* and Linda Greenlaw on the *Hannah Boden.* There's also a 150-foot Japanese longliner named the *Eishin Maru 78.* The *Eishin Maru* is carrying a Canadian Fisheries observer, Judith Reeves, who is the only person on board who has a survival suit or knows how to speak English. The *Mary T* is on her way out, and another boat named the *Laurie Dawn 8* has just arrived in New Bedford to gear-up.

Billy's at 41 degrees west, way out on the edge. He's almost off the fishing charts. The weather has turned raw and blustery and the men work in layers of sweatshirts and overalls and rubber slickers. It's the end of the season, their last chance for a decent trip. They just want to get this thing done.

THE FLEMISH CAP

And I saw as it were a sea of glass mingled with fire . . .

—*Revelation* 15

New Englanders started catching swordfish in the early 1800s by harpooning them from small sailboats and hauling

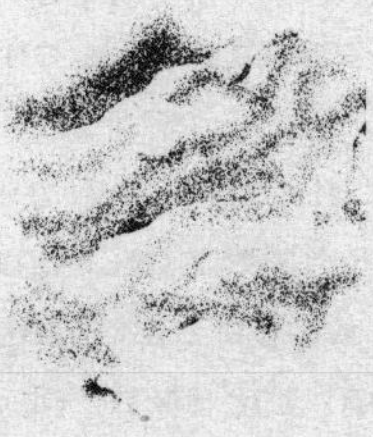

them on board. Since swordfish don't school, the boats would go out with a man up the mast looking for single fins lolling about in the glassy inland waters. If the wind sprang up, the fins were undetectable, and the boats went in. When the lookout spotted a fish, he guided the captain over to it, and the harpooner made his throw. The throw had to take into account the roll of the boat, the darting of the fish, and the refraction of light through water. Giant bluefin tuna are still hunted this way, but fishermen use spotter planes to find their prey and electric harpoons to kill them. Giant bluefin are a delicacy in Japan; they are air-freighted over and get up to eighty dollars a pound. A single bluefin might go for thirty or forty thousand dollars.

Spotter planes were introduced to New England fishermen in 1962, but it was the longline that really changed the fishery. For years the Norwegians had caught mako on longlines, along with a few swordfish, but they had never gone after swordfish exclusively. Then, in 1961, Canadian fishermen made some alterations to the gear and nearly tripled the total northeastern sword catch. The boom didn't last long, though; ten years later the U.S. Food and Drug Administration determined that swordfish carried a dangerous amount of mercury in them, and both the American and Canadian governments banned sale of the fish. Some longliners went out after swordfish anyway, but they risked having their catch seized and tested by the F.D.A.

Finally, in 1978, the U.S. government relaxed the standards for acceptable mercury contamination in fish, and the gold rush was on. In the interim fishing had changed, though; boats were using satellite navigation, electronic fish finders, temperature-depth gauges. Radar reflectors were used to track gear, and new monofilament made it possible to set thirty or forty miles of line at a time. By the mid-eighties, the U.S. swordfish fleet alone was up to 700 boats fishing around fifty million hooks a year. "The technological change appears to be bumping up against the limits of the resource," as one government study put it at the time.

Until then the fishery had been relatively unregulated, but a new drift-entanglement net in the early eighties finally got the wheels of bureaucracy turning. The nets were a mile long, ninety-feet wide, and set out all night from the stern of a converted longliner. Although the large mesh permitted juveniles to escape, the National Marine Fisheries Service was still leery of its impact on the swordfish population. They published a management plan for the North Atlantic swordfish that suggested numerous regulatory changes, including limiting the use of drift nets, and invited responses from state and federal agencies, as well as individual fishermen. A series of public hearings were held up and down the East Coast throughout 1983 and 1984, and fishermen who couldn't attend—those who were fishing, in other words—sent in letters. One of the people who responded was Bob Brown, who explained in a barely-legible scrawl that he'd made fifty-two sets that year and there seemed to be plenty of mature fish out there, they just stayed in colder water than people realized. Alex Bueno of the *Tiffany Vance* wrote a letter pointing out, among other things, that draggers weren't likely to switch over to drift nets because they cost too much, and that swordfish population estimates were inaccurate because they didn't take into account fish outside the two-hundred-mile limit. Sportsfishermen accused commercial fishermen of raping the oceans, commercial fishermen accused sportsfishermen of squandering a resource, and almost everyone accused the government of gross incompetence.

In the end, the Fishery Management Plan did not include a catch quota for Atlantic swordfish, but it required all sword boats to register with the National Marine Fisheries Service, a division of the Department of Commerce. Boat owners who had never swordfished in their lives scrambled for permits just to keep their options open, and the number of boats nearly doubled while, by all indications, the swordfish stock continued to decline. From 1987 to 1991, the total North Atlantic swordfish catch went from 45 million pounds to 33 million pounds, and their average size dropped from 165 pounds to 110. This was what resource management experts know as *tragedy of the commons,* a reference to overgrazing in eighteenth-century England. "In the case of common grazing areas," explained one fisheries-management pamphlet, "grass soon disappeared as citizens put more and more sheep on the land. There was little incentive to conserve or invest in the resource because others would then benefit without contributing."

That was happening throughout the fishing industry: haddock landings had plummeted to one-fiftieth of what they were in 1960, cod landings had dropped by a factor of four. The culprit—as it almost always has been in fishing—was a sudden change in technology. New quick-freeze techniques allowed boats to work halfway around the world and process their fish as they went, and this made the three-mile limit around most countries completely ineffectual. Enormous Russian factory ships put to sea for months at a time and scoured the bottom with nets that could take thirty tons of fish in a single haul. They fished practically within sight of the American coast, and within years the fish populations had been staggered by fifty-percent losses. Congress had to take action, and in 1976 they passed the Magnuson Fishery Conservation and Management Act, which extended our national sovereignty to two hundred miles offshore. Most other nations quickly followed suit.

Of course, the underlying concern wasn't for fish populations, it was for the American fleet. Having chased out the competition, America set about constructing an industry that could scrape Georges Bank just as bare as any Russian factory ship. After the passage of the Magnuson Act, American fishermen could take out federally-guaranteed loans and set themselves up for business in quarter-million dollar steel boats. To make matters worse, the government established eight regional fishing councils that were exempt from conflict-of-interest laws. In theory, this should have put fisheries management in the hands of the people who fished. In reality, it showed the fox into the chicken coop.

Within three years of Magnuson, the New England fleet had doubled to 1,300 boats. Better equipment resulted in such huge takes that prices dropped and fishermen had to resort to more and more devastating methods just to keep up. Draggers raked the bottom so hard that they actually levelled outcrops and filled in valleys—the very habitats where fish thrived. A couple of good years in the mid-eighties masked the overall decline, but the end was near, and many people knew it. The first time anyone—at least any fisherman—suggested a closure was in 1988, when a Chatham fisherman named Mark Simonitsch stood up to speak at a New England Fisheries Council meeting. Simonitsch had fished off Cape Cod his whole life; his brother, James, was a marine safety consultant who had worked for Bob Brown. Both men knew fishermen, knew fish, and knew where things were headed.

Simonitsch suggested that Georges Bank be closed to all fishing, indefinitely. He was shouted down, but it was the beginning of the end.

The swordfish population didn't crash as fast as some others, but it crashed all the same. By 1988, the combined North Atlantic fleet was fishing over one hundred million hooks a year, and catch logs were showing that the swordfish population was getting younger and younger. Finally, in 1990, the International Commission for the Conservation of Tunas suggested a fishing quota for the North Atlantic swordfish. The following year the National Marine Fishery Service implemented a quota of 6.9 million pounds of dressed swordfish for U.S.-licensed sword boats, roughly two-thirds of the previous year's catch. Every U.S.-licensed boat had to report their catch when they arrived back in port, and as soon as the overall quota was met, the entire fishery was shut down. In a good year the quota might be met in September; in bad years it might not be met at all. The result was that not only were fishing boats now racing the season, they were racing each other. When the *Andrea Gail* left port on September 23, she was working under a quota for the first time in her life.

Albert Johnston has the *Mary T* back out on the fishing grounds by October 17th and his gear in the water that night. He's a hundred miles south of the Tail, right on the edge of the Gulf Stream, around 41 north and 51 west. He's after big-eye tuna and doing really well—"muggin' 'em," as swordfishermen say. One night they lose $20,000 worth of big-eye to a pod of killer whales, but otherwise they're pulling in four or five thousand pounds of fish a night. That's easily enough to make a trip in ten sets. They're in the warm Gulf Stream water and the rest of the fleet's off to the east. "At that time of the year it's nice to fish down by the Gulf," Johnston says. "You get a little less bad weather—the lows tend to ride the jetstream off to the north. You could still get the worst storm there ever was, but the average weather's a little better."

Like most of the other captains out there, Johnston started commercial fishing before he could drive. He was running a boat by age nineteen and bought his first one at twenty-nine. Now, at thirty-six, he has a wife and two children and a small business back in Florida. He sells fishing tackle to commercial boats. There comes a point in every boat owner's life—after the struggles of his twenties, the terror of the initial investment—when he realizes he can relax a bit. He doesn't need to take late-season trips to the Banks, doesn't need to captain the boat month in and month out. At thirty-six, it's time to start letting the younger guys in, guys who have little more than a girlfriend in Pompano Beach and a pile of mail at the Crow's Nest Inn.

Of course, there's also the question of odds. The more you go out, the more likely you are never to come back. The dangers are numerous and random: the rogue wave that wipes you off the deck; the hook and leader that catches your palm; the tanker that plots a course through the center of your boat. The only way to guard against these dangers is to stop rolling the dice, and the man with a family and business back home is more likely to do that. More people are killed on fishing boats, per capita, than in any other job in the United States. Johnston would be better off parachuting into forest fires or working as a cop in New York City than longlining off the Flemish Cap. Johnston knows many fishermen who have died and more than he can count who have come horribly close. It's there waiting for you in the middle of a storm or on the most cloudless summer day. Boom—the crew's looking the other way, the hook's got you, and suddenly you're down at the depth where swordfish feed.

Back in 1983, a friend of Johnston's ran into a fall gale in an 87-foot boat called the *Canyon Explorer.* Three lows merged off the coast and formed one massive storm that blew one hundred knots for a day and a half. The seas were so big that Johnston's friend had to goose the throttle just to keep from sliding backward down their faces. The boat was forced sixty miles backward—despite driving full-steam ahead—because the whole surface of the ocean had been set in motion. At one point the captain glanced out the window and saw an enormous wave coming at them. Hey Charlie, look at this! he shouted to another crew member who was down below. Charlie sprinted up the companionway but didn't get to the wheelhouse in time; the wave bore down on them, slate-colored and foaming, and blew the wheelhouse windows out.

That happened to be a particularly severe storm, and it devastated the rest of the fleet. A boat named the *Lady Alice* had her wheelhouse knocked in and a crew member paralyzed for life. The *Tiffany Vance,* which had just transferred fisheries observer Joseph Pelczarski to the *Andrea Gail* the week before, nearly went down with her sister ship, the *Rush.* The two boats were a mile apart when the storm hit, way out on the Flemish Cap, and both lost their port-side stabilizing birds. The bird on the *Tiffany Vance* was hung from chain, and without two hundred pounds of steel to keep it down, the chain started slamming against the boat. It had to be cut; Alex Bueno, the captain, stripped to his underwear, tied a rope around his waist and waded out onto the deck with a welding torch. There was so much water coming over the deck that he had trouble keeping the torch lit. He finally managed to burn the chain free, and then he went back inside and waited for the boat to sink. "We didn't even bother calling the Coast Guard, we were just too far out," he says. "There's really nothing to do but rely on the other guys around you."

Unfortunately, the *Rush* was in even more trouble than the *Tiffany Vance.* She had cable on her birds instead of chains, and the broken cable managed to wrap itself around the drive shaft and freeze the propeller. The boat went dead in the water and immediately turned side-to in the waves—in "a beam sea," as it's called. A boat in a beam sea can count her future in hours, maybe minutes. Wayne Rushmore, her captain, got on the radio and told Bueno he was going down and needed help, but Bueno radioed back that he was going down, too. The *Rush's* crew went back out on deck and, taking extraordinary risks, managed to pull the cable free of the propeller. For the next several days the two boats rode the storm out side by side; at one point the sun came out, and Bueno noticed that the larger waves put his wheelhouse in shadow. They blocked out the sun.

BY ALL reports, Billy's having a terrible trip. After fourteen sets he only has about 20,000 pounds of fish in the hold, which is barely enough to cover expenses, much less compensate six men for a month of their life. When Linda Greenlaw arrives on the fishing grounds Billy tells her that he's disgusted and is going to need more fuel if they want to make any money at all. Sword boats lend each other supplies all the time on the high seas, but Billy has a particular reputation for pushing things to the limit. This is not the first time Linda has bailed him out. The two boats rendezvous south of the Flemish Cap, and Linda drops a tow line and refuelling hose over the side. Billy comes up bow to stern and ties off the tow line, and the boats chug along, the *Hannah Boden* pulling the *Andrea Gail*, while the fuel gets pumped into Billy's tanks. It's a dangerous maneuver—with any other boat, Bob Brown would insist that Linda just tie floats to fuel drums and drop them over the side—but sister ships are a different matter. They'll do almost anything to give themselves an edge over the rest of the fleet. When they're finished, Linda hauls her lines back and the two crews wave goodbye as the boats draw apart. Half an hour later they're just white squares on each other's radar screens.

The fuel is just the beginning of Billy's problems, though. Throughout the trip he's been having trouble getting the ice machine to work properly. Ordinarily it's supposed to pump out three tons of ice a day, but the compressor is malfunctioning and cannot even handle half that. Day by day, in other words, the quality of the fish is starting to drop; a loss of just fifty cents a pound would mean $20,000 off the value of the catch. That could only be offset by catching more fish, which in turn means staying out even longer. It's a classic cost-benefit dilemma that fishermen have agonized over for centuries.

And then there's the crew. They get ugly at about the same rate as badly-iced fish. By the end of a long trip they may be picking fights with one another, hoarding food, ostracizing the new members—acting, in short, like men in prison, which in some ways they are. There are stories of sword boats coming into port with crew members manacled to their bunks or tied to the headstay with monofilament line. It's a kind of Darwinism that keeps the boats stocked with rough, belligerent men who have already established themselves in the hierarchy. Billy would never permit that sort of viciousness on his boat—the crew are all friends, more or less, and he intends to keep it that way—but he knows you can lock six men together for only so long before someone gets crazy. They've been at sea three weeks and are looking at a minimum of two more. If they're going to salvage anything from the trip, they've got to catch some fish in a hurry.

Billy keeps talking with the other captains, studying surface temperature charts, analyzing the water column with his Doppler. He's looking for that temperature discontinuity, that concentration of plankton, mackerel, and squid. In five good sets they could turn this trip around. He knows it. Ice or no ice, he's not going back in until they do.

BILLY TYNE has the only private room on the *Andrea Gail*, which is standard for the captain. On some boats the captain's quarters are upstairs behind the bridge, but Billy's is in a small room next to the head; it's about the size of a private sleeper on an Amtrak train. There's a seabag full of dirty clothes and a few photos taped to the wall. The photos are of his two daughters, Erica and Billie Jo. Seven years ago, when Billie Jo was born, Billy stayed home to take care of her while his wife worked. Billie Jo got used to having a father around and took it hard when he went back on the boat. Erica was born four years later and has never known anything different; as far as she's concerned, fathers are men who go away for weeks at a time and come home smelling of fish.

The rest of the crew are wedged into a dark little room across from the galley. The bunks are stacked along the inner wall and the starboard hull, and the floor is covered with the detritus that accumulates around young men—clothes, cassette tapes, beer cans, cigarettes, magazines. Along with the magazines are dozens of books, including a few ragged paperbacks by Dick Francis. Francis writes about horse racing, which seems to appeal to swordfishermen because it's another way to win or lose huge amounts of money. The books get passed around the fleet "at about four hundred miles an hour," as one swordfisherman put it, and they've probably been to the Grand Banks more times than the men themselves. Most fishermen tape photos of their girlfriends to the wall, alongside pages ripped from *Penthouse* and *Playboy,* and the crew of the *Andrea Gail* are undoubtedly no different.

The galley is the largest room on the boat, other than the fish hold. At first glance it could almost be a kitchen in a house trailer: wood veneer, fluorescent panel lights, cheap wood cabinets. There's a four-burner gas stove, an industrial stainless-steel refrigerator, and a Formica table angled into the forward wall. A bench runs along the length of the port side, and there's a single porthole above the bench. It's too small for a man to wiggle out of. A door at the aft end of the galley exits into a small holding area and a companionway that goes down into the engine room. The companionway is protected by a watertight door that screws down securely with four steel dogs. The fo'c'sle and pilothouse doors are watertight as well; in theory, the entire forward end of the boat can be sealed off, with the crew inside.

The engine, an eight-cylinder, 365-horsepower turbocharged diesel, is slightly more powerful than the largest tractor-trailer rigs on the highway. The engine was refurbished in 1989 because the boat flooded at dock after a discharge pipe froze, cracking the weld. The engine drives a propellor shaft that runs through a cut-out in the aft bulkhead of the compartment and through the fish hold to the stern of the boat. Most boats have a gasket that seals the prop as it passes through the bulkhead, but the *Andrea Gail* does not. This is a weak point; flooding in the fish hold could conceivably slosh forward and kill the engine, crippling the boat.

The machinery room sits just forward of the engine and is crammed with tools, spare parts, lumber, old clothes, a backup generator, and three bilge pumps. The job of the pumps is to lift water out of the hold faster than it comes in; in the old days crews would be at the hand-pumps for days at a stretch, and ships went down when the storms outlasted the men. The tools are stored in metal lock-boxes on the floor and include just about everything you'd need to rebuild the engine—vice grips, pry bar, hammer, crescent wrenches, pipe wrenches, socket wrenches, allen wrenches, files, hacksaw, channel-lock pliers, bolt cutters, ball peen hammer. Spare parts are packed in cardboard boxes and stacked on wooden shelves: Starter motor, cooling pump, alternator, hydraulic hoses and fittings, v-belts, jumper wires, fuses, hose clamps, gasket material, nuts and bolts, sheet metal, silicone rubber, plywood, screw gun, duct tape, lube oil, hydraulic oil, transmission oil, and fuel filters.

Boats try at all costs to avoid going into Newfoundland for repairs. Not only does it waste valuable time, but it costs obscene amounts of money—one infamous repair bill amounted to $50,000 for what should've been a $3,500 job.

(The machinists had reportedly run their lathes at 46 rpms rather than 400 in order to rack up overtime.) As a result, sword boat captains help each other out on the high seas whenever they can; they lend engine parts, offer technical advice, donate food or fuel. The competition between a dozen boats rushing a perishable commodity to market fortunately doesn't kill an inherent sense of concern for each other. This may seem terrifically noble, but it's not—or at least not entirely. It's also self-interested. Each captain knows he may be the next one with the frozen injector or the leaking hydraulics.

Diesel fuel on the *Andrea Gail* is carried in a pair of 2,000-gallon tanks along either side of the engine room, and in two 1,750-gallon tanks at the stern. There are also thirty plastic drums lashed to the whaleback with another 1,650 gallons of fuel. Each one has *AG* painted on them in white lettering. Two thousand gallons of fresh water are stored in two fore-peak tanks, and another 500 gallons or so are stored in drums up on deck, along with the oil. There's also a "water-maker" that purifies saltwater by forcing it through a membrane at 800 pounds per square inch. The membrane is so fine that it even filters out bacteria and viruses. The boat butcher—who is constantly covered in fish guts—gets to shower every day. The rest of the crew showers every two or three.

The fish hold is gained by a single steel ladder that drops steeply down from a hatch in the middle of the deck. During storms, the hatch is covered and lashed down so that big seas can't pry it off—although they still manage to. The hold is divided by plywood penboards that keep the load from shifting; a shifted load can put a boat over on her side and keep her there until she sinks. There's an industrial freezer in the stern where the food is stored, and then another compartment called the lazarette. The lazarette is where the steering mechanism is housed; like the engine room, it's not sealed off from the rest of the boat.

Up on deck, immediately forward of the fish hold, is the

tool room. Six leader carts, spools as big as car tires, are lined up behind the staircase that rises to the whaleback deck. The men hang their foul weather gear along the wall behind the spools, along with anything else that could get swept away on deck. An overhang in the whaleback protects the Lindegren longline reel, and the port-side bulwark has been raised to the height of the whaleback and extended eighteen feet aft. Huddled up against it are bins full of ball drops, high-flyers, radio beacons—everything that hangs off a longline.

At the stern of the boat is the setting-out house, a frame-and-plywood shed that gives some shelter to the men when they're baiting the line. A big sea across the stern might take out the setting-out house; otherwise it would probably be protected by the pilothouse up front. The deck is steel and covered with no-skid tiles. The gunwales are waist-high and have gaps in them, called scuppers, or freeing ports, that allow boarding seas to drain off the deck. The scuppers are normally blocked by scupper-plates that prevent fish and gear from sliding out to sea, but when the weather gets dangerous the plates are taken out. Or should be.

The ability of a boat to clear her decks is one of the most crucial aspects of her design. A boarding sea is like putting a swimming pool on the deck; the boat wallows, loses her steerage, and for a few moments is in extreme danger. One longline fisherman, a Gloucester local named Chris, was almost lost in such a situation. The boat he was on was running down-sea when she took "one wicked sea from hell." The stern lifted, the bow dropped, and they started surfing down the face of the wave. When they got to the bottom there was nowhere to go but down, and the crest of the breaking wave drove them like a piling. Chris looked out the porthole, and all he could see was black.

If you look out the porthole and see whitewater, you're still near the surface and relatively safe. If you see greenwater, at least you're in the body of the wave. If you see blackwater, you're a submarine. "I felt the boat come to a complete stop," says Chris. "I thought, 'My God we're goin' down.' We hung there a moment and then the buoyancy caught and it was as if she'd been thrown into reverse. We plowed right back out the way we came."

Any number of things could have happened to Chris's boat at that moment. The breather pipes could have gotten stuffed and killed the engine. The fish hatch could have given way and filled the hold. A tool could have gotten loose and knocked out some machinery. The wheelhouse windows could have exploded, a bulkhead could have failed, or thirty tons of ice and fish could have shifted in the hold. But even assuming the boat popped up like a cork, she would still be laboring under a crushing load of water. If anything were caught in the scuppers—a hatch cover, an old sleeping bag—the water would have been impeded as it drained off. All it takes is a moment of vulnerability for the next wave to roll you over: props in the air, crew on their ass, cargo avalanching. It's the end.

Every boat has a degree of roll from which she can no longer recover. The *Queen Mary* came within a degree or two of capsizing off Newfoundland when a rogue wave burst her pilothouse windows ninety feet up; she sagged on her beam ends for an agonizing minute before regaining her trim. Two forces are locked in combat for a ship like that: the downward push of gravity and the upward lift of buoyancy. Gravity is the combined weight of the vessel and everything on it—crew, cargo, fishing gear—seeking the center of the earth. Buoyancy is the force of all the enclosed air in the hull trying to rise above water level.

On a trim and stable ship, these two forces are equal and cancel each other out along the centerline; but all this changes when a boat gets shoved over onto her side. Instead of being lined up, the two forces are now laterally offset. The center of gravity stays where it is, but the center of buoyancy migrates to the submerged side, where proportionally more air has been forced below the waterline. With gravity pushing down at the center and buoyancy pushing up from the submerged side, the ship pivots on her center and returns to an even keel. The more the ship heels, the farther apart the two forces act and the more leverage the center of buoyancy has. To greatly simplify, the lateral distance between the two forces is called the *righting arm,* and the torque they generate is called the *righting moment.* Boats want a big righting moment. They want something that will right them from extreme angles of heel.

The righting moment has three main implications. First of all, the wider the ship, the more stable she is. (More air is submerged as she heels over, so the righting arm is that much longer.) The opposite is also true: The taller the ship, the more likely she is to capsize. The high center of gravity reduces what is called the metacentric height, which determines the length of the righting arm. The greater the metacentric height, the less leverage there is with which to overcome the downward force of gravity. Finally, there always comes a point where the boat can no longer right herself. Logically, this would happen when her decks have gone past vertical and the center of gravity falls *outside* the center of buoyancy—the "zero-moment" point. But in reality, boats get into trouble a lot sooner than that. Depending on the design, an angle of about sixty or seventy degrees starts to put a vessel's lee gunwales under water. That means there's greenwater on deck, and the righting moment has that much more weight to overcome. The boat may eventually recover, but she's spending more and more time under water. The deck is subject to the full fury of the waves and a hatch might come loose, a bulkhead might fail, a door might burst open because someone forgot to dog it down. Now she's not just sailing, she's sinking.

The problem with a steel boat is that the crisis curve starts out gradually and quickly becomes exponential. The more trouble she's in, the more trouble she's likely to get in, and the less capable she is of getting out of it, which is an acceleration of catastrophe that is almost impossible to reverse. With the boat's bilge partially flooded, she sits lower in the water and takes more and more prolonged rolls. Longer rolls mean less steerage; lower buoyancy means more damage. If there's enough damage, flooding may overwhelm the pumps and short out the engine or gag its air intakes. With the engine gone, the boat has no steerageway at all and turns broadside to the seas. Broadsides exposes her to the full force of the breaking waves, and eventually a part of her deck or wheelhouse lets go. After that, downflooding starts to occur.

Downflooding is the catastrophic influx of ocean water into the hold. It's a sort of death rattle at sea, the nearly-vertical last leg of an exponential curve. In Portland, Maine, the Coast Guard Office of Marine Safety has a video clip of a fishing boat downflooding off the coast of Nova Scotia. The boat was rammed amidship by another boat in the fog, and the video starts with the ramming boat backing full-screw astern. It's all over in twenty seconds: the crippled vessel settles in her stern, rears bow-up, and then sinks. She goes down so fast that it looks as if she's getting yanked under by some huge hand. The last few moments of the film show the crew diving off the upended bow and trying to swim to the other boat fifty feet away. Half of them make it, half of them don't. They're sucked down by the vacuum of a large steel boat making for the deep.

Very few boats ever get to that point, of course. They might take water in the hold or lose their antennas or windows, but that's it. The result, fortunately, is that their stability limits are rarely tested in a real-life situation. The only way to know the stability profile for each boat is to perform a standard dockside test on her. A 5,000-pound weight is put on deck, ten feet off the centerline, and the resulting angle of heel is run through a standard formula that gives the righting moment. So many things can affect the stability of a boat, though, that even the Coast Guard considers these tests to be of limited value. Load a few tons of gear onto the deck, take a little water in her bilge, shift from longlining to dragging to gillnetting, and the dynamics of the ship change completely. As a result, stability tests are mandatory only for vessels over 79 feet. At deck height, the *Andrea Gail* measures seventy-two.

When the *Andrea Gail* was overhauled in 1986, Bob Brown simply pulled her out of the water and started welding; no stability tests were performed, no marine architect was consulted. In the trade this is known as "eyeball engineering," and it includes the *Andrea Gail* in an overwhelming majority of the commercial fleet that has been altered without plans. The work was done at St. Augustine Trawlers in St. Augustine, Florida; in all, eight tons of machinery and structural changes were added to the boat, including the fuel and water drums on her whaleback deck.

After the work was finished, marine surveyor James Simonitsch—whose brother, Mark, would propose shutting down Georges Bank the following year—flew to Florida to reinspect the *Andrea Gail*. Two years earlier he'd appraised both the *Hannah Boden* and *Andrea Gail* for the settlement of Bob Brown's divorce, and the *Andrea Gail* had been valued at $400,000. Simonitsch surveyed her again in January, 1987, and wrote a letter to Bob Brown with some minor suggestions: Loosen the dogs on one of the watertight doors and provide flotation collars and lights for the survival suits. Otherwise the vessel seemed ship-shape. "The modifications and additional furnishings will increase the vessel's ability to make longer trips and return with a high-quality product," Simonitsch concluded. The question of stability never came up.

In 1990, St. Augustine Shipyards was sold by the Internal Revenue Service for non-payment of taxes. In October of that year Simonitsch visited the *Andrea Gail* in Gloucester and made a few more suggestions: professionally service the six-man life raft, replace a dead battery in the Class B EPIRB, and install a flare kit in the wheelhouse. Again, there was no mention of stability tests, but the vessel was well within the law. Bob Brown also neglected to refile documentation for the *Andrea Gail* after altering her hull, although neither discrepancy was Simonitsch's problem. He was paid to look at a boat and evaluate what he saw. In November, 1990, the principal surveyor for Marine Safety Consultants, Inc., the company that employed Simonitsch, inspected the *Andrea Gail* one last time. "The vessel is well suited for its purpose," he wrote. "Submitted without prejudice, David C. Dubois."

If Billy Tyne were inclined to worry, though, there were a number of things about the *Andrea Gail* that might have given him pause. First of all, according to Tommy Barrie of the *Allison,* she had a boxy construction and a forward wheelhouse that took the seas hard. She was a rugged boat that didn't concede much to the elements. And then there were the St. Augustine alterations. The extended whaleback deck was burdened with the weight of an icemaker and three dozen 55-gallon drums, so her center of gravity had been raised and she would recover from rolls a little more slowly. Only a couple of other boats in the fleet—the *Eagle Eye,* the *Sea Hawk*—store fuel oil on their upper decks. The portside bulwark on the *Andrea Gail* could be a problem, too. It had been raised and extended to protect the fishing gear, but it also tended to hold water on deck. A few years earlier, she'd taken a big sea over the stern and was pushed so far over that her rudder came part-way out of the water. Bob Brown was on board, and he sprinted up to the wheelhouse and put the helm around; at the same moment the boat rode up the face of another big sea. Slowly, the *Andrea Gail* righted herself and cleared her decks; everything was fine except that the bulwark had been flattened like a tin can.

One could argue that if a wave takes a piece of a boat out, maybe it shouldn't be there. Or one could argue that that's just what waves do—tear down what men put up. Either way, the incident was unsettling. Brown blamed it on the inexperience of the man at the helm and said that it was his own quick action that saved the boat. The crew didn't see it that way. They saw a boat pinned on her port side by a mass of water and then righted by freak wave action. In other words, they saw bad luck briefly followed by good. The bulwark was replaced as soon as they got in, and nobody mentioned it again.

Bob Brown's reputation in Gloucester is a complex one. On the one hand he's a phenomenally successful businessman who started with nothing and still works as hard as any crew member on any of his boats. On the other hand, it's hard to find a fisherman in town who has anything good to say about him. Fishing's a marginal business, though, and people don't succeed in it by being well-liked, they succeed by being tough. Some—such as Gloucester fisherman "Hard" Bob Millard—are tough on themselves, and some are tough on their employees. Brown is tough on both. When he was a young man, people called him Crazy Brown because he took such horrific risks, tub-trawling for cod and haddock in an open wooden boat all winter long. He had no radio, loran, or fathometer and worked alone because no one would go with him. He remembers winter days when he had to slide a skiff out across the harbor ice just to get to his mooring. "I had a family to feed and I was intent upon doing that," he says.

Only once in his life did he work for someone else, a six-month stint with a company that was exploring the lobster population on the continental shelf. That was in 1966; three years later he was working two hundred miles offshore in a forty-foot wooden boat. "Never so much as cracked a pane of glass," he says. "Bigger doesn't always mean better." Eventually he was running four or five sword boats out of Gloucester and pulling in hundreds of thousands of dollars a year. One winter he and his son started accumulating ice on deck on their way back from Georges Bank. "If you're making ice on Georges you know you're going to be in real trouble closer to land," he says. "We went back out and that night it blew a hundred from the northwest and snowed. The wind gauge only goes to a hundred and it was pegged for three days straight—pegged like it was broken. We were in a steel boat and it didn't seem so bad, we were comfortable enough. Steel is tough compared to wood, don't let anyone tell you different. Anyone tells you different, they're a romanticist. Steel goes down faster, though. It goes down . . . well, like a load of steel."

The bad feeling between Bob Brown and the town of Gloucester hit bottom in 1980, when Brown lost a man off a boat named the *Sea Fever.* The *Sea Fever* was a fifty-foot wooden boat with a crew of three that was hauling lobster traps off Georges Bank. It was late November and the Weather Service predicted several days of moderate winds, but they were catastrophically wrong. One of the worst storms on record had just drawn a deep breath off the Carolinas. It screamed northward all night and slammed into Georges Bank around dawn, dredging up seventy-foot waves in the weird shallows of the continental shelf. To make matters worse, a crucial offshore data buoy had been malfunctioning for the past two and a half months, and the Weather Service had no idea what was going on out there. The men on the *Sea Fever* and on another boat, the 55-foot *Fair Wind,* woke up to find themselves in a fight for their lives.

The *Fair Wind* got the worse end of the deal. She flipped end over end in an enormous wave and her four crew were trapped in the flooded pilothouse. One of them, a shaggy 33-year-old machinist named Ernie Hazard, managed to gulp some air and pull himself through a window. He burst to the surface and swam to a self-inflating life raft that had popped up, tethered, alongside the boat. The *Fair Wind* continued to founder, hull-up, for another hour, but the rest of the crew never made it out, so Hazard finally cut the tether and set himself adrift. For two days he scudded through the storm, capsizing over and over, until a Navy P-3 jet spotted him and dropped an orange smoke marker. He was picked up by a Coast Guard cutter and then rushed by helicopter to a hospital on Cape Cod. He had survived two days in his underwear on the North Atlantic. Later, when asked how long it took him to warm up after his ordeal, he said, without a hint of irony, "Oh, three or four months."

The *Sea Fever* fared a little better, but not much. She took a huge sea and lost all her windows; the half-inch safety glass burst as if it had been hit by a wrecking ball. The captain, who happened to be Bob Brown's son, turned down-sea to avoid any more flooding, but the wave put them on their beam ends and swept one of the crew out of the wheelhouse and over the side. The man's name was Gary Brown (no relation); while one of the remaining crew scrambled below deck to restart the engine, the other threw a lifesaver overboard to save Brown. It dropped right in front of him but he made no attempt to grab it. Brown just drifted away, a dazed look in his eyes.

The other two men called a mayday, and an hour later a Coast Guard helicopter was pounding overhead in the wild dark. By then the two men on board the *Sea Fever* had righted her and pumped her out. *Do you wish to remain with your vessel, or do you wish to be taken off by hoists?* the helicopter pilot asked over the radio. *We'll stay with the boat,* they radioed back. The pilot lowered a bilge pump and then veered back towards shore because he was running out of fuel. On the way back he turned on his "Night Sun" search light to look for Gary Brown, but all he could see were the foam-streaked waves. Brown had long since gone under.

Four years later, U.S. District Judge Joseph Tauro in Boston ruled that the National Weather Service was negligent in their failure to repair the broken data buoy. Had it been working, he wrote, the Weather Service might have predicted the storm; and furthermore, they failed to warn fishermen that they were making forecasts with incomplete information. This was the first time the government had ever been held responsible for a bad forecast, and it sent shudders of dread through the federal government. Every plane crash, every car accident could now conceivably be linked to weather forecasting. The National Oceanic and Atmospheric

Administration appealed the decision, and it was quickly overturned by a higher court.

None of this was Bob Brown's fault, of course. There's nothing irresponsible about going to Georges in November—he'd done it his whole life, and worse—and the storm was completely unforecast. Moreover, a larger steel-hulled boat sank while the *Sea Fever* remained afloat; that said a lot about her crew and general state of repair. Still, a man had died on one of Bob Brown's boats, and that was all a lot of people needed to know. A story went around about how Bob Brown once spotted the biggest wave of his life—an enormous Grand Banks rogue—and didn't even stop fishing, he just kept hauling his gear. People started calling him "Suicide" Brown, because working for him meant risking your life. And then it happened again.

It was the mid-eighties and boats were making a million dollars a year. Brown was out on the Grand Banks on the *Hannah Boden*, and he found himself having to haul back a full set of gear in a sixty-knot breeze. At one point a wave swept the deck, and when the boat climbed back out of the whitewater, two men had gone overboard. They were wearing rain gear and thigh-high rubber boots and could hardly move in the freezing Newfoundland water. One of them went under immediately, but the other man was smashed back against the hull, and a quick-thinking member of the crew extended a gaff hook over the side for him to grab. The hook went through the man's hand, but the situation was too desperate to worry about it and they hauled him on board anyway. They had to steam four hundred miles just to get him to within helicopter range to be taken to a hospital.

Brown's reputation is no concern of Billy's, though. Brown's not on the boat, he's twelve hundred miles away in Gloucester, and if Billy doesn't want him in his life, he just doesn't pick up the radio mike. Furthermore, Billy's making money hand over fist on his boat, and that makes Brown's scruples—or his judgment—or his lack of empathy—all but irrelevant. All Billy needs is five men, a well-maintained boat, and enough fuel to get to and from the Flemish Cap.

The first five sets of Johnston's trip are on what's called the "frontside" of the moon, the quarters leading up to full. Boats that fish the frontside tend to get small males on the line; boats that fish the backside get large females. Johnston's record is twenty-seven consecutive hooks with a fish on each, mostly small males. On the day of the full moon the catch abruptly switches over to huge females and stays that way for a couple of weeks. "You might go from an average weight of seventy pounds, all males, to four or five 800-pounders, all females," Johnston says. "They lose their heads on the full moon, they feed with reckless abandon."

The full moon is on October 23rd, and Johnston has timed his trip to straddle that date. There are captains who will cut a good trip short just to stay on the lunar cycle. The first four or five sets of Johnston's trip are spare, but then he starts to get into the fish. By the 21st, he's landing six or seven thousand pounds of big-eye a day, enough to make his trip in a week. The weather has been exceptionally good for the season, and Johnston gets on the VHF every night to give the rest of the fleet a quick update. As the western-most boat, the fleet relies on him to decide how much gear to fish. They don't want forty miles of line hanging out there with a storm coming on. On October 22nd, the *Laurie Dawn 8,* a converted oil boat captained by a quiet Texan named Larry Davis, leaves New Bedford for the Grand Banks. She's the last boat of the season to head out to the fishing grounds. The same day a containership named the *Contship Holland* leaves the port of Le Havre, France, for New York City. Her voyage is a classic rhumbline course from the English Channel straight through the fishing grounds. Scattered south of the Flemish Cap are the *Hannah Boden*, the *Allison,* the *Miss Millie,* and the *Seneca.* The *Mary T* and the *Mr. Simon* are southwest of the Tail, right on the edge of the Gulf Stream, and Billy Tyne is nearly six hundred miles to the east.

Billy's been out through the dark of the moon, which may explain his bad luck, but things start to change around the 18th. The whole fleet, in fact, starts to get into a little more fish with the approach of the full moon. Tyne doesn't tell anyone how much he's catching, but he's rapidly making up for three weeks of thin fishing. He's probably pulling in swordfish at the same rate Johnston's pulling in big-eye, five or six thousand pounds a day. By the end of the month he has 40,000 pounds of fish in his hold, worth around $160,000. "I talked with Billy on the 24th and he said he'd hatched his boat," Johnston says. "He was headed in while the rest of us were just starting our trips. You could just tell he was happy."

Billy finishes up his last haul around noon on the 25th and—the crew still stowing their gear—turns his boat for home. They'll be one of the only boats in port with a load of fish, which means a short market and a high price. Captains dream of bringing 40,000 pounds into a short market. The weather is clear, the blue sky brushed with cirrus and a solid northwest wind spackling the waves with white. A long heavy swell rolls under the boat from a storm that passed far off to the south. Billy has a failing ice machine and a twelve hundred mile drive ahead of him. He'll be heading in while the rest of the fleet is still in mid-trip, and he'll make port just as they're finishing up. He's two weeks out of synch. Ultimately, one could blame some invisible contortion of the Gulf Stream for this: The contortion disrupts the swordfish, which adds another week or two to the trip, which places the *Andrea Gail* on the Flemish Cap when she should already be heading in. The circumstances that place a boat at a certain place at a certain time are so random that they can't even be catalogued, much less predicted, and a total of fifty or sixty more people—swordfishermen, mariners, sailors—are also converging on the storm grounds of the North Atlantic. Some of these people have been heading there, unavoidably, for months; others made a bad choice just a few days ago.

IN EARLY September, a retired sailor named Ray Leonard started asking around Portland, Maine, for a crew to help him sail his 32-foot Westsail sloop to Bermuda. Portland is a big sailing town—people race J-boats in the summer, crew on in the Caribbean in the winter, squeeze in a little skiing between seasons—and Leonard was quickly introduced to Karen Stimson, one of the most experienced sailors in the harbor. Stimson, 42, started crewing on boats as a teenager, graduated from maritime academy in her thirties, and has crossed the ocean several times on oil tankers. Between sailing trips she and another woman, Sue Bylander, 38 years old, worked as graphic designers for a friend of Leonard's. Leonard offered them both a place on his boat if they would fly themselves home from Bermuda, and their boss said that they were free to take the time off if they wanted. They accepted, and a departure date was set for the last weekend in October. One month later the sloop *Satori* cast off from the Great Bay Marina in Portsmouth, New Hampshire, and motored slowly down the Piscataqua River toward open ocean.

The weather was so warm that the crew were in t-shirts on deck and the sky was the watery blue of Indian summer. A light wind came in from the west, a backing wind. The *Satori* ran down the Piscataqua under power, rendezvoused with another boat, cleared Kittery Point, and then bore away to the east. The two boats were headed for the Great South Channel between Georges Bank and Cape Cod, and from there they would sail due south for Bermuda. Bylander stayed below to sort out the mountain of food and gear in the cabin while Stimson and Leonard sat above deck and talked. Fog rolled in before they'd even cleared Isle of Shoals, and by dark the *Satori* was alone on a strangely quiet sea.

When Bylander finished stowing the supplies, the crew squeezed around a small dinette table in the cabin and ate lasagna baked by Stimson's mother. Stimson has straw-blonde hair and a sort of level, grey-eyed look that seems to assess a situation, run the odds, and make a decision all in the same moment. She's no romantic—"if you're looking for enlightenment it's not going to happen on a oil tanker"—but she's deeply in love with the ocean. She's not married and has no children. She's the perfect crew for a late-season run south.

So, Ray, have you listened to a weather forecast lately? she asked at one point during dinner.

Leonard nodded his head.

Did you hear there's a front coming through?

It shouldn't be a problem, he says. We can always cut into Buzzard's Bay.

Buzzard's Bay is at the western end of the Cape Cod Canal. One could, if the weather were bad enough, go nearly all the way from Boston to New York City by protected waterways. It's not particularly beautiful, but it's safe. "Ray was used to sailing solo, so having me on board may have made him feel more invulnerable," Stimson says. "And there's a point at which you're so far out that you don't want to turn back, you just run offshore. In the future *I* will listen to the weather forecast, *I* will decide, as crew, whether I'm willing to keep sailing. It will be immaterial to me the level of experience of the owner-captain."

The date was October 26. The lives of Stimson, Bylander, and Leonard were about to converge with several dozen others off the New England coast.

BILLY, like Leonard, has undoubtedly heard the forecast, but he's even less inclined to do anything about it than Leonard is. The lead time for an accurate forecast is only two or three days, and it takes twice that long for a sword boat to make port. Weather reports are vitally important to the fishing, but not so much for heading home; when the end of the trip comes, captains generally just haul their gear and go.

Because errors compound, the longer the trip, the more careful the captain has to be when he sets his initial heading for home. An error of just one degree puts a boat thirty miles off-course by the time she gets back to Gloucester; a captain could add a day to each trip with a month of such errors. When Billy Tyne starts for home, a bearing of 260 degrees would run him straight into Cape Ann, but it would also shave too close to Sable Island, which presents a ghastly hazard to shipping. ("I try to avoid it by at least forty or fifty miles," says Charlie Reed.) The channel between Sable and Nova Scotia is blessed with a good, cold counter-current that starts in Labrador and hugs the coast all the way down to Hatteras, but for some reason Billy decides not to take it. He decides to cross the Tail around 44 degrees north—his "waypoint"—and then, once clear of Sable, shoot a course almost due west for Gloucester.

Fishing boats use a global positioning system for bluewater navigation. GPS, as it's called, fixes a position relative to military satellites circling the earth and then converts it to longitude and latitude. It's accurate to within fifteen feet. The Department of Defense intentionally distorts the signals because they're worried about the misuse of such precise information, but the standards of accuracy on a sword boat are loose enough so that it doesn't matter. Fishermen generally use GPS to back up a loran system, which works by measuring the time it takes for two separate low-frequency radio signals to reach the vessel from broadcasting stations on shore. Charts are printed with numbered lines radiating out from the signal sources, and a loran reading identifies which lines correspond to the vessels's position.

Even with two electronic systems, though, mistakes happen—iron-bearing landmass, electrical interference, all kinds of things skew the output. Furthermore, the plotter gives you a pure direction, as if you could slice right through the curvature of the earth, but boats must follow an arc from point to point—the "Great Circle" route. The Great Circle route requires a correction of about eleven degrees north between Gloucester and the Flemish Cap. On the night of October 24th, Billy Tyne punches in the loran coordinates for his waypoint on the Tail of the Banks and reads a bearing of 250 degrees on his video plotter. On a Great Circle route, the compass heading and the actual heading are identical at the start of a trip, gradually diverge until the half-way point, and then converge again as the boat nears its destination.

Having determined his Great Circle route and plugged the heading into the autopilot, Tyne then goes over to the chart drawer and pulls out a ten-dollar nautical chart called INT 109. He lines up a course of 250 degrees to his waypoint on the Tail and then walks his way down the map with a set of hinged parallel rules. He rechecks the bearing at the compass rose at the bottom and then adjusts by 20 degrees for the local magnetic variation. (The earth's magnetic field doesn't line up exactly with the axis of the earth; in fact it doesn't even come close.) That should bring him to his waypoint on the Tail in about three days. From there he'll come up fourteen degrees and take another Great Circle route into Gloucester.

INT 109 is one of the few charts that shows the full width and breadth of the summer swordfishing grounds, and is carried by every sword boat in the Banks. It has a scale of one to three-and-a-half-million; on a diagonal it stretches from New Jersey almost to Greenland. Land on 109 is depicted the way mariners must see it, a blank, featureless expanse with a scattering of towns along a minutely-rendered coast. The lighthouses are marked by fat exclamation points and jut from every godforsaken headland between New York City and South Wolf Island, Labrador. Water depth is given in meters and shallow areas are shaded in blue. Georges Bank is clearly visible off Cape Cod, an irregular shape about the size of Long Island and rising to a depth of nine feet. To the west of Georges is the Great South Channel; beyond are the Nantucket Shoals and an area peppered with old ordnance: *Sub-*

merged torpedo, Unexploded depth charges, Unexploded bombs. The Two Hundred Fathom line is the chart's most prominent feature, echoing the coastline in broad strokes like a low-angle shadow. It swings north around Georges, skirts Nova Scotia a hundred miles offshore and then runs deep up the St. Lawrence Seaway. East of the Seaway are the old fishing grounds of Burgeo and St. Pierre Banks, and then the line makes an enormous seaward loop to the southeast. The Grand Banks.

The Banks are a broad flat plateau that extend hundreds of miles southeast from Newfoundland before plunging off the continental shelf. A clump of terrors known as the Virgin Rocks lurk seventy miles east of St. Johns, but otherwise there are no true shoals to speak of. A sheet of cold water called the Labrador Current flows over the northern edge of the Banks, injecting the local food chain with plankton; and a sluggish warm-water flow called the North Atlantic Current creeps toward Europe east of the Flemish Cap. Bending around the Tail of the Banks is something called Slope Water, a cold half-knot current that feeds into the generally-eastward movement of the area. Below Slope Water is the Gulf Stream, trundling across the Atlantic at speeds of up to three or four knots. Eddies sometimes detach themselves from the Gulf Stream and spin off into the North Atlantic, dragging entire ecosystems with them. These eddies are called warm core rings. When the cores fall apart, the ecosystems die.

Billy wants to run a slot between the Gulf Stream to the south and Sable Island to the north. It's a relatively straight shot that doesn't buck the warm head-current or come too close in to Sable. Steaming around the clock, he's looking at a one-week trip; maybe he even takes one bird out of the water to speed things up. The diesel engine has been throbbing relentlessly for a month now and, without the distraction of work, it suddenly seems hellishly loud. There's no way to escape the noise—it gets inside your skull, shakes your stomach lining, makes your ears ring. If the crew weren't so sleep-deprived it might even bother them; as it is they just wallow in their bunks and stand watch at the helm twice a day. After two-and-a-half days the *Andrea Gail* has covered about 450 miles, right to the edge of the continental shelf. The weather is fair and there's a good rolling swell from the northeast. At 3:15 on the afternoon of October 27, Billy Tyne raises the Canadian Coast Guard on his single sideband to tell them he's entering Canadian waters. *This is the American fishing vessel Andrea Gail, WYC 6681,* he says. *We're at 44.25 north, 49.05 west, bound for New England. All our fishing gear is stowed.*

The Canadian Coast Guard at St. Johns gives him the go-ahead to proceed. Most of the sword fleet is a couple of hundred miles to the east, and Albert Johnston is the same distance to the south. Sable Island is no longer in the way, so Billy comes up fourteen degrees and puts Gloucester right in his gunsights. They're heading almost due west and running a Great Circle route on auto-pilot. Around nightfall a Canadian weather map creaks out of the satellite fax. There's a hurricane off Bermuda, a cold front coming down off the Canadian Shield and a storm brewing over the Great Lakes. They're all heading for the Grand Banks. A few minutes after the fax, Linda Greenlaw calls.

Billy, you seen the chart? she asks.

Yeah I saw it, he says.

What do you think?

Looks like it's gonna be wicked.

They agree to talk the next day so Billy can give her a list of supplies he's going to need. He has no desire at all to talk to Bob Brown. They sign off, and then Billy hands the helm off to Murph and goes below for dinner. They're in a big steel boat with 40,000 pounds of fish in the hold, plus ice. It takes a lot to sink a boat like that. Around nine o'clock, a half-moon emerges off their port quarter. The air is calm, the sky is full of stars. Two thousand miles away, weather systems are starting to collide.

THE BARREL OF THE GUN

The men could only look at each other through the falling snow, from land to sea, from sea to land, and realize how unimportant they all were.

—Ship on the rocks, Newburyport, Massachusetts, 1839, no survivors.
(*Sidney Perley,* Historic Storms of New England, 1891)

There's a certain amount of denial in swordfishing. The boats claw through a lot of bad weather, and the crews generally just batten down the hatches, turn on the VCR, and put their faith in the tensile strength of steel. Still, every man on a sword boat knows there are waves out there that can crack them open like a coconut. Oceanographers have calculated that the maximum theoretical height for wind-driven waves is 198 feet; a wave that size could put down a lot of oil tankers, not to mention a 72-foot sword boat.

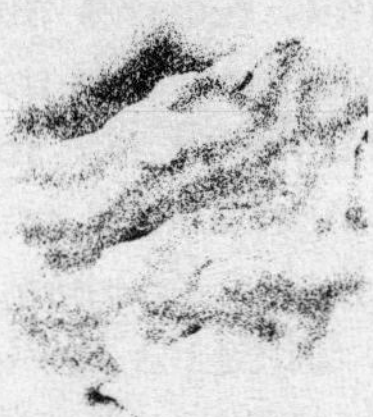

Once you're in the denial business, though, it's hard to know when to stop. Captains routinely overload their boats, ignore storm warnings, stow their life rafts in the wheelhouse, and disarm their emergency radio beacons. Coast Guard inspectors say that going down at sea is so unthinkable to many owner-captains that they don't even take basic precautions. "We don't need an EPIRB because we don't plan on sinking," is a sentence that Coast Guard inspectors hear a lot. One of the videos on file with the Portland Coast Guard—shown as often as possible to local fishermen—was shot from the wheelhouse of a commercial boat during a really bad blow. It shows the bow rising and falling, rising and falling over mammoth, white-streaked seas. At one point the captain says, a little smugly, "Yep, this is where you wanna be, right in your wheelhouse, your own little domain—."

At that moment a wall of water the size of a house fills the screen. It's no bigger than the rest of the waves but it's solid and foaming and absolutely vertical. It engulfs the bow, the foredeck, the wheelhouse, and then blows all the windows out. The last thing the camera sees is whitewater coming at it like a big wet fist.

The farther you work from shore, the less smug you can afford to be. Any weekend boater knows the Coast Guard will pluck him out of whatever idiocy he gets himself into, but sword boats don't have that option. They're working four or five hundred miles from shore, way beyond helicopter range. So Billy—any bluewater fisherman—has a tremendous respect for the big wet fist. When Billy receives the weather chart off the fax machine, he undoubtedly tells the crew that there's something very heavy on the way. There are specific things you can do to survive a storm at sea and whether the crew does them, and how well they do them, depends on how jaded they all are. Billy has fished his whole life. Maybe he thinks nothing can sink him; or maybe the sea is every nightmare he's ever had.

A good, worried crew starts by dogging down every hatch, porthole, and watertight door on the boat. That keeps breaking waves from busting things open and flooding the hold. They check the hatches on the lazarette, where the steering mechanism is housed, and make sure they're secure. A lot of boats founder when the lazarette floods. They check the bilge pump filters and fish out any debris floating in the bilgewater.

They clear everything off the deck—fishing gear, gaff pikes, oil slickers, boots—and put them down the fishhole. They remove the scupper plates so the boat can clear her decks. They tighten the anchor fastenings. They double-lash the fuel and water barrels on the whaleback. They shut off the gas cocks on the propane stove. They lash down anything in the engine room that might break loose and cause damage. They press down the fuel tanks so that some are empty and others are as full as possible. That reduces something called free surface effect—liquid sloshing around in tanks, changing the center of gravity.

Some boats pay one crew member a bit extra to oversee the engine, but the *Andrea Gail* doesn't have such a position; Billy takes care of it himself. He climbs down the engine room companionway and runs through the checklist: engine oil, hydraulics, batteries, fuel lines, air intakes, injectors. He makes sure the fire and high-water alarms are on and the bilge pumps are working. He tests the back-up generator. He hands out seasick pills. If one of the steel birds is out of the water, he puts it back in. He fixes his position on the chart and calculates how the weather will affect his drift. He reckons their course in his head in case a wave takes out their electronics. He checks the emergency lighting. He checks the survival suits. He checks the photos of his daughters. And then he settles down to wait.

So far the weather has been overcast but calm, light winds out of the northwest and a little bit of sea. Before the Portland Gale of 1898, one captain reported that it was "the greasiest evening you ever saw," and a few hours later 450 people were dead. It's not quite that calm, but almost. The wind hovers around ten knots and a six-foot swell rolls lazily under the boat. The *Andrea Gail* passes just north of Albert Johnston during the night, and by dawn they've almost made the western edge of the Banks, around 52 degrees west. They're half-way home. Dawn creeps in with a few shreds of salmon-pink sky, and the wind starts to inch into the southeast. That's called a backing wind; it goes counterclockwise around the compass and usually means bad weather is coming. A backing wind is an ill wind; it's the first distant touch of a low-pressure system going into its cyclonic spin.

Then another weather fax comes in:

> HURRICANE GRACE MOVING WILL TURN NE AND ACCELERATE. DEVELOPING DANGEROUS STORM MOVING E 35 KTS WILL TURN SE AND SLOW BY 12 HOURS. FORECAST WINDS 50 TO 65 KTS AND SEAS 22 TO 32 FEET WITHIN 400 NM SEMICIRCLE.

It reads like an inventory of things fishermen don't want to hear. An accompanying chart shows Hurricane Grace as a huge swirl around Bermuda, and the developing storm as a tightly-jammed set of barometric lines just north of Sable Island. Every boat in the swordfish fleet receives this information. Albert Johnston, south of the Tail, decides to head northwest into the cold water of the Labrador Current. Cold water is heavier, he says, and seems to lay better in the wind; it doesn't produce such volatile seas. The rest of the sword fleet stays far to the east, waiting to see what the storm does. They couldn't make it into port in time anyway. The *Contship Holland*, a hundred miles south of Billy, heads straight into the teeth of the thing. Two hundred miles east, another containership, the Liberian-registered *Zarah*, also heads for New York. Ray Leonard on the sloop *Satori* has decided not to head for port; he holds to a southerly course for Bermuda. The *Laurie Dawn 8* keeps plowing out to the fishing grounds and the *Eishin Maru 78*, 150 miles due south of Sable Island, makes for Halifax harbor to the northeast. Billy can either waste several days trying to get out of the way, or he can stay on-course for home. The fact that he has a hold full of fish, and not enough ice, must figure into his decision.

"He did what ninety percent of us would've done—he battened down the hatches and hung on," says Tommy Barrie, captain of the *Allison*. "He'd been gone well over a month. He probably just said, 'Screw it, we've had enough of this shit,' and kept heading home."

THE Boston office of the National Weather Service occupies the ground floor of a low brick building along a gritty access road in back of Logan Airport. Heavy glass windows allow a tinted view of the USAir shuttle terminal and a wasteland of gravel piles and rebar. Weather Service meteorologists can look up from their radar screens and watch USAir jets taxi back and forth behind a grey jet-blast barrier. Only their stabilizers stick up above it; they cruise like silver sharks across a concrete sea.

Weather generally moves west-to-east across the country with the jet stream. In a very crude sense, forecasting simply means calling up someone to the west of you and asking them to look out their window. In the early days—just after the Civil War—the National Weather Service was under the auspices of the War Department, because that was the only agency that had the discipline and technology to relay information eastward faster than the weather moved. After the novelty of telegraph wore off, the Weather Service was shifted over to the Department of Agriculture, and it ultimately wound up in the Department of Commerce, which oversees aviation and interstate trucking. Regional Weather Service offices tend to be in very grim places, like industrial parks bordering metropolitan airfields. They have sealed windows and central air-conditioning. Very little of the air being studied actually gets inside.

October 28 is a sharp, sunny day in Boston, temperatures in the fifties with a stiff wind blowing off the ocean. A senior meteorologist named Bob Case is crisscrossing the carpeted room, consulting with the various meteorologists on duty that day. Most of them are seated at heavy blue consoles staring resolutely at columns of numbers—barometric pressure, dewpoint, visibility—scrolling down computer screens. Behind the aviation desk is a bank of hotline phones: State Emergency Management, Regional Circuit, and Hurricane. Twice a day the State Emergency Management phone rings and someone in the office sprints to pick it up. It's the state testing its ability to warn people of a nuclear strike.

Case is a fit, balding man in his mid-fifties. A satellite photo of a hurricane about to clobber the coast of Maryland hangs in his office. He is responsible for issuing regional forecasts based on satellite imagery and a nationwide system called the Limited Fine Mesh, a grid superimposed on a map of the country where the corners represent data-collection points. Twice a day hundreds of LFM weather balloons are released to measure temperature, dewpoint, barometric pressure, and windspeed, and relay the information back by theodolite. The balloons rise to 60,000 feet and then burst, allowing the instruments to float back to earth on parachutes. When people find them, they mail them back to the Weather Service. The data from the LFM, plus input from a thousand or so other ground sites around the country, is fed into huge Cray computers at the National Meteorological Center in Camp Springs, Maryland. The computers run numerical models of the atmosphere and then spit forecasts back out to regional offices, where they are amended by local meteorologists. Humans still "add value" to a forecast, as meteorologists say. There is an intuitive element to forecasting that even the most powerful computers cannot duplicate.

Since early the previous day, Case has been watching something called a "short-wave trough aloft" slide eastward from the Great Lakes. On satellite photos it looks like an S-curve in the line of clear dry air moving south from Canada. Cold air is denser than warm air, and huge, slow undulations develop along the boundary between them and roll eastward—on their side, as it were—much like an ocean swell. The undulation gets more and more pronounced until the "crest" gets separated from the rest of the warm front and just starts to spin around itself. This is called a cut-off low, or an occluded front. Air gets sucked in toward the center, the system spins faster and faster, and within hours you have a storm.

The mechanics of a hurricane are fundamentally the same as a cut-off low, but their origins differ: hurricanes brew in the lukewarm waters around the equator. When the sun hits the equator it hits it dead-on, a square-foot beam of light heating up exactly one square foot of water. The farther north or south you are, the lower the angle of the sun and the more water a square-foot of sunlight must heat up; as a result the water doesn't heat up as much. The equatorial sea cooks all summer and evaporates huge amounts of water into the air. Evaporated water is unstable and contains energy in the same way that a boulder on top of a hill does—one small push unleashes a huge destructive force. Likewise, a drop in air temperature causes water vapor to precipitate out as rain and release its latent energy back into the atmosphere. The air above one square-foot of equatorial water contains enough latent energy to drive a car two miles. A single thunderstorm could supply four days' worth of the electrical power needed by the United States.

Warm air is less dense than cool air; it rises off the surface of the ocean, cools in the upper atmosphere, and then dumps its moisture before rushing back to earth. Huge cumulus clouds develop over the zones of rising air, with thunder, lightning, and terrifically strong rain. As long as there's a supply of warm water, the thunderstorm sustains itself, converting moisture into sheeting rain and downdraft winds. Other thunderclouds might line up along the leading edge of a cold front into a "squall line," a towering convective engine that stretches from horizon to horizon.

Hurricanes start when a slight kink—a disturbance in the trade winds, a dust storm blowing out to sea off the Sahara—develops in the upper-level air. The squall line starts to rotate around the kink, drawing in warm, volatile air and sending it up the gathering vortex at its center. The more air that gets drawn in, the faster it spins, and the more water is evaporated off the ocean. The water vapor rises up the core of the system and releases rain and latent heat. Eventually the system starts spinning so fast that inward-spiralling air can no longer overcome the centrifugal force and make it into the center. The eye of the storm has formed, a column of dry air surrounded by a solid wall of wind. Tropical birds get trapped inside and cannot escape. A week later, after the system has fallen apart, frigate birds and egrets might find themselves over Newfoundland, say, or New Jersey.

A mature hurricane is by far the most powerful event on earth; the combined nuclear arsenals of the United States and the former Soviet Union don't contain enough energy to keep a hurricane going for one day. A typical hurricane encompasses a million cubic miles of atmosphere and could provide all the electric power needed by the United States for three or four years. During the Labor Day Hurricane of 1935, winds surpassed 200 miles an hour and people caught outside were sandblasted to death. Rescue workers found nothing but their shoes and belt buckles. So much rain can fall during a hurricane—up to five inches an hour—that the soil liquifies. Hillsides slump into valleys and birds drown in flight, unable to shield their upward-facing nostrils. In 1970, a hurricane drowned half a million people in what is now Bangladesh. In 1938, a hurricane put downtown Providence, Rhode Island, under ten feet of ocean. The waves generated by that storm were so huge that they literally shook the earth; seismographs in Alaska picked up their impact five thousand miles away.

A lesser version of that is heading toward the Grand Banks: Hurricane Grace, a late-season fluke that still contains enough energy to crank another storm system off the chart. Ordinarily, Grace would come ashore somewhere in the Carolinas, but the same cold front that spawned the short-wave trough aloft also blocks her path on shore. (Cold air is very dense, and warm weather systems tend to bounce off them like beach balls off a brick wall.) According to atmospheric models generated by the Cray computers in Maryland, Grace will collide with the cold front and be forced northward, straight into the path of the short-wave trough. Wind is simply air rushing from an area of high pressure to an area of low; the greater the pressure difference, the faster it blows. An Arctic cold front bordering a hurricane-fortified low will create a pressure gradient that meteorologists may not see in their lifetime.

Ultimately, the engine behind all of this activity is the jet stream, a river of cold upper-level air that screams around the globe at thirty or forty thousand feet. Storms, cold fronts, short-wave troughs—they're all dragged eastward sooner or later by upper-level winds. The jet stream is not steady; it convulses like a loose firehose, careening off mountains, veering across plains. These irregularities create continent-sized eddies that come ballooning out of the Arctic as deep cold fronts. They are called anticyclones because the cold air in them flows outwards and clockwise, the opposite of a low. It is along the leading edge of these anticyclones that low-pressure waves sometimes develop; occasionally, one of these waves will intensify into a major storm. Why, and when, is still beyond the powers of science to predict. It typically happens over areas where a leg of the jet stream collides with subtropical air—the Great Lakes, the Gulf Stream off Hatteras, the southern Appalachians. Since air flows counterclockwise around these storms, the winds come out of the northeast as they move offshore. For that reason they're known as "nor'easters." Meteorologists have another name for them. They call them "bombs."

The first sign of the storm comes late on October 26, when satellite images reveal a slight bend in the leading edge of the cold front over western Indiana. The bend is a pocket of low barometric pressure—a short-wave trough—imbedded in the wall of the cold front at around 20,000 feet. It's the embryo of a storm. The trough moves east at forty miles an hour, strengthening as it goes. It follows the Canadian border to Montreal, cuts east across northern Maine, crosses the Bay of Fundy, and traverses Nova Scotia throughout the early hours of October 28th. By dawn an all-out gale is raging north of Sable Island. The upper-level trough has disintegrated, to be replaced by a sea-level low, and warm air is rising out the top of the system faster than it can be sucked in at the bottom. That is the definition of a strengthening storm. The barometric pressure is dropping more than a millibar an hour, and the Sable Island storm is sliding away fast to the southeast with 65-knot winds and thirty-foot seas. It's a tightly-packed low that Billy Tyne, two hundred miles away, can't even feel yet.

The Canadian Government maintains a data buoy seventy miles east of Sable Island, at 43.8 north and 57.4 west, just short of Billy's position. It is simply known as buoy #44139; there are eight others like it between Boston and the Grand Banks. They relay oceanographic information back to shore on an hourly basis. Throughout the day of October 28th, buoy #44139 records almost no activity whatsoever—dingy-sailing weather on the high seas. At two o'clock the needle jumps, though: suddenly the seas are twelve feet and the winds are gusting to fifteen knots. That in itself is nothing, but Billy must know he has just seen the first stirrings of the storm. The wind calms down again and the seas gradually subside, but a few hours later another weather report creaks out of the radiofax:

> WARNINGS. HURRICANE GRACE MOVING E 5 KTS MXIMUM WINDS 65 KTS GUSTING TO 80 NEAR CENTER. FORECAST DANGEROUS STORM WINDS 50 TO 75 KTS AND SEAS 25 TO 35 FT.

Billy's at 44 north, 56 west and heading straight into the mouth of meteorological hell. For the next hour the sea is calm, horribly so. The only sign of what's coming is the wind direction; it shifts restlessly from quadrant to quadrant all afternoon. At four o'clock it's out of the southeast. An hour later it's out of the south-southwest. An hour after that it's backed around to due north. It stays that way for the next hour, and then right around seven o'clock it starts creeping into the northeast. And then it hits.

It's a shear change; the *Andrea Gail* enters the Sable Island storm the way one might step into a room. The wind is instantly forty knots and parting through the rigging with an unnerving scream. Fishermen say they can gauge how fast the wind is—and how worried they should be—by the sound it makes against the wire stays and outrigger cables. A scream means the wind is around Force 9 on the Beaufort Scale, forty or fifty knots. Force 10 is a shriek. Force 11 is a moan. Over Force 11 is something fishermen don't want to hear. Linda Greenlaw, captain of the *Hannah Boden*, was in a storm where the wind registered a hundred miles an hour before it tore the anemometer off the boat. The wind, she says, made a sound she'd never heard before, a deep tonal vibration like a church organ. There was no melody, though; it was a church organ played by a child.

By eight o'clock the barometric pressure has dropped to 996 millibars and shows no sign of levelling off. That means the storm is continuing to strengthen and create an even greater vacuum at its center. Nature, as everyone knows, abhors a vacuum, and will try to fill it as fast as possible. The waves catch up with the wind speed around 8 PM and begin increasing exponentially; they double in size every hour. After nine o'clock every graph line from data buoy 44139 starts climbing almost vertically. Maximum wave heights peak at forty-five feet, drop briefly, and then nearly double to seventy. The wind climbs to fifty knots by 9 PM and gradually keeps increasing until it peaks at 58 knots. The waves are so large that they block the anemometer, and gusts are probably reaching ninety knots. That's 104 miles an hour—Gale Force 12 on the Beaufort Scale. The cables are moaning.

Minutes after the evening weather report, Tommy Barrie raises Tyne on the single sideband. Barrie's from Florida, a solid, square-shouldered guy with slicked-back hair and a voice like a box of rocks. He wants to know, of all things, how much gear to fish that night. He's six hundred miles to the east and figures he might as well squeeze in as much fishing as he can. The conversation, as Barrie remembers it, is brief and to-the-point:

We're over here around the forty-six, Billy. What's it look like?

It's blowin' fifty to eighty and the seas are thirty feet. It was calm for a while, but now it's startin' to come on pretty good. I'm 130 miles east of Sable.

Okay, we're gonna keep the gear in the boat but let's talk at eleven. Maybe we'll throw a little bit of gear in late.

All right, I'll give you a check after the weather. I'll tell you what's goin' on out here.

We'll be standin' by.

After talking to Barrie, Billy picks up the microphone on his single sideband and issues one last message to the fleet: *She's comin' on boys, and she's comin' on strong.* The position he'd given Linda Greenlaw on the *Hannah Boden*—44 north, 56.4 west—is a departure from his original heading. It appears to be more the heading of a man bound for Halifax, Nova Scotia, or maybe even Louisbourg, Cape Breton Island, than Gloucester, Massachusetts. Louisbourg is only 250 miles to the northeast, a 24-hour drive with the seas at their stern. Maybe Billy, having looked down the barrel of the gun, has decided to dodge north like Johnston. Or maybe he's worried about fuel, or needs to pick up ice, or decides that the cold countercurrent inside Sable is starting to look pretty good.

Whatever the reason, Billy changes course sometime before 6 PM and neglects to tell the rest of the fleet. They all assume he's headed straight for Gloucester. Albert Johnston on the *Mary T,* Tommy Barrie on the *Allison,* and Linda Greenlaw on the *Hannah Boden* all hear Billy Tyne's six o'clock bulletin on the weather. Only Linda is worried—"Those boys sounded scared and we were scared for them," she says. The rest of the fleet is more nonchalant. "We live in this stuff for years and years," says Barrie. "You have to look at the charts, listen to the weather, talk to the other boats, and make a decision on your own. You can't just go out there and wait for nice weather."

The storm is centered around Sable Island, but its far western edges are already brushing the New England coast. The *Satori*—now too far offshore to abort the trip—starts to feel the storm as early as Sunday morning. Another wall of fog moves in from Georges Bank and the barometer starts a slow downward slide that can only mean something very big is on the way. The *Satori* is at the top of the Great South Channel, off Cape Cod, and working her way through an increasingly restless and uneasy sea. Stimson mentions the weather forecasts again, but Leonard insists there's no reason to worry. By Sunday morning the swells start to mound up in ominous, chaotic ways, and that afternoon, when Stimson tunes in to the NOAA weather broadcast, she feels the first stabs of fear: NORTHEAST WIND 30 TO 40 KNOTS, AVERAGE SEAS EIGHT TO FIFTEEN FEET, VISIBILITY UNDER TWO MILES IN RAIN.

By nightfall the wind swings out of the northeast, as predicted, and starts to climb steadily up the Beaufort scale. It's clear that both the *Satori* and the boat she left Portsmouth with are in for a bad night. The two crews talk every hour or so over the VHF, but by midnight on Sunday, the air is so highly charged that the radios are useless. Around eleven o'clock Stimson takes one last call from the other boat—*We're having a rough time and have lost gear on deck*—and they're not heard from again. The *Satori* heads alone into the night, straining crazily up the swells and struggling to maintain steerageway.

Monday dawns a full gale, the seas building to twenty feet and the wind shearing ominously through the rigging. The sea takes on a grey, marbled look, like bad meat. Stimson tells Leonard that she really thinks it's going to be a bad one, but he insists it'll blow itself out in twenty-four hours. I don't think so, Ray, Stimson tells him, I've got a bad feeling. She and Leonard and Bylander eat chili cooked by Stimson's mother and spend as much time as possible below deck, out of the weather. The navigation table is across from the galley on the starboard side, and Bylander sets herself up as the communications person, monitoring the radar and weather forecasts and tracking their position by GPS. A dash into shore would be risky now, across shipping lanes and dangerous shoal waters, so they reef down the sails and keep to open sea.

Monday night the storm crosses offshore and the "first stage wind surge" passes over the *Satori.* NOAA weather radio reports that conditions will ease off briefly and then deteriorate again as the storm swings back toward the coast. By then, though, the *Satori* might be far enough south to escape its full wrath. They wallow on through Monday night, the barometer rising slightly and the wind easing off to the northeast; but then late that night, like a bad fever, it comes on again. The wind climbs to fifty knots and the seas rise up in huge dark mountains behind the boat. The crew take turns at the helm, clipped into a safety line, and occasionally take a breaking sea over the cockpit. The barometer crawls downward all night, and by dawn the conditions are worse than anything Stimson has ever seen in her life. For the first time, she starts thinking seriously about dying at sea.

Meanwhile, five hundred miles to the east, the sword fleet is getting slammed. On Albert Johnston's boat, the crew is so terrified that they just watch videos. Johnston stays at the helm and drinks a lot of coffee; like most captains, he's loath to relinquish the helm unless the weather calms down a bit. On the *Andrea Gail,* Billy probably takes the helm while the rest of the crew go below and try to forget about it. Some guys get stoned, which keeps them calm, and some sleep, or try to. Others just lie on their bunks and think about their families, or their girlfriends, or how much they wish this wasn't happening.

"I picture it like this," says Charlie Reed, trying to imagine the last evening aboard the *Andrea Gail.* "The guys are down below readin' books, and every now and then the boat takes a big sea on the side. They run up to the wheelhouse and ask, 'Hey, what's goin' on, Cap?' and Billy says something like, 'Well, we're gettin' there, boys, we're gettin' there.' If Billy's goin' downsea it has to be an awful frightening ride. Sometimes you come off the top of one of those waves and it just kinda leaves out from under you. The boat just drops. It's better to take the seas head-on—at least that way you can see what's comin' at you. That's about all you can do."

Of the men on the boat, Bugsy, Murph, and Billy have the most time at sea—34 years, all told, much of it together. At home Billy has a photo of the three of them at sea with a gigantic swordfish. He has hip boots on, rolled down to his shins, and he's sitting on a hatchcover pulling open the fish's mouth with a steel hook. He's staring straight into the camera. Bugsy's just behind Billy, head cocked to one side, looking as gaunt and ethereal as Christ on the Shroud of Turin. Murph's in back, squinting into the sea glare and noticeably huge even beneath a bulky pair of Farmer-John waders.

All these men have seen their share of close-calls at sea, but Murph's record is the worst. He's six-foot-two, 250 pounds, covered in tatoos and, apparently, extremely hard to kill. Once a mako shark clamped its jaws around his arm on deck and his friends had to beat it to death. The Coast Guard helicoptered him out. Another time he was laying out the longline when an errant hook went into his palm, out the other side and into a finger. No one saw it happen, and he was dragged off the back of the boat and down into the sea. All he could do was watch the hull of his boat get smaller and smaller above him and hope someone noticed he was gone. Luckily another crew member turned around a few seconds later, understood what was happening, and hauled him in like a swordfish. I thought I was gone, Mom, he told his mother later. I thought I was dead.

The worst accident occurred on a sticky, windless night off Cape Canaveral. Murph tried sleeping up on deck but it was too hot, so he went below to see if it was any better down there. The air-conditioning was broken, though, so he went back up on deck. He was half asleep when a tremendous shriek of metal brought him to his feet. The boat lurched to one side and water started pouring into the hold. A sleek dark shape loomed in the water off their bow. After the bilge pumps kicked in and the boat stabilized, they turned their searchlights on it: they'd been run down by the conning tower of a British nuclear submarine. It had ripped a hole in the hull and crushed Murph's bunk like a beer can.

With all this catastrophe in his life Murph had two choices—decide either that he was blessed or that his death was only a matter of time. He decided it was only a matter of time. When he met his wife, Debra, he told her flat-out he wasn't going to live past thirty; she married him anyway. They had a baby, Dale Junior, but the marriage broke up because Dale Senior was always at sea. And a few weeks before signing onto the *Andrea Gail*, Murph had stopped by his parents' house in Bradenton for a somewhat unsettling goodbye. His mother reminded him that he needed to keep up on his life insurance policy—which included burial coverage—and he just shrugged.

Mom, I wish you'd quit worryin' about burying me, he said. I'm going to die at sea.

His mother was taken aback, but they talked a bit longer, and at one point he asked whether she still had his high school trophies. Of course I do, she said.

Well, make sure you keep them for my son, he said, and kissed her goodbye.

"It took my breath away," says his mother. "And then he was gone—I mean one minute he was there, the next he was out the door. I didn't even have time to think. He was a rough, tough man. He wasn't exactly a house person."

Murph left for Boston in late June by train. (He was scared of flying.) He brought with him *The Joy of Cooking*, which his mother had given him, because he loved to cook on board the boats. He had taken his sea blanket to Debra's to wash but forgot to retrieve it, and so Debra folded it and put it up for his return. He'd told her he'd be home by November 2nd to take her out to dinner on her birthday. You'd better be, she said. After the first trip he called her and said he'd made over six thousand dollars and that he was going to send a package down for Dale Junior. He didn't call his parents because Debra said she'd call for him. He talked to his son for a while and then said goodbye to Debra and hung up the phone.

That was September 23. The *Andrea Gail* was due to leave within hours.

By ten o'clock average windspeed is forty knots out of the north-northeast, spiking to twice that and generating a huge sea. The *Andrea Gail* is a square-transom boat, meaning the stern is not tapered or rounded, and she tends to ride up the face of a following sea rather than slice through it. Every time a large sea rises to her stern, the *Andrea Gail* slews to one side and Billy must fight the wheel to keep from broaching. Broaching is when the boat turns broadside to the seas and rolls over. Fully-loaded steel boats don't recover from broachings; they downflood and sink.

If Billy's still running with the weather, he's taking seas almost continually over his stern and running a real risk of having a hatchcover or watertight door tear loose. And to make matters worse, the waves have an exceptionally short period; instead of coming every fifteen seconds or so, the waves now come every eight or nine. The shorter the period, the steeper the wave faces and the closer they are to breaking; 45-foot breaking waves are much more destructive than rolling swells twice that size. According to buoy 44139, maximum wave heights for October 28th coincide with exceptionally low periods right around ten o'clock. It's a combination that a boat the size of the *Andrea Gail* couldn't take for long. Certainly by ten—if not earlier, but no later than ten—Billy Tyne must have decided to bring his boat around into the seas.

If there's a maneuver that raises the hairs on the back of a captain's neck, it's coming around in large seas. The boat is broadside to the waves—"beam-to"—for half a minute or so, which is easily long enough to get rolled over. Even aircraft carriers are at risk when they're beam-to in a big sea. If Billy attempts to come around that late in the storm, he'd make sure the decks were cleared and give her full power on the way around. The *Andrea Gail* would list way over and Billy would peer out of the windows to see what was bearing down on them. With luck, he'd pick a lull between the waves and they'd round up into the weather without any problem.

Billy's been through a lot of storms, though, and he's probably brought her around earlier in the evening, maybe even before talking to Barrie. Either way, it's a significant moment; it means they've stopped steaming home and are simply trying to survive. In a sense Billy's no longer at the helm, the conditions are, and all he can do is react. If danger can be seen in terms of a narrowing range of choices, Billy Tyne's choices have just racheted down a notch. A week ago he could have headed in early. A day ago he could have run north like Johnston. An hour ago he could have radioed to see if there were any other vessels around. Now the electrical noise has made the VHF practically useless, and the single sideband only works for long range. These aren't mistakes so much as an inability to see into the future. No one, not even the Weather Service, knows for sure what a storm's going to do.

There are distinct drawbacks to heading into the weather, though. The windows are exposed to breaking seas, the boat uses more fuel, and the bow tends to catch the wind and drag the boat to leeward. The *Andrea Gail* has a high bow that would force Billy to oversteer simply to stay on course. One can imagine Billy standing at the helm and gripping the wheel with the force and stance one might use to carry a cinder block. It would be a confused sea, mountains of water converging, diverging, piling up on themselves from every direction. A boat's motion can be thought of as the instantaneous integration of every force acting upon it in a given moment, and the motion of a boat in a storm is so chaotic as to be almost without pattern. Billy would just keep his bow pointed into the worst of it and hope he doesn't get blindsided by a freak wave.

The degree of danger Billy's in can be gauged from the beating endured by the *Contship Holland,* two hundred or so miles to the east. The *Holland* is a big ship—542 feet and 10,000 tons—and capable of carrying almost seven hundred land/sea containers on her decks. She could easily take the *Andrea Gail* as cargo. From her daily log, October 29–30:

0400—Ship labors hard in very high following seas.
1200—Ship labors in very high stormy seas (hurricane gusts), water over deck and deck cargo. Ship strains heavily, travel reduced.
0200—Steering weather-dependent course. Ship no longer obeys rudder. Ship strains hard and lurches heavily.
0400—Containers are missing from Bay 6.

In other words, Billy's riding out a storm that has forced a 10,000-ton containership to abandon course and simply steer to survive. The next High Seas report comes in at 11 PM, and Tommy Barrie mulls it over while waiting for Billy to call. The storm is supposed to hit just west of the Tail, around the 42 and the 55, but the Weather Service doesn't always know everything. The 42 and the 55 are only about a hundred miles southeast of Billy, so he's a much more reliable source for local conditions than the weather radio. It's possible, Barrie thinks, that the *Allison* could get away with fishing a little gear that night. Two sections, maybe eight miles of line. Barrie's the westernmost boat of the main fleet, so whatever is on the way is going to hit him first; but first of all it's going to hit Billy Tyne. Barrie waits twenty, thirty minutes, but Billy never calls. That's not as bad as it sounds—we're all big boys out there, as Barrie says, and can take care of ourselves. Maybe Billy's got his hands full, or maybe he went below to take a nap, or maybe he simply forgot.

Finally, around midnight, Barrie tries to raise Billy himself. He can't get through, though, which is more serious. It means the *Andrea Gail* has sunk, has lost her antennas, or there's such pandemonium on board that no one can get to the radio. Barrie guesses it's the antennas—they're bolted to a steel mast behind the wheelhouse, and although they're high up, they're fragile. Most sword boats have lost them at one point or another, and there's not much that can be done about it until the weather calms down. You can't even survive a walk across the deck during Force 12 conditions, much less a trip up the mast.

Losing the antennas would seriously affect the *Andrea Gail:* it would mean they'd lost their GPS, radio, weatherfax, and loran. And a wave that had taken out their antennas may well have also stripped them of their radar, running lights, and floodlight. Not only would Billy not know where he was, he wouldn't be able to communicate with anyone or detect other boats in the area; he'd basically be back in the nineteenth century. There's not much he could do at this point but keep the *Andrea Gail* pointed into the seas and hope the windows don't get blown out. They're half-inch Lexan, but there's a limit to what they can take; the *Contship Holland* took waves over her decks that peeled land/sea containers open like sardine cans, forty feet above the surface. The *Andrea Gail*'s pilothouse is half that high.

Around midnight a curious thing happens: The Sable Island storm eases up a bit. The winds drop a few knots and maximum wave heights fall about ten feet. Their periods lengthen as well, meaning there are fewer breaking waves; instead of crashing through walls of water, the *Andrea Gail* rises up the face of each wave and plunges down its backside.

Forty-five foot waves have an angled face of sixty or seventy feet, which is nearly the length of the boat. On exceptionally big waves, the *Andrea Gail* has her stern in the trough and her bow still climbing toward the crest.

The lull, such as it is, lasts until one AM. At that point the center of the low is directly over the *Andrea Gail*. It's possible that the low, with its ferocious winds and extremely tight pressure gradient, has developed an eye similar to that of a hurricane. Two days later, satellite photographs will show clouds swirling into its center like water down a drain. Dry arctic air wraps one-and-a-half times around the low before finally making it into the center—an indication of how fast the system is spinning. On October 28th the center isn't that well defined, but it may serve to take the edge off the conditions just a bit. The reprieve doesn't last long, though; within a couple of hours the waves are back up to seventy feet. A seventy-foot wave has an angled face of well over a hundred feet. The sea state has reached levels that no one on the boat, and few people on earth, have ever seen.

When the *Contship Holland* finally limped into port several days later, one of her officers stepped off and swore he'd never set foot on another ship again. She'd lost 36 land/sea containers over the side, and the ship's owners promptly hired an American meteorological consultant to help defend them against lawsuits. "The storm resulted in large-scale destruction of offshore shipping and coastal installations from Nova Scotia to Florida," wrote Bob Raguso of *Weathernews New York*. "It was called an extreme nor'easter by U.S. scientists and ranked as one of the five most intense storms from 1899-1991. It had the highest significant wave heights either arrived at by measurement or calculation. Some scientists termed it the hundred year storm."

The *Andrea Gail* is at the epicenter of this storm and almost on top of the Sable Island shoals. It's very likely she has lost her antennas, or Billy would have radioed Tommy Barrie that things looked bad—and definitely don't fish any gear that night. On the other hand, it's debatable whether the sea-state could have overwhelmed Billy's boat that early in the evening; the 55-foot *Fair Wind* didn't flip until winds hit a hundred knots and the waves were running seventy feet. A more likely scenario is that Billy manages to get through the ten o'clock spike in weather conditions but takes a real beating—the windows are out, the electronics are dead, and the crew is terrified.

For the first time they are completely, irrevocably on their own.

GRAVEYARD OF THE ATLANTIC

In a few days the El Dorado expedition went into the patient wilderness, that closed upon it like the sea closes over a diver. Long afterwards the news came back that all the donkeys were dead.

—*JOSEPH CONRAD,* Heart of Darkness

ALBERT JOHNSTON:

I was the first one to know how bad it was really gonna be. Halifax called for twenty meter seas and when we heard that we thought, Oh boy. You don't really have time to run to land so we tried to get into the coldest water we could find. The colder the water, the denser it is and the waves don't get as big. Also, I knew we'd get a northeast-northwest wind. I wanted to make as much headway as possible 'cause the Gulf Stream was down south and that's where the warm water and fast current are.

There was an awful lot of electrical noise along the leading edge of this thing, there was so much noise you couldn't hear anything on the radio. I was up in the wheelhouse, when it's bad like that I usually stay up there. If it looks like it's settlin' down a bit and I can grab a little sleep, then I will. The crew just racks out and watches videos. Everybody acknowledged this was the worst storm they'd ever been in—you can tell by the size of the waves, the motion of the boat, the noise, the crashing. There's always a point when you realize that you're in the middle of the ocean and if anything goes wrong, that's it. You see so much bad weather that you kind of get used to it. But then you see *really* bad weather. And that, you never get used to.

They had ship reports of thirty meter seas. That's ninety feet. I would imagine—truthfully, in retrospect—that if the whole U.S. swordfish fleet had been caught in the center of that thing, everybody would've gone down. We only saw, I don't know, maybe fifty foot waves, max. We went into it until it started to get dark, and then we turned around and went with it. You can't see those rogue waves in the dark and you don't want to get blasted and knock your wheelhouse off. We got the RPM tuned in just right to be in synch with the waves; too fast and we'd start surfing, too slow and the waves would just blast right over the whole boat. The boat was heavy and loaded with fish, very stable. It made for an amazingly good ride.

JOHNSTON had finished his last haul late in the afternoon of the 28th: nineteen swordfish, twenty big-eye, twenty-two yellowfin, and two mako. He immediately started steaming north and by morning he was approaching the Tail of the Banks, winds out of the northeast at 100 knots and seas twenty to thirty feet. Several hundred miles to the west, though, conditions have gone off the chart. The Beaufort Wind Scale defines a Force 12 storm as having 73-mile-an-hour winds and 45-foot seas. Due south of Sable Island, data buoy 44137 starts notching 75-foot waves on the afternoon of the 29th and stays up there for the next seventeen hours. Significant wave height—the average of the top third, also known as HSig—tops fifty feet. The first hundred-foot wave spikes the graph at 8 PM, and the second one spikes it at midnight. For the next two hours, peak wave heights stay at a hundred feet and winds hit eighty miles an hour. The waves are blocking the data buoy readings, though, and the wind is probably hitting 120 or so. Eighty-mile-an-hour wind can suck fish right out of bait barrels. Hundred-foot waves are fifty percent higher than the most extreme sizes predicted by computer models. They are the largest waves ever recorded on the Scotian Shelf. They are among the very highest waves measured anywhere in the world, ever.

Scientists understand how waves work, but not exactly how *huge* ones work. There are rogue waves out there, in other words, that seem to exceed the forces generating them. For all practical purposes, though, heights of waves are a function of how hard the wind blows, how long it blows for, and how much sea room there is—"speed, duration, and fetch," as it's known. Force 12 winds over Lake Michigan would generate wave heights of 35 feet after ten hours or so, but the waves couldn't get any bigger than that because the fetch—the amount of open water—isn't great enough. The waves have reached what is called a "fully-developed sea state." Every wind speed has a minimum fetch and duration to reach a fully-developed sea state; waves driven by a Force 12 wind reach their full potential in three or four days. A gale blowing across a thousand miles of ocean for sixty hours would generate significant wave heights of 97 feet; peak wave heights would be more than twice that. Waves that size have never been recorded, but they must be out there. It's possible that they would destroy anything in a position to measure them.

All waves, no matter how huge, start as rough spots—cats' paws—on the surface of the water. The cats' paws are filled with diamond-shaped ripples, called capillary waves, that are weaker than the surface tension of water and die out as soon as the wind stops. They give the wind some purchase on an otherwise glassy sea, and at winds over six knots, actual waves start to build. The harder the wind blows, the bigger the waves get and the more wind they are able to "catch." It's a feedback loop that has wave height rising exponentially with wind speed.

Such waves are augmented by the wind but not dependent on it; were the wind to stop, the waves would continue to propagate by endlessly falling into the trough that precedes them. Such waves are called gravity waves, or swells; in cross-section they are symmetrical sine curves that undulate along the surface with almost no energy loss. A cork floating on the surface moves up and down but not laterally when a swell passes beneath it. The higher the swells, the farther apart the crests and the faster they move. Antarctic storms have generated swells that are half a mile or more between crests and travel thirty or forty miles an hour; they hit the Hawaiian islands as breakers forty feet high.

Unfortunately for mariners, the total amount of wave energy in a storm doesn't rise linearly with wind speed, but to its fourth power. The seas generated by a forty-knot wind aren't twice as violent as those from a twenty-knot wind, they're seventeen times as violent. A ship's crew watching the anemometer climb even ten knots could well be watching their death sentence. Moreover, high winds tend to shorten the distance between wave crests and steepen their faces. The waves are no longer symmetrical sine curves, they're sharp peaks that rise farther above sea level than the troughs fall below it. If the height of the wave is more than one seventh the distance between the crests—the "wavelength"—the waves become too steep to support themselves and start to break. In shallow water, waves break because the underwater turbulence drags on the bottom and slows the waves down, shortening the wavelength and changing the ratio of height to length. In open ocean the opposite happens: wind builds the waves up so fast that the distance between crests can't keep up, and they collapse under their own mass. Now, instead of propagating with near-zero energy loss, the breaking wave is suddenly transporting a huge amount of water. It's cashing in its chips, as it were, and converting all its potential and kinetic energy into water displacement.

A general rule of fluid dynamics holds that an object in the water tends to do whatever the water it replaces would have done. In the case of a boat in a breaking wave, the boat will effectively become part of the curl. It will either be flipped end over end or shoved backward and broken on. Instantaneous pressures of up to six tons per square foot have been measured in breaking waves. Breaking waves have lifted a 2,700-ton breakwater, *en masse,* and deposited it inside the harbor at Wick, Scotland. They have blasted open a steel door 195 feet above sea level at Unst Light in the Shetland Islands. They have heaved a half-ton boulder 91 feet into the air at Tillamook Rock, Oregon.

There is some evidence that average wave heights are slowly rising, and that freak waves of eighty or ninety feet are becoming more common. Wave heights off the coast of England have risen an average of 25 percent over the past couple of decades, which converts to a twenty-foot increase in the highest waves over the next half-century. One cause may be the tightening of environmental laws, which has reduced the amount of oil flushed into the oceans by oil tankers. Oil spreads across water in a film several molecules thick and inhibits the generation of capillary waves, which in turn prevent the wind from getting a "grip" on the sea. Plankton releases a chemical that has the same effect, and plankton levels in the North Atlantic have dropped dramatically. Another explanation is that the recent warming trend—some call it the greenhouse effect—has made storms more frequent and severe. Waves have destroyed docks and buildings in Newfoundland, for example, that haven't been damaged for decades.

As a result, stresses on ships have been rising. The standard practice is to build ships to withstand what is called a 25-year stress—the most violent condition the ship is likely to experience in 25 years. The wave that flooded the wheelhouse of the *Queen Mary,* ninety feet up, must have nearly exceeded her 25-year stress. North Sea oil platforms are built to accommodate a 111-foot wave beneath their decks, which is calculated to be a one-hundred-year stress. Unfortunately, the 25-year stress is just a statistical concept that offers no guarantee about what will happen next year, or next week. A ship could encounter several 25-year waves in a month or never encounter any at all. Naval architects simply decide what level of stress she's likely to encounter in her lifetime and then hope for the best. It's economically and structurally impractical to construct every boat to hundred-year specifications.

Inevitably, then, ships encounter waves that exceed their stress rating. In the dry terminology of naval architecture, these are called "non-negotiable waves." Mariners call them "rogue waves" or "freak seas." Typically they are very steep and have an equally steep trough in front of them—a "hole in the ocean" as some witnesses have described it. Ships cannot get their bows up fast enough, and the ensuing wave breaks their back. Maritime history is full of encounters with such waves. When Sir Ernest Shackleton was forced to cross the South Polar Sea in a 22-foot open life boat, he saw a wave so big that he mistook its foaming crest for a moonlit-cloud. He only had time to yell, "Hang on, boys, it's got us!" before the wave broke over his boat. Miraculously, they didn't sink. In February 1883, the 320-foot steamship *Glamorgan* was swept bow-to-stern by an enormous wave that ripped the wheelhouse right off the deck, taking all the ship's officers with it. She later sank. In 1966, the 44,000-ton *Michelangelo,* an Italian steamship carrying 775 passengers, encountered a single massive wave in an otherwise unremarkable sea. Her bow fell into a trough and the wave stove in her bow, flooded her wheelhouse, and killed a crewman and two passengers. In 1976, the oil tanker *Cretan Star* radioed, " . . . vessel was struck by a huge wave that went over the deck . . . " and was never heard from again. The only sign of her fate was a four-mile oil slick off Bombay.

South Africa's "wild coast," between Durban and East London, is home to a disproportionate number of these monsters. The four-knot Agulhas Current runs along the continental shelf a few miles offshore and plays havoc with swells arriving from Antarctic gales. The current shortens their wavelengths, making the swells steeper and more dangerous, and bends them into the fastwater the way swells are bent along a beach. Wave energy gets concentrated in the center of the current and overwhelms ships that are there to catch a free ride. In 1973 the 12,000-ton cargo ship *Bencruachan* was cracked by an enormous wave off Durban and had to be towed into port, barely afloat. Several weeks later the 12,000-ton *Neptune Sapphire* broke in half on her maiden voyage after encountering a freak sea in the same area. The crew were hoisted off the stern section by helicopter. In 1974, the 132,000-ton Norwegian tanker *Wilstar* fell into a huge trough ("There was no sea in front of the ship, only a hole," said one crew member) and then took an equally huge wave over her bow. The impact crumpled inch-thick steel plate like sheet-metal and twisted railroad-gauge I-beams into knots. The entire bow bulb was torn off.

The biggest rogue on record was during a Pacific gale in 1933, when the 478-foot Navy tanker *Ramapo* was on her way from Manila to San Diego. She encountered a massive low-pressure system that blew up to 68 knots for a week straight and resulted in a fully-developed sea that the *Ramapo* had no choice but to take on her stern. (Unlike today's tankers, the *Ramapo*'s wheelhouse was slightly forward of amidships.) Early on the morning of February seventh, the watch officer glanced to stern and saw a freak wave rising up behind him that lined up perfectly with a crow's nest above and behind the bridge. Simple geometry later showed the wave to be 112 feet high.

Rogue waves such as that are thought to be several ordinary waves that happen to get "in step," forming highly-unstable piles of water. Others are waves that overlay long-distance swells from earlier storms. Such accumulations of energy can travel in threes—a phenonemon called "the three sisters"—and are so huge that they can be tracked by radar. There are cases of the three sisters crossing the Atlantic Ocean and starting to shoal along the 100-fathom curve off the coast of France. One hundred fathoms is six hundred feet, which means that freak waves are breaking over the continental shelf as if it were a shoreline sandbar. Most people don't survive encounters with such waves, and so firsthand accounts are hard to come by, but they do exist. An Englishwoman named Beryl Smeeton was rounding Cape Horn with her husband in the 1960s when she saw a shoaling wave behind her that stretched away in a straight line as far as she could see. "The whole horizon was blotted out by a huge grey wall," she writes in her journal. "It had no curling crest, just a thin white line along the whole length, and its face was unlike the sloping face of a normal wave. This was a wall of water with a completely vertical face, down which ran white ripples, like a waterfall."

The wave flipped the 46-foot boat end over end, snapped Smeeton's harness, and threw her overboard.

Tommy Barrie had a similar experience off Georges Bank. He was laying-to in a storm when a wave clobbered him out of nowhere, imploding his windows. "There was this 'boom' and the Lexan window was blown right off," he says. "The window hit the clutch and so the clutch was pinned and we couldn't get her into gear. The boat's over a bit, layin' in a beam sea and shit flyin' everywhere—things that have never moved on that boat before goin' all over the place. The wave ripped the life raft off its mount and blew the front hatch open. It was dogged down, but there was so much water it blew it open anyway. I came up quick and radioed the *Miss Millie:* 'Larry we took a hell of a wave, stand by, I'm here.' I took the boat downsea and about ten minutes later the same wave hit him. His bird came out of the water and the hull took a big dent."

If a wave takes Billy's windows out, it would be similar to the one experienced by Smeeton or Barrie—big, steep, and unexpected. It's an awful scene to imagine: water knee-deep in the wheelhouse, men scrambling up the companionway, wind screaming through the blown-out window. If enough water gets in, it can make its way down to the engine room, soak the wiring, and take on an electric charge. The entire boat gets electrified; anyone standing in water gets electrocuted. A boat that loses her windows can start filling up with water in minutes, so two men tie safety lines to their waists and crawl out onto the whaleback deck with sheets of marine plywood. "The plywood acts like a kite, you have to manhandle the sonofabitch," says Charlie Reed. "It's a horrible thought, someone out there in that weather. As captain, it's your worst fear, someone goin' over the side."

It's hard to find a more dangerous job than venturing onto the whaleback during a storm to do a little carpentry. On land a 100-knot wind reduces people to a crawl; at sea it knocks you flat. The decks are awash, the boat is rolling, the spray is raking you like grapeshot. You work in the calm of the wave troughs and flatten yourself at the crests to keep from being blown off the boat. One man holds the plywood against the window while the other lines up a power drill with the holes in the wheelhouse and starts drilling. He drills one hole, hammers a bolt through, and then someone in the wheelhouse threads on the nut while the men on the outside keep drilling and bolting, drilling and bolting until the plywood is screwed down tight. Some captains put a piece of inner tube between the wood and steel to make it waterproof.

Although it's a suicidal job, crews that lose their windows almost always manage to get some plywood up, even if it means turning downsea to do it. After the plywood is bolted down, the crew starts bucket-bailing the wheelhouse and putting the cabin back in order. Maybe someone tries to wire the loran or radio up to a battery to see if he can get a signal. Billy starts shifting fuel from one tank to another, trying to trim the boat. Someone probably checks the engine room and work deck—are the scuppers clearing their water? Are the birds down? Is the fish hatch secure?

There's not much they can do at this point but head into the storm and hope they don't take any more big waves. If waves keep taking out their windows they could turn around and go downsea, but that generates a whole new set of problems. Several large waves could simply bury them, or the lazarette could flood, or sediment could get stirred up in the tanks and clog the fuel filters. If the ship motion is violent enough, the crew has to change the filters non-stop—pull them out, flush the sediment, put them back in again, over and over, as fast as they can. Or the engine stops and the boat goes over.

There's no question Billy would radio for help now if he had the capability. All he'd have to do is say "mayday," on channel 16 or 2182 kilohertz, and give his coordinates. Sixteen and 2182 are monitored by the Coast Guard, the military, and all ocean-going vessels; according to maritime law, any vessel that picks up a mayday must respond immediately, unless their own lives would be put in danger. The Coast Guard would send out an Aurora rescue plane to locate the *Andrea Gail* and circle her. A rescue-swimmer and helicopter crew would be placed on standby at the airbase outside Halifax. The Canadian Coast Guard cutter *Edward Cornwallis* would start steaming east out of Halifax on what would probably be a 36-hour trip. The *Triumph C,* an ocean-going tug based at a drilling platform off Sable Island, would put to sea as well. The *Contship Holland,* the *Zarah,* and possibly the *Mary T,* would all try to converge on Billy. Once there, they wouldn't be able to leave until the Coast Guard signs them off.

Presumably, then, Billy's radios are out. The Coast Guard never receives a call. Now his only link to the rest of the world is his EPIRB, which sits outside in a plastic holster on the whaleback deck. It's about the size of a bowling pin and has a ring switch that can be set to "off," "on," or "armed." EPIRBs are kept permanently in the "armed" position, and if the boat goes down, a water-sensitive switch triggers a radio signal that gets relayed by satellite to listening posts on shore. The Coast

Guard immediately knows the name of the boat, the location, and that something has gone disastrously wrong. If a boat loses her radios before actually sinking, though, the captain can send a distress signal by just twisting the ring switch to the "on" position. It's the same as screaming "mayday" into the radio.

Billy doesn't do it, though; he never trips the switch. This can only mean one thing: that he's hopeful about their chances right up until the moment when they have no chance at all. He must figure that the kind of sea that took out their windows probably won't hit again—or that, if it does, they'll be able to take it. Statistically a forty-knot wind generates thirty- or forty-foot breaking sea every six minutes or so—greenwater over the bow and whitewater over the house. Every hour, perhaps, Billy might get hit by a breaking fifty-footer. That's probably the kind of wave that blew out the windows. And every 100 hours, Billy can expect to run into a non-negotiable wave—a breaking seventy-footer that could flip the boat end over end. He's got to figure the storm's going to blow out before his hundred hours are up.

Everyone on a sinking boat reacts differently. A man on one Gloucester boat just curled up and started to cry while his shipmates worked untethered on deck. The *Andrea Gail* crew, all experienced fishermen, are probably trying to shrug it off as just another storm—they've been through this before, they'll go through it again, and at least they're not puking. Billy's undoubtedly working too hard at the helm to give drowning much thought. Ernie Hazard claims it was the last thing on his mind. "There was no conversation, just real business-like," he says of going down off Georges Bank. "You know, 'Let's just get this thing done.' Never any overwhelming sense of danger. We were just very, very busy."

Be that as it may, certain realities still must come crashing in. At some point Tyne, Shatford, Sullivan, Moran, Murphy, and Pierre must realize there's no way off this boat. They could trigger the EPIRB, but a night rescue in these conditions would be virtually impossible. They could deploy the life raft, but they probably wouldn't survive the huge seas. If the boat goes down, they go down with it, and no one on earth can do anything about it. Their lives are utterly and completely in their own hands.

That fact must settle into Bobby Shatford's stomach like a bad meal. It was he, after all, who had those terrible misgivings the day they left. That last afternoon on the dock he came within a hair's breadth of saying no—just telling Chris to start up the car and drive. They could have gone back to her place, or up the coast, or anywhere at all. It wouldn't have mattered; he wouldn't be in this storm right now, and neither would the rest of them. It would have taken Billy at least a day to replace him, and right now they'd still be east with the rest of the fleet.

The previous spring Bobby and Chris rented a movie called *The Fighting Sullivans,* about five brothers who died on a U.S. Navy boat during World War Two. It was Ethel's favorite movie. Sitting there with Chris, watching the movie, and thinking about his brothers, Bobby started to cry. He was not a man who cried easily and Chris was unsure what to do. Should she say something? Pretend not to notice? Turn off the T.V.? Finally, Bobby said that he was upset by the idea of all his brothers fishing, and that if anything happened to *him,* he wanted to be buried at sea. Chris said that nothing was going to happen to him, but he insisted. Just bury me at sea, he said. Promise me that.

And now here he is, getting buried at sea. The conditions have degenerated from bad to unspeakable, Beaufort Force 10 or 11. The British *Manual of Seamanship* describes a Force 10 gale as: "Foam is in great patches and is blown in dense white streaks along the direction of the wind. The rolling of the sea becomes heavy and shock-like." Force 11 is even worse: "Exceptionally high waves, small or medium-sized ships might be lost from view behind them. The sea is completely covered with long patches of white foam." Hurricane Grace is still working her way north, and when she collides with the Sable Island storm—probably in a day or so—conditions will get even more severe, maybe as high as Force 12. Very few boats that size can withstand a Force 12 gale.

Since Billy presumably can't use his radio, there's no way to know how things are going aboard the *Andrea Gail.* A fairly good idea, though, can be had from the *Eishin Maru 78,* the Japanese longliner two hundred miles to the southwest. The *Eishin Maru* has a Canadian observer on board, Judith Reeves, who is charged with making sure the vessel abides by Canadian fishing regulations. The storm hits the *Eishin Maru* around the same time as the *Andrea Gail,* but not as abruptly; buoy 44137, sixty miles to the south, shows a slow, gradual increase in windspeed starting at 5 PM on the 28th. By dawn on the 29th, the wind is forty knots gusting to fifty, and peak wave heights are only 45 feet. That's considerably less than what Billy is experiencing, but it just keeps getting worse. By midnight sustained windspeeds are fifty knots, gust are hitting sixty, and peak wave heights are over one hundred feet. At ten past eight at night, October 29th, the first big wave hits the *Eishin Maru.*

It blows out a port-side window with the sound of a shotgun going off. Water inundates the bridge and barrels down the hallway into Reeves's room. She hears panicked shouts from the crew and then orders that she doesn't understand. Men scramble to board up the window and bail out the water, and within an hour the captain has regained control of the bridge. The boat is taking a horrific beating, though. She's 150 feet long—twice the size of the *Andrea Gail*—and waves are completely burying her decks. There are no life jackets on hand, no survival suits, and no EPIRB. Just before dawn, the second wave hits.

It blows out four windows this time, including the one with plywood over it. "All the circuits went, there was smoke and wires crackling," says Reeves. "We crippled the ship. The VHF, the radar, the internal communication system, the navigation monitors, they were all rendered inoperable. That's when the radio operator came to me and said—in sign language—that he wanted me to go into the radio room."

The radio operator had managed to contact the ship's agent by satellite phone, and Reeves is put on the line to explain what kind of damage they've sustained. While she's talking, Coast Guard New York breaks in; they've been listening in on the conversation and want to know if the *Eishin Maru* needs help. Reeves says they've lost most of their electronics and are in serious trouble. New York patches her through to the Coast Guard in Halifax, and while they're discussing how to get people off the boat, the radio operator interrupts her. He's pointing to a sentence in an English phrase book. Reeves leans in close to read it: "We are helpless and drifting. Please render all assistance." (Unknown to Reeves, the steering linkage has just failed, although the radio operator doesn't know how to explain that to her.) It's at this moment that Reeves realizes she's going down at sea.

"We had no steerage and we were right in the eye of the storm," she says. "It was a confused sea, all the waves were coming from different directions. The wind was picking up the tops of the waves and slinging them so far that when the search-and-rescue plane arrived, we couldn't even see it. The whole vessel would get shoved over on its side, so that we were completely upside-down. If you get hit by one wave and then hit by another, you can drive the vessel completely down into the water. And so that second before the vessel starts to come up you're just holding your breath, waiting."

They're dead in the water, taking the huge waves broadside. According to Reeves, they are doing 360-degree barrel rolls and coming back up. Four boats try to respond to her mayday, but three of them have to stand down because of the weather. They cannot continue without risking their own lives. The ocean-going tug *Triumph C* leaves Sable Island and claws her way southward, and the Coast Guard cutter *Edward Cornwallis* is on her way from Halifax. The crew of the *Eishin Maru,* impassive, are sure they're going to die. Reeves is too busy to think about it; she has to look for the life jackets, work the radio and satellite phone, flip through the Japanese phrase book. Eventually she has a moment to consider her options.

"Either I jump ship, or I go down with the ship. As for the first possibility, I thought about it for a while until I realized that they'd hammered all the hatches down. I thought, 'God, I'll never get off this friggin' boat, it will be my tomb.' So I figured I'd do whatever I had to do at the time, and there was no point in really thinking about it because it was just too frightening. I was just gripped by this feeling that I was going to have to do something very unpleasant. You know, like drowning is *not* going to be pleasant. And it wasn't until the moment we lost steerage that I actually thought we were going to die. I mean, I knew there was a real possibility, and I was going to have to face that."

Soon after losing steerage, a communications officer in New York asks Reeves how it's going. Not too well, she says. Is your survival suit out? Yeah, it's here, she says. Well, how many Japanese can you fit into it? Reeves laughs; even that slight joke is enough to ease the desperateness of the situation. A couple of hours later the satellite phone rings. Improbably, it's a Canadian radio reporter who wants to interview her. His name is Rick Howe.

Miss Reeves, is it rough out there? Howe asks, over the static and wind-shriek.

It's pretty rough.

What about the trawler, what's the problem?

It's not a trawler, it's a longliner. The problem is we took three windows out of the bridge earlier this morning and lost all our instrumentation.

Are you in any danger or are you confident everything's going to work out all right?

Well, we're in danger, definitely we're in danger. We're

drifting in 12 meter swells and between 50 and 60 knot winds. If we get any more water coming through the bridge that's gonna wipe out any communication that we have left. So we're definitely in danger right now.

Do you know how close the nearest ship to you is?

We're looking at about a hundred miles. If we have to abandon ship there are helicopters that can be here in three-and-a-half hours. Unfortunately they won't be able to come in the dark, so if anything happens in the dark, we're goners.

You mentioned that you expect the weather to clear up later in the day. What more can you tell us about that?

The swell size is supposed to go down to five to eight meters and the winds come around to the east, 25 to 35 knots. So that will take a lot of the edge off the fear I have right now, which is of sustaining a direct hit. If we take a direct hit, and the boat goes over, and we take another hit, the boat goes down. And we're all shored up here, everything is battened down, hatched and practically nailed shut. If she goes over there's no way anybody's gonna get out, over.

Now is there a point where you may have to abandon ship, and is the crew and yourself prepared for that eventuality?

Well, to tell you the absolute truth I don't think the crew is very prepared for an emergency. They have no emergency beacon and don't seem very up on their emergency procedure, which is a little frightening. I'm the only one who has a survival suit. But, in a swell like we have today, it wouldn't do me much good.

Yeah, right. Well, listen, I thank you for talking to us, and the whole of the province is praying for your safe return.

Thank you.

With that, Reeves turns back to the business at hand.

AFTER talking to Tommy Barrie, Billy is probably able to steam northwest another two or three hours before the seas get too rough to take on his stern. That would place him just north of data buoy 44139 and on the edge of Banquereau, one of the old fishing grounds off Nova Scotia. The 200-fathom line turns a corner at Banquereau, running north up the St. Lawrence Channel and south-southwest to Sable Island. About sixty miles due east is an underwater canyon called "The Gully," and then the Sable Island shallows start.

Sable Island is a twenty-mile sandbar that extends another forty or fifty miles east-west below water. From a distance, the surf that breaks on the shoals looks like a white sand cliff. Mariners have headed for it in storms, thinking they might save themselves by driving their boat onto the beach, only to be pounded to pieces by twenty-foot waves on the outer bar. Sable Island historian George Patterson writes, in 1894: "From the east end a bar stretches northeasterly for seventeen miles, of which the first four are dry in fine weather, the next nine covered with heavy breakers and the last four with a heavy cross-sea. The island and its bar present a continuous line of upwards of fifty miles of terrific breakers. The currents around the island are terribly conflicting and uncertain, sometimes passing around the whole circuit of the compass in 24 hours. An empty cask will be carried round and round the island, making the circuit several times, and the same is the case with bodies from wrecks."

The island prowls restlessly around the Scotian Shelf, losing sand from one end, building it up on the other, endlessly, throughout the centuries. Since 1873 it has melted away beneath the foundations of six lighthouses. Herds of wild horses live on the island, the descendants of tough Breton mountain horses left there by the French. Nothing but marran grass holds the dunes in place, and cranberries, blueberries, and wild roses grow in the inland bogs. The Gulf Stream and the glacial Labrador Current converge at Sable, frequently smothering the island in fog. Five thousand men are said to have drowned in its shallows, earning it the name "The Graveyard of the Atlantic," and at least that many have been pulled to safety by lifesaving crews that have been maintained there since 1801. "We have had a tolerable winter, and no wrecks, except the hull of the schooner Juno, of Plymouth," one island-keeper recorded in 1820. "She came ashore without masts, sails or rigging of any description, and no person on board except one dead man in the hold."

In bad weather, horsemen circled the island looking for ships in distress. If any were spotted, the horsemen rushed back for the surf boat and rowed out through the breakers to save anyone who was still alive. Sometimes they were able to fire rockets with a line attached and rig up a breeches buoy. After the storm died down they'd salvage the cargo and saw the ship timber up for firewood or construction material. People pulled from sinking ships often spent the entire winter on the island. Sometimes two or three hundred people would be camped out in the dunes, waiting for a relief ship to arrive in the spring.

Today there are two lighthouses, a Coast Guard station, a meteorological station, and several dozen oil and natural gas wells. There's a sixty-foot shoal thirty miles to the northwest and a 45-foot shoal twenty miles to the east. They mark the western and eastern ends of the sandbar, respectively. Billy isn't right on top of the bars yet, but he's getting close. In the old days it was known that most shipwrecks on Sable occurred because of errors in navigation; the westerly current was so strong that it could throw boats off by sixty to a hundred miles. If Billy has lost his electronics—his GPS, radar, and loran—he's effectively back in the old days. He'd have a chart of the Grand Banks on the chart table and would be estimating his position based on compass heading, forward speed, and wind conditions. This is called dead reckoning. Maybe the currents and the storm winds push Billy farther west than he realizes, and he gets into the shallows around Sable. Maybe he has turned downsea on purpose to keep water out of the wheelhouse, or to save fuel. Or maybe their steering's gone and, like the *Eishin Maru,* they're just careening westward on the weather.

Whatever it is, one thing is known for sure. Around midnight on October 28th—when the storm is at its height off Sable Island—something catastrophic happens aboard the *Andrea Gail*.

THE ZERO-MOMENT POINT

Behold a pale horse, and his name who sat
on him was Death, and Hell followed with him.

—*Revelation* 6:8

In the 1950s and 1960s, the U.S. Government decided to detonate a series of nuclear devices in the Pacific Ocean. The

thinking was that deep water would absorb the shock-wave and minimize the effect on the environment, while still allowing scientists to gauge the strength of the explosions. But an oceanographer named William Van Dorn, associated with the Scripps Institute in La Jolla, California, warned them that a nuclear explosion in the wrong place "could convert the entire continental shelf into a surf zone."

Concerned, the Navy ran a series of wave tank tests to see what kind of stresses their fleet could take. (They'd already lost three destroyers to a typhoon in 1944. Before going down the ships had radioed that they were rolling through arcs of 140 degrees. They downflooded through their stacks and sank.) The Navy subjected model destroyers and aircraft carriers to various kinds of waves and found that a single nonbreaking wave—no matter how big it was—was incapable of sinking a ship. A single *breaking* wave, though, would flip a ship end over end if it was higher than the ship was long. Typically, the ship would climb the wave at an angle of 45 degrees, fail to gain the top, and then slide back down the face. Her stern would bury itself into the trough, and the crest of the wave would catch her bow and flip her over. This is called pitch-poling; Ernie Hazard was pitch-poled on Georges Bank. It's one of the few motions that can end ship-to-shore communication instantly.

Another is a succession of waves that simply drives the boat under—"founders," as mariners say. The dictionary defines founder as "to cave in, sink, fail utterly, collapse." On a steel boat the windows implode, the hatches fail, and the boat starts to downflood. The crew is prevented from escaping by the sheer force of the water pouring into the cabin—it's like walking into the blast of a firehose. In that sense, pitch-poling is better than foundering because an overturned boat traps air in the hold and can stay afloat for an hour or more. That might allow members of the crew to swim out a doorway and climb into a life raft. The rafts are designed to inflate automatically and release from the boat when she goes down. In theory the EPIRB floats free as well, and begins signalling to shore. All the crew has to do is stay alive.

By the late hours of October 28th the sea state is easily high enough to either pitch-pole the *Andrea Gail* or drive her under. And if she loses power—a clogged fuel filter, a fouled prop—she could slew to the side and roll. The same rule applies to capsizing as to pitch-poling: the wave must be higher than the boat is wide. The *Andrea Gail* is twenty feet across her beam. But even if the boat doesn't get hit by a non-negotiable wave, the rising sea state allows Billy less and less leeway to maneuver. If he maintains enough speed to steer, he beats the boat to pieces; if he slows down, he loses rudder control. This is the end result of two days of narrowing options; now the only choice left is whether to go upsea or down, and the only outcome is whether they sink or float. There's not much in between.

If the conditions don't subside, the most Billy can realistically hope for is to survive until dawn. Then at least they'll have a chance of being rescued—now it's unthinkable. "In violent storms there is so much water in the air, and so much air in the water, that it becomes impossible to tell where the atmosphere stops and the sea begins," writes Van Dorn. "That may literally make it impossible to distinguish up from down." In such conditions a helicopter pilot could never pluck six people off the deck of a boat. So, for the next eight hours, the crew of the *Andrea Gail* must keep the pumps and engine running and just hope they don't encounter any rogue waves. Seventy-footers are roaming around the sea state like surly giants and there's not much Billy can do but take them head-on and try to get over the top before they break. If his floodlights are out he wouldn't even have that option—he'd just feel a drop into the trough, a lurch, and the boat starting up a slope way too steep to survive.

"Seventy foot seas—I'd be puttin' on my diapers at that point," says Charlie Reed. "I'd be quite nervous. That's higher than the highest point on the *Andrea Gail.* I once came home from the Grand Banks in 35-foot seas. It was a scary fuckin' thought—straight up, straight down, for six days. My guess is that Billy turned side-to and rolled. You come off one of those seas cocked, the next one comes at a different angle, it pushes the boat around and then you roll. If the boat flips over—even with everything dogged down—water's gonna get in. The boat's upside-down, the plywood's buckling, that's the end."

When Ernie Hazard went over on Georges Bank in 1982, the motion wasn't a violent one so much as a huge, slow somersault that laid the boat over on her back. Hazard remembers one wave spinning them around and another lifting them end over end. It wasn't like rolling a car at high speeds, it was more like rolling a house. Hazard was 33 at the time; three years earlier he'd answered a newspaper ad and got a job on the *Fair Wind,* a lobster boat out of Newport, Rhode Island. The storm hit on their last trip of the year, late November. The crew were all good friends; they celebrated the end of their season at a steakhouse and then left for Georges Bank late the next morning. The winds were light and the forecast called for several more days of fair weather. By dawn it was blowing a hundred:

> We were driving the boat well. You point the boat into the sea and try to hold your own until it blows out—stay there, take your pounding. You balance the boat, flood the tanks, try to save what you have on deck. There was the typical howling of wind in the wires and there was a lot of foam because of the wind, yellow foam, spindrift. We'd lose power on the waves because they were more foam than water, the propeller just couldn't bite.
>
> It happened quick. We were close to the edge of the continental shelf and the seas were getting large, starting to break. Cresting. I remember looking out the pilothouse and this monster wave came and broke over the bow and forced us backwards. There was nothing to hold us there and we must have dug the stern in and then spun around. Now we're in a full following sea. We never went more than one more wave when we buried our bow in the trough and flipped over. There was the wave breaking and then a sensation of the boat turning, and the next thing I knew we were upside-down. Floating inside the boat.
>
> I happened to surface in a small air pocket and I didn't know if I was upside down or standing on the walls or what. I made a dive into the pilothouse and I could see some light—it could have been a window or a porthole, I don't know—and when I got back up into the wheelhouse there was no more air. It was all gone. I was thinking, "This is it. Just take a mouthful of water and it's over." It was very matter-of-fact. I was at a fork in the road and there was work to do—swim or die. It didn't scare me, I didn't think about my family or anything. It was more business-like. People think you always have to go for life, but you don't. You can quit.

For reasons that he still doesn't understand, Hazard didn't quit. He made a guess and swam. The entire port side of the cabin was welded steel and he knew if he picked that direction, he was finished. He felt himself slide through a narrow opening—the door? a window?—and suddenly he was back in the world. The boat was hull-up, sliding away fast, and the life raft was convulsing at the end of its tether. It was his only hope; he wriggled out of his clothes and started to swim.

Whether the *Andrea Gail* rolls, pitch-poles, or gets driven down, she winds up, one way or another, in a position from which she cannot recover. Among marine architects this is known as the zero-moment point—the point of no return. The transition from crisis to catastrophe is fast, probably under a minute, or someone would've tripped the EPIRB. (In fact the EPIRB doesn't even signal when it hits the water, which means it has somehow malfunctioned. In the vast majority of cases, the Coast Guard knows when men are dying offshore.) There's no time to put on survival suits or grab a life vest; the boat's moving through the most extreme motion of her life and there isn't even time to shout. The refrigerator comes out of the wall and crashes across the galley. Dirty dishes cascade out of the sink. The T.V., the washing machine, the VCR tapes, the men, all go flying. And, seconds later, the water moves in.

When a boat floods, the first thing that happens is that her electrical system shorts out. The lights go off, and for a few moments the only illumination is the frenetic blue of sparks arcing down into the water. It's said that people in extreme situations perceive things in distorted, almost surreal ways, and when the wires start to crackle and burn, perhaps one of the crew thinks of fireworks—of the last Fourth of July, walking around Gloucester with his girlfriend and watching colors blossom over the inner harbor. There'd be tourists shuffling down Rogers Street and fishermen hooting from bars and the smell of gunpowder and fried clams drifting through town. He'd have his whole life ahead of him, that July evening; he'd have every choice in the world.

And he wound up swordfishing. He wound up, by one route or another, on this trip, in this storm, with this boat filling up with water and one or two minutes left to live. There's no going back now, no rescue helicopter that could possibly save him. All that's left is to hope it's over fast.

When the water first hits the trapped men, it's cold but not paralyzing, around 52 degree. A man can survive up to four hours in that temperature if something holds him up. If the boat rolls or flips over, the men in the wheelhouse are the first to drown. Their experience is exactly like Hazard's except that they don't make it out of the wheelhouse to a life raft; they inhale and that's it. After that the water rises up the companionway, flooding the galley and berths, and then starts up the inverted engine room hatch. It may well be pouring in the aft door and the fish hatch, too, if either failed during the sinking. If the boat is hull-up and there are men in the engine room, they are the last to die. They're in absolute darkness, under a landslide of tools and gear, the water rising up the companionway and the roar of the waves probably very muted through the hull. If the water takes long enough, they might attempt to escape on a lungful of air—down the companionway, along the hall, through the aft door and out from under the boat—but they don't make it. It's too far, they die trying. Or the water comes up so hard and fast that they can't even think. They're up to their waists and then their chests and then their chins and then there's no air at all. Just what's in their lungs, a minute's worth or so.

The instinct not to breathe underwater is so strong that it overcomes the agony of running out of air. No matter how desperate the drowning person is, he doesn't inhale until he's on the verge of losing consciousness. At that point there's so much carbon dioxide in the blood, and so little oxygen, that chemical sensors in the brain trigger an involuntary breath whether he's underwater or not. That is called the "break point"; laboratory experiments have shown the break point to come after 87 seconds. It's a sort of neurological optimism, as if the body were saying, *Holding our breath is killing us, and breathing in might not kill us, so we might as well breathe in.* If the person hyperventilates first—as free divers do, and as a frantic person might—the break point comes as late as 140 seconds. Hyperventilation initially flushes carbon dioxide out of the system, so it takes that much longer to climb back up to critical levels.

Until the break point, a drowning person is said to be undergoing "voluntary apnea," choosing not to breathe. Lack of oxygen to the brain causes a sensation of darkness closing in from all sides, as in a camera aperture stopping down. The panic of a drowning person is mixed with an odd incredulity that this is actually happening. Having never done it before, the body—and the mind—do not know how to die gracefully. The process is filled with desperation and awkwardness. "So *this* is drowning," a drowning person might think. "So *this* is how my life finally ends."

Along with the disbelief is an overwhelming sense of being wrenched from life at the most banal, inopportune moment imaginable. "I can't die, I have tickets to next week's game," is not an impossible thought for someone who is drowning. The drowning person may even feel embarrassed, as if he's squandered a great fortune. He has an image of people shaking their heads over his dying so senselessly. The drowning person may feel as if it's the last, greatest act of stupidity in his life.

These thoughts shriek through the mind during the minute or so that it takes a panicked person to run out of air. When the first involuntary breath occurs most people are still conscious, which is unfortunate, because the only thing more unpleasant than running out of air is breathing in water. At that point the person goes from voluntary to involuntary apnea, and the drowning begins in earnest. A spasmodic breath drags water into the mouth and windpipe, and then one of two things happen. In about ten percent of people, water—anything—touching the vocal cords triggers an immediate contraction in the muscles around the larynx. In effect, the central nervous system judges something in the voice box to be more of a threat than low oxygen levels in the blood, and acts accordingly. This is called a laryngospasm. It's so powerful that it overcomes the breathing reflex and eventually suffocates the person. A person with laryngospasm drowns without any water in his lungs.

In the other ninety percent of people, water floods the lungs and ends any waning transfer of oxygen to the blood. The clock is running down now; half-conscious and enfeebled by oxygen depletion, the person is in no position to fight his way back up to the surface. The very process of drowning makes it harder and harder not to drown, an exponential disaster curve similar to that of a sinking boat.

Occasionally someone makes it back from this dark world, though, and it's from these people that we know what drowning feels like. In 1892 a Scottish doctor named James Lowson was on a steamship bound for Colombo, Sri Lanka, when they ran into a typhoon and went down in the dead of night. Most of the 150 people on board sank with the ship, but Lowson managed to fight his way out of the hold and over the side. The ship sank out from under his feet, dragging him down, and the last thing he remembers is losing consciousness underwater. A few minutes later the buoyancy of his life vest shot him to the surface, though, and he washed up on an island and lived to write about his experiences in the *Edinburgh Medical Journal.* He attributed the clarity of his recollection to the "preternatural calm" of people facing death. It's as close as one is going to get to the last moments of the *Andrea Gail:*

> All afternoon the hammering of the big seas on the doomed vessel went on, whilst night came only to add darkness to our other horrors. Shortly before ten o'clock three tremendous seas found their way down the stokehole, putting out the fires, and our situation was desperate. The end came shortly before mid-

night, when there was a heavy crash on the reef, and the vessel was lying at the bottom of the Straits of Formosa in under a minute.

With scarcely time to think I pulled down the life-belts and, throwing two to my companions, tied the third on myself and bolted for the companionway. There was no time to spare for studying humanity at this juncture, but I can never forget the apparent want of initiative in all I passed. All the passengers seemed paralyzed—even my companions, some of them able military men. The stewards of the ship, uttering cries of despair and last farewells, blocked the entrance to the deck, and it was only by sheer force I was able to squeeze past them. Getting out on deck, a perfect mountain of water seemed to come from overhead, as well as from below, and dashed me against the bridge companionway. The ship was going down rapidly, and I was pulled down with her, struggling to extricate myself.

I got clear under water and immediately struck out to reach the surface, only to go farther down. This exertion was a serious waste of breath, and after ten or fifteen seconds the effort of inspiration could no longer be restrained. It seemed as if I was in a vice which was gradually being screwed up tight until it felt as if the sternum and spinal column must break. Many years ago my old teacher used to describe how painless and easy a death by drowning was—"like falling about in a green field in early summer"—and this flashed across my brain at the time. The "gulping" efforts became less frequent, and the pressure seemed unbearable, but gradually the pain seemed to ease up. I appeared to be in a pleasant dream, although I had enough will power to think of friends at home and the sight of the Grampians, familiar to me as a boy, that was brought into my view. Before losing consciousness the chest pain had completely disappeared and the sensation was actually pleasant.

When consciousness returned, I found myself at the surface, and managed to get a dozen good inspirations. Land was about four hundred yards distant, and I used a bale of silk and then a long wooden plank to assist me to shore. On landing, and getting behind a sheltering rock, no effort was required to produce copius emesis. After the excitement, sound sleep set in, and this sleep lasted three hours, when a profuse diarrhea came on, evi-

> dently brought on by the sea water ingested. Until morning broke all my muscles were in a constant tremor which could not be controlled. (Several weeks later) I was sleeping in a comfortable bed and, late in the evening, a nightmare led to my having a severe struggle with the bedroom furniture, finally taking a "header" out of the bed and coming to grief on the floor.

Lowson guesses that laryngospasm prevented water from entering his lungs when he was unconscious. The crew of the *Andrea Gail* either have laryngospasms or completely inundated lungs. They are suspended, open-eyed and unconscious, in the flooded enclosures of the boat. The darkness is absolute and the boat may already be on her way to the bottom. At this point only a massive amount of oxygen could save these men. They have suffered, at most, a minute or two. Their bodies, having imposed increasingly drastic measures to keep functioning, have finally started to shut down. Water in the lungs washes away a substance called surfactant, which enables the alvioli to leech oxygen out of the air. The alvioli themselves, grape-like clusters of membrane on the lung wall, collapse because blood cannot get through the pulmonary artery. The artery has constricted in an effort to shunt blood to areas of the lungs where there is more oxygen. Unfortunately, those don't exist. The heart labors under critically low levels of oxygen and starts to beat erratically—"like a bag full of worms," as one doctor says. This is called ventricular fibrillation. The more irregularly the heart beats, the less blood it moves and the faster life-functions decline. Children—who have proportionally stronger hearts than adults—can maintain a heartbeat for up to five minutes without air. Adults die faster. The heart beats less and less effectively until, after several minutes, there's no movement at all. Only the brain is alive.

The central nervous system does not know what has happened to the body; all it knows is that not enough oxygen is getting to the brain. Orders are still being issued—*Breathe! Pump! Circulate!*—that the body cannot obey. If the person were defibrillated at that moment, he might possibly survive. He could be given cardiopulmonary resuscitation, put on a respirator, and coaxed back to life. Still, the body is doing everything it can to delay the inevitable. When cold water touches the face, an impulse travels along the trigeminal nerve to the central nervous system and lowers the metabolic rate. The pulse slows down and the blood pools where it's needed most, in the heart and skull. It's a sort of temporary hibernation that drastically reduces the body's need for oxygen. Nurses will splash ice water on the face of a person with a racing heart to trigger the same reaction.

The diving reflex, as this is called, is compounded by the general effect of cold temperature on tissue—it preserves it. All chemical reactions, and metabolic processes, become honey-slow, and the brain can get by on less than half the oxygen it normally requires. There are cases of people spending forty or fifty minutes under lake ice and surviving. The colder the water, the stronger the diving reflex, the slower the metabolic processes, and the longer the survival time. The crew of the *Andrea Gail* do not find themselves in particularly cold water, though; it may add five or ten minutes to their lives. And there is no one around to save them anyway. The electrical activity in their brain gets weaker and weaker until, after fifteen or twenty minutes, it ceases altogether.

The body could be likened to a crew that resorts to increasingly desperate measures to keep their vessel afloat. Eventually the last wire has shorted out, the last bit of decking has settled under the water. Tyne, Pierre, Sullivan, Moran, Murphy, and Shatford are dead.

THE WORLD OF THE LIVING

The sea had kept his finite body up, but drowned the infinite of his soul. He saw God's foot upon the treadle of the loom, and spoke it; and his shipmates called him mad.

—*Herman Melville,* Moby Dick

Albert Johnston, fifty miles south of the Tail on the *Mary T*, gets hit a few hours after the *Andrea Gail* but just as hard. The first sign of the storm is a massive amount of static over the VHF, and then the wind comes: thirty, forty, fifty knots, and finally it tears the anemometer off buoy #44138. The buoy is about fifty miles northwest of Johnston's position and pegs 56 knots before flatlining at the bottom of the chart. Wind speeds above the interference of the wave crests are probably half again as high. The center of the low slides past Johnston late on the 28th and continues curving back around toward the coast throughout the next day. That motion spares Johnston the worst of the storm. It also, as far as he's concerned, spares him his life.

Johnston jogs into the wind and seas until night falls and then turns around and goes with it. He doesn't want to take the chance of running into a rogue wave in the dark and blowing his windows out. Throughout the early hours of October 29th, he surfs downwind on the backs of the huge seas, following a finger of cold Labrador Current, and when dawn breaks he turns around and fights his way northward again. He wants to gain enough sea-room so that he won't hit the Gulf Stream when he runs south again the following night. On the second day the crew fight their way onto the deck to check the fishhold and lazarette hatches and tighten the anchor fastenings. The sun has come out, glancing dully off the green ocean, and the wind screams out of the east, setting the cables to moaning and sending long streaks of foam scudding through the air. Radio waves become so bogged down in the saturated air that the radar stops working; at one point an unidentified Japanese sword boat appears out of nowhere, searchlight prying into the gloom, and passes within a few hundred yards of the *Mary T.* On the steeper seas she can't get her bow up in time and plunges straight through the wall of water. Nothing but her wheelhouse shows and then slowly, unstoppably, her bow rises back up. The two vessels pass by each other without a word or a sign, unable to communicate, unable to help each other, navigating their own courses through hell.

Except for that one expedition on deck to check the fishhold, the crew keep to their bunks and Johnston stays bolted to the wheelhouse floor, wrestling the helm and jotting down notes in the ship log. His entries are terse, bullet descriptions of the unending chaos outside. *"NE 80-100 winds came on as we passed through west side of eye,"* he records on the 29th. *"Seas 20-30 feet. Dangerous Storm to move E 15 kts become station drift SW & merge with Grace."* Johnston is one of the most meteorologically-inclined captains of the sword fleet, and he's been keeping a weather eye on Hurricane Grace, which has been quietly slipping up the coast. At 8 AM on the 29th, Grace collides with the cold front, as predicted, and goes reeling back out to sea. She's moving extremely fast and packing eighty-knot winds and thirty-foot seas. She's a player now, an important—if dying—element in the atmospheric machinery assembling itself south of Sable. Grace crosses the 40th parallel that afternoon, and at 8 PM on October 29th, Hurricane Grace runs into the Sable Island storm.

The effect is instantaneous. Tropical air is a sort of meteorological accelerant that can blow another storm system through the roof, and within hours of encountering Hurricane Grace, the pressure gradient around the storm forms the equivalent of a cliff. Weather charts plot barometric pressure the way topographical maps plot elevation, and in both cases, the closer together the lines are, the steeper the change. Weather charts of the Grand Banks for the early hours of October 30th show isobaric lines converging in one black mass on the north side of the storm. A storm with tightly-packed isobaric lines is said to have a steep pressure gradient, and the wind will rush downhill, as it were, with particular violence. In the case of the storm off Sable Island, the wind starts rushing into the low at speeds up to a hundred miles an hour. As a NOAA disaster report put it blandly a year later, "The dangerous storm previously forecast was now fact."

The only good thing about such winter gales, as far as coastal residents are concerned, is that they tend to travel west-to-east offshore. That means their forward movement is subtracted from their windspeed: A seventy-knot wind from a storm moving away at twenty knots effectively becomes a fifty-knot wind. The opposite is also true—forward movement is added to wind speed—but that almost never happens on the East Coast. The atmospheric movement is all west-to-east in the midlatitudes, and it's nearly impossible for a weather system to overcome that. Storms may wobble northeast or southeast for a while, but they never really buck the jet stream. It takes a freakish alignment of variables to permit that to happen, a third cog in the huge machinations of the sky.

Generally speaking, it takes a hurricane.

By October 30th, the Sable Island storm is firmly imbedded between the remnants of Hurricane Grace and the Canadian high. Like all large bodies, hurricanes have a hard time slowing down, and her counterclockwise circulation continues long after her internal structures have fallen apart. The Canadian high, in the meantime, is still spinning clockwise with dense, cold air. These two systems function like huge gears that catch the storm between their teeth and extrude it westward. This is called a retrograde; it's an act of meteorological defiance that might happen in a major storm only every hundred years or so. As early as October 27th, NOAA's Cray computers in Maryland were saying that the storm would retrograde back toward the coast; two days later Bob Case was in his office watching exactly that happen on GOES satellite imagery. Meteorologists see perfection in strange things, and the meshing of three completely independent weather systems to form a hundred-year event is one of them. My God, thought Case, this is the perfect storm.

As a result of this horrible alignment, the bulk of the sword fleet—way out by the Flemish Cap—is spared the brunt of the storm, while everyone closer to shore gets pummeled. The 105-foot *Mr. Simon,* a hundred miles west of Albert Johnston, gets her aft door blown in, her wheelhouse flooded, and her anchor fastenings torn off. The anchor starts slamming around on deck and a crewman has to go out and cut it free. The *Laurie Dawn 8* loses her antennas and then takes a wave down her breather pipes that stuffs one of her engines. Farther south down the coast the situation is even worse. A bulk carrier named the *Eagle* finds herself in serious trouble off the Carolinas, along with a freighter named the *Star Baltic,* and both struggle into port badly damaged. The 90-foot schooner *Anne Khristine,* built 123 years ago, sinks off the coast of Delaware and her crew has to be saved by Coast Guard helicopters. The bulk carrier *Zarah,* just fifty miles south of the *Andrea Gail,* takes ninety-foot seas over her decks that shear off the steel bolts holding her portholes down.

Thirty tons of water flood the crew mess, continue into the officer's mess, explode a steel bulkhead, tear through two more walls, flood the crew's sleeping quarters, course down a companionway, and kill the ship's engine. The *Zarah* is 550 feet long.

And the sailing vessel *Satori,* alone at the mouth of the Great South Channel, is starting to lose the battle to stay afloat. Karen Stimson crouches miserably by the navigation table and listens to the Tuesday morning NOAA forecast: ONE OF THE WORST STORMS SINCE THE BLIZZARD OF '78, ALREADY THREE DOZEN BOATS BEACHED OR SUNK AT NAUSET BEACH. SHIP REPORTS OF 63 FOOT SEAS, WHICH IS PROBABLY HIGH BUT A SIGN OF PROBLEMS UPCOMING. HEAVY SURF ADVISORY BEING ISSUED DESPITE TEMPORARY LULL IN THE WIND FIELD.

Instead of abating, as Leonard insisted, the storm just keeps getting worse; the seas are thirty feet and the winds are approaching hurricane force. The boat rolls helplessly on her beam-ends every time a wave catches her on the side. "We were taking *such* a hammering—real neck-snapping violence," says Stimson. "Things were flying, every wave was knocking us across the cabin. It was only a matter of time before the boat started to break up." Bylander refuses to go on deck, and Leonard curls up on his bunk, sullen and silent, sneaking gulps off a whiskey bottle. Stimson puts on every piece of clothing she has, climbs the narrow companionway and clips herself onto the lifeline.

No matter what she does—lashing the tiller, running downwind, showing less jib—she can't control the boat. Several times she's snapped to the end of her tether by boarding seas. Stimson knows that if they don't keep their bow to the weather they'll roll, so she decides they have no choice but to run the engine. She goes belowdeck to ask Leonard how much fuel they have, but he gives a different answer each time she asks. That's a bad sign for both the fuel level and Leonard's state of mind. But fuel isn't their only problem,

Leonard points out; there's also the propeller itself. In such chaotic seas the prop keeps lifting out of the water and revving too high; eventually the bearings will burn out.

While Leonard is explaining the subtleties of prop cavitation, the first knockdown occurs. A wave catches the *Satori* broadsides and puts her mast in the water; the entire crew crashes against the far wall. Canned food rockets across the galley and water starts pouring into the cabin. At first Stimson thinks the hull has opened up—a death sentence—but the water has just burst through the main hatch. Debris and splintered glass litter the cabin, and the nav table is drenched. The single sideband is dead, and the VHF looks doubtful.

Most of Stimson's experience is with wooden boats; in rough weather they tend to spring their caulking and sink. Fiberglass is a lot stronger but it, too, has limits. Stimson just doesn't know what those limits are. There seems to be no way to keep the boat pointed into the seas, no way to minimize the beating they're taking. Even if the VHF can transmit a mayday—and it's impossible to know that for sure—it only has a range of several miles. They're fifty miles out at sea. Between waves, between slammings, Stimson shouts, I think we should prepare a survival bag! In case we have to abandon ship!

Bylander, grateful for something to do, sorts through the wreckage on the floor and stuffs tins of food, bottled water, clothes, and a wire cheese slicer into a sea bag. Sue, we don't need the slicer, we can bite the cheese! Stimson says, but Bylander just shakes her head. I've read about this and it's the little niceties that make the difference! Ray, where are the boat cushions? While preparing their emergency bag, they get knocked over a second time. This one is even more violent than the first, and the boat is a long time in coming back up. Stimson and Leonard pick themselves off the floor, bruised and dazed, and Bylander sticks her head out the hatch to check for damage on deck. My God, Karen! she screams. The life raft's gone!

"I was in a corner and I covered myself with soft things," says Stimson, "and with a flashlight I took about ten minutes and wrote some goodbyes and stuck it in a ziplock bag and put it in my clothing. That was the lowest point. We had no contact with anyone, it was the dark of the night—which brings its own kind of terror—and I had a sense that things were going to get worse. But it's a strange thing. There was no sentiment there, no time for fear. To me, fear is two AM, walking down a city street and someone's following me—that to me is a terror beyond words. What was happening was not a terror beyond words. It was a grim sense of reality, a scrambling to figure out what to do next, a determination to stay alive and keep other people alive, and an awareness of the dark noisy slamming of the boat. But it wasn't a terror beyond words. I just had an overwhelming sense of knowing we weren't going to make it."

Stimson doesn't know it, but Bylander tapes her passport to her stomach so her body can be identified. Both women, at this point, are prepared to die. After Stimson finishes writing her goodbyes, she tells Leonard that it's time to issue a mayday. Mayday comes from the French *venez m'aidez*—come help me!—and essentially means that those on board have given up all hope. It's up to someone else to save them. Leonard is motionless on his berth. Okay, he says. Stimson forces her way out to the cockpit and Bylander sits down at the nav table to see if she can coax the VHF back to life.

At 11:15 PM, October 29th, a freighter off Long Island picks up a woman's terrified voice on the VHF: *This is the* Satori, *the* Satori, *39:49 north and 69:52 west, we are three people, this is a mayday. If anyone can hear us, please pass our position on to the Coast Guard. Repeat, this is a mayday, if anyone can hear us, pass our position on to the Coast Guard . . .*

The freighter, the *Gold Bond Conveyor,* relays the message to Coast Guard operations in Boston, which in turn contacts the Coast Guard cutter *Tamaroa* in Provincetown Harbor. The *Tamaroa* has just come off Georges Bank, where she was conducting spot checks on the fishing fleet, and now she's waiting out the weather inside Cape Cod's huge flexed arm. A small Falcon jet scrambles from Air Station Cape Cod and the *Tamaroa*, 1,600 tons and 205 feet, weighs anchor at midnight and heads down the throat of the storm.

The crew of the *Satori* have no way of knowing whether the radio is working, they just have to keep repeating the mayday and hope for the best. And even if the radio *is* working, they still have to be within two or three miles of another vessel for the signal to be heard. That's a lot to ask for on a night like this. Bylander, wedged behind the nav table, broadcasts their name and position intermittently for half an hour without any response at all; they're alone out there, as far as she can tell. She keeps trying—what else is there to do?—and Stimson goes back on deck to try to keep the *Satori* pointed into the seas. She's not there long when she hears the sound of an airplane fading in and out through the roar of the storm. She looks around frantically in the darkness, and a minute later a Falcon jet, flying low under the cloud cover, shrieks overhead and raises Bylander on the VHF. "Sue was so excited she was giddy," Stimson says, "but I wasn't. I remember not feeling elated or relieved so much as like, instantly, I'd rejoined the world of the living."

The Falcon pilot circles just below cloud level and discusses what to do next over the VHF with Bylander. The *Tamaroa* won't be there for another twelve hours, and they've got to keep the boat afloat until then, even if that means burning out the engine. They can't afford to risk any more knockdowns. Bylander, against Leonard's wishes, finally toggles the starter switch, and to her amazement it turns over. With the storm jib up and the prop turning away they can now get a few degrees to the weather. It's not a lot, but it's enough to keep from getting broached by the seas.

Throughout the night the Falcon pilot flies over them, reassuring Bylander that they're going to come out of this alive. Stimson stays at the helm and Leonard lies on his bunk contemplating the impending loss of his boat. When the *Tamaroa* arrives he'll have to abandon ship, which is an almost unthinkable act for a captain. The *Satori* is his home, his life, and if he allows himself to be taken off by the Coast Guard he'll probably never see her again. Not intact, anyway. At some point that night, lying on his bunk waiting for dawn, Ray Leonard decides he won't get off the boat. The women can leave if they want to, but he'll see the vessel into port.

Throughout that night the *Tamaroa* slugs her way through the storm. She's a bulldog of a vessel, built to salvage crippled battleships in World War Two, and she can "tow anything afloat," according to her literature. The sea state is so high, though, that the most she can make is three or four knots—roughly walking pace. On the larger swells she plunges into the crest, stalls, and launches out the far side, spray streaming off her bridge and greenwater sheeting out her scuppers. She crosses Cape Cod Bay, threads the canal, leaves the Elizabeth Islands to starboard, and finally turns the corner around Martha's Vineyard. Commander Lawrence Brudnicki, chief officer on board, estimates that they'll arrive on-scene late the next afternoon; the *Satori* crew has to stay afloat until then. They have no life raft or survival suits on board, and the nearest helicopter base is an hour away. If the *Satori* goes down, the crew is dead.

Brudnicki can't speak directly to the *Satori,* but he can relay messages via the Falcon that's circling above them. Both ship and plane are also in contact with the First District Command Center in Boston—D1 Comcen, as it's referred to in Coast Guard reports. D1 Comcen is responsible for coordinating all the Coast Guard vessels and aircraft on the rescue, and developing the safest strategy for taking the people off the boat. Every decision has to be approved by them. Since the *Satori* isn't sinking yet, they decide to have the Falcon fly cover until the *Tamaroa* arrives, and then take the crew off by raft. Air rescue in such conditions can be riskier than actually staying with the the boat, so it's used as a last resort. As soon as day breaks, the Falcon will be relieved by an H-3 rescue helicopter, and H-3's will fly cover in shifts until the *Tamaroa* shows up. Helicopters have a limited amount of flying time—generally about four hours—but they can pluck people out of the water if need be. Falcon jets can't do much for people in the water except circle them and watch them drown.

From the incident log, D1 Comcen:

2:30 AM—s/v [sailing vessel] is running out of fuel, recommend we try to keep Falcon o/s [on-scene] until Tamaroa arrives.
5:29 AM—Falcon has lost comms [communication] with vessel, vessel is low on battery power and taking on water. Pumps are keeping up but are run by ele [electric].
7:07 AM—Falcon o/s, vessel has been located. Six hours fuel left. People on board are scared.

The H-3 arrives on scene around 6:30 and spends half an hour just trying to locate the *Satori.* The conditions are so bad that she's vanished from the Falcon's radar, and the H-3 pilot is almost on top of her before spotting her in the foam-streaked seas. The Falcon circles off to the southwest to prepare a life-raft drop while the H-3 takes up a hover directly over the boat. In these conditions the Falcon pilot could never line up on something as small as a sailboat, so the H-3 acts as a stand-in. The Falcon comes back at 140 knots, radar locked onto the helicopter, and at the last moment the H-3 falls away and the jet makes the drop. The pilot comes screaming over the *Satori*'s mast and the copilot pushes two life-raft packages out a hatch in the floorboards. The rafts are linked by a long nylon tether, and as they fall they cartwheel apart, splashing down well to either side of the *Satori.* The tether, released at two hundred feet into a hurricane-force wind, drops right into Bylander's hand.

The H-3 hovers overhead while the *Satori* crew haul in the packages, but both rafts have exploded on impact. There's nothing at either end of the line. The *Tamaroa* is still five hours away and the storm has retrograded to within a couple of hundred miles of the coast; over the next twenty-four hours it will pass directly over the *Satori*. A daylight rescue in these conditions is difficult, and a nighttime rescue is out of the question. If the *Satori* crew is not taken off in the next few hours, there's a good chance they won't be taken off at all. Late that morning the second H-3 arrives and the pilot, Lieutenant Klosson, explains the situation to Ray Leonard. Leonard radios back that he's not leaving the boat.

It's unclear whether Leonard is serious or just trying to save face. Either way, the Coast Guard is having none of it. Two helicopters, two Falcon jets, a medium-range cutter, and a hundred air- and seamen have already been committed to the rescue; the *Satori* crew are coming off now. *"Owner refuses to leave and says he's sailed through hurricanes before,"* the Comcen incident log records at 12:24 that afternoon. *"Tamaroa wants manifestly unsafe voyage so that o/o [owner-operator] can be forced off."*

A "manifestly unsafe voyage" means that the vessel has been deemed an unacceptable risk to her crew or others, and the Coast Guard has the legal authority to order everyone off. Commander Brudnicki gets on the radio with District One and requests a manifestly unsafe designation for the *Satori*, and at 12:47 it is granted. The *Tamaroa* is just a couple of miles away now, within VHF range of the *Satori*, and Brudnicki raises Leonard on the radio and tells him he has no choice in the matter. Everyone is leaving the boat. At 12:57 in the afternoon, thirteen hours after weighing anchor, the *Tamaroa* plunges into view.

There's a lot of hardware circling the *Satori*. There's the Falcon, the H-3, the *Tamaroa*, and the freighter *Gold Bond Conveyor*, which has been cutting circles around the *Satori* since the first mayday call. Hardware is not the problem, though; it's time. Dark is only three hours away, and the departing H-3 pilot doesn't think the *Satori* will survive another night. She'll run out of fuel, start getting knocked down, and eventually break apart. The crew will be cast into the sea, and the helicopter pilot will refuse to drop his rescue swimmer because he can't be sure of getting him back. It would be up to the *Tamaroa* to maneuver alongside the swimmers and pull them on board, and in these seas it would be almost impossible. It's now or never.

The only way to take them off, Brudnicki decides, is to shuttle them back to the *Tamaroa* in one of the little Avons. The Avons are 21-foot inflatable rafts with rigid hulls and outboard engines; one of them could make a run to the *Satori,* drop off survival suits and then come back again to pick up the three crew. If anyone wound up in the water, at least they'd be insulated and afloat. It's not a particularly complicated maneuver, but no one has done it in conditions like this before. No one has even *seen* conditions like this before. At 1:23 PM the *Tamaroa* crew gathers at the port davits, three men climb aboard the Avon, and they lower away.

It goes badly from the start. What passes for a lull between waves is in fact a crest-to-trough change of thirty or forty feet. Chief bosun Thomas Amidon lowers the Avon half way down, gets lifted up by the next wave, can't keep up with the trough and freefalls to the bottom of the cable. The lifting eye gets ripped out of its mount and Amidon almost pitches overboard. He struggles back into position, finishes lowering the boat, and makes way from the *Tamaroa.*

The seas are twice the size of the Avon raft. With excruciating slowness it fights its way to the *Satori,* comes up bow-to-stern, and a crew member flings the three survival suits on deck. Stimson grabs them and hands them out, but Amidon doesn't back out in time. The sailboat rides up a sea, comes down on the Avon, and punctures one of her air bladders. Things start to happen very fast now: the Avon's bow collapses, a wave swamps her to the gunwales, the engine dies, and she falls away astern. Amidon tries desperately to get the engine going again and finally manages to, but they're up to their waists in water and the raft is crippled. There's no way they can even get themselves back onto the *Tamaroa,* much less save the crew of the *Satori.* Six people, not just three, now need to be rescued.

The H-3 crew watches all this incredulously. They're in a two o'clock hover with their jump door open, just over the tops of the waves. They can see the raft dragging heavily through the seas, and the *Tamaroa* heaving through 90-degree rolls. Pilot Claude Hessel finally gets on the radio and tells Brudnicki and Amidon that he may have another way of doing this. He can't hoist the *Satori* crew directly off their deck, he says, because the mast is flailing too wildly and might entangle the hoist. That would drag the H-3 right down on top of the boat. But he could drop his rescue swimmer, who could take the people off the boat one at a time and bring them up on the hoist. It's the best chance they've got, and Brudnicki knows it. He consults with District One and then gives the okay.

The rescue swimmer on Hessel's helicopter is Dave Moore, a three-year veteran who has never been on a major rescue. ("The good cases don't come along too often—usually someone beats you to them," he says. "If a sailboat gets in trouble far out we usually get a rescue, but otherwise it's just a lot of little stuff.") Moore is handsome in a baby-faced sort of way—square-jawed, blue-eyed, and a big open smile. He has a dense, compact body that is more seal-like than athletic. His profession of rescue swimmer came about when a tanker went down off New York in the mid-1980s. A Coast Guard helicopter was hovering overhead, but it was winter and the tanker crew were too hypothermic to get into the lift basket. They all drowned. Congress decided they wanted something done, and the Coast Guard adopted the Navy rescue program. Moore is 25 years old, born the year Karen Stimson graduated from high school.

Moore is already wearing a neoprene wetsuit. He puts on socks and hood, straps on swim fins, pulls a mask and snorkel down over his head, and then struggles into his neoprene gloves. He buckles on a life vest and then signals to flight engineer Vriesman that he's ready. Vriesman, who has one arm extended, gate-like, across the jump door, steps aside and allows Moore to crouch by the edge. That means that they're at "ten and ten"—a ten foot hover at ten knots. Moore, who's no longer plugged into the intercom, signals final corrections to Vriesman with his hands, who relays them to the pilot. This is it; Moore has trained three years for this moment. An hour ago he was in the lunch line back on base. Now he's about to drop into the maelstrom.

Hessel holds a low hover with the boat at his two o'clock. Moore can see the crew clustered together on deck and the *Satori* making slow, plunging headway into the seas. Vriesman is seated next to Moore at the hoist controls, and avionicsman Ayres is behind the copilot with the radio and search gear. Both wear flightsuits and crash helmets and are plugged into the internal communication system in the wall. The time is 2:07 PM. Moore picks a spot between waves, takes a deep breath, and jumps.

It's a ten-foot fall and he hits feet-first, hands at his side. He comes up, clears his snorkel, settles his mask, and then strikes out for the *Satori.* The water is lukewarm—they're in the Gulf Stream—and the seas are so big they give him the impression he's swimming uphill and downhill rather than over individual waves. Occasionally the wind blows a crest off, and he has to dive under the cascade of whitewater before setting out again. The *Satori* appears and disappears behind the swells and the H-3 thunders overhead, rotors blasting a lily-pad of flattened water into the sea. Vriesman watches anxiously through binoculars from the jump door, trying to gauge the difficulty of getting Moore back into the helicopter. Ultimately, as flight engineer, it's his decision to deploy the swimmer, his job to get everyone safely back into the aircraft. If he has any doubts, Moore doesn't jump.

Moore swims hard for several minutes and finally looks up

at Vriesman, shaking his head. The boat's under power and there's no way he's going to catch her, not in these seas. Vriesman sends the basket down and Moore climbs back in. Just as he's about to ride up, the wave hits.

It's huge and cresting, fifty or sixty feet. It avalanches over Moore and buries both him and the lift basket. Vriesman counts to ten before Moore finally pops up through the foam, still inside the basket. It's no longer attached to the hoist cable, though; it's been wrenched off the hook and is just floating free. Moore has such tunnel vision that he doesn't realize the basket has come off; he just sits there, waiting to be hoisted. Finally he understands that he's not going anywhere, and swims the basket over to the cable and clips it on. He climbs inside, and Vriesman hauls him up.

This time they're going to do things differently. Hessel banks the helicopter to within fifty feet of the *Satori* and shows a chalk board that says, "Channel 16." Bylander disappears below, and when Hessel has her on the VHF, he tells her they're going to do an in-the-water pick-up. They're to get into their survival suits, tie the tiller down, and then jump off the boat. Once they're in the water they are to stay in a group and wait for Moore to swim over to them. He'll put them into the hoist basket and send them up one at a time.

Bylander climbs back up on deck and gives the instructions to the rest of the crew. Moore, looking through a pair of binoculars, watches them pull on their suits and try to will themselves over the gunwale. First, one of them puts a leg over the rail, then another does, and finally all three of them splash into the water. It takes four or five minutes for them to work up the nerve. Leonard has a bag in one hand, and as he goes over he loses his grip and leaves it on deck. It's full of his personal belongings. He claws his way down the length of the hull and finally punches himself in the head when he realizes he's lost it for good. Moore takes this in, wondering if Leonard is going to be a problem in the water.

Moore sheds his hood and gloves because the water's so

warm and pulls his mask back down over his face. This is it; if they can't do it now, they can't do it at all. Hessel puts the *Satori* at his six o'clock by lining them up in a little rearview mirror and comes down into a low hover. It's delicate flying. He finally gives Moore the go-ahead, and Moore breathes in deep and pushes off. "They dropped Moore and he just skimmed over the top of the water, flying towards us," says Stimson. "When he gets there he says, 'Hi, I'm Dave Moore your rescue swimmer, how are you?' And Sue says, 'Fine, how are you?' It was very cordial. Then he asks who's going first, and Sue says, 'I will.' And he grabbed her by the back of the survival suit and skimmed back across the water."

Moore loads Bylander into the rescue basket, and twenty seconds later she's in the helicopter. Jump to recovery takes five minutes (avionicsman Ayres is writing everything down in the hoist log). The next recovery, Stimson's, takes two minutes, and Leonard's takes three. Leonard is so despondent that he's deadweight in the water, Moore has to wrestle him into the basket and push his legs in after him. Moore's the last one up, stepping back into the aircraft at 2:29. They've been on-scene barely two hours.*

Moore starts stripping off his gear, and he's got his wet-suit half-way off when he realizes the helicopter isn't going

* Ray Leonard was unavailable for interviews with the media after the storm, and he was unavailable to the author until after this book's first publication. However, he has since denied the accuracy of this account of the *Satori*'s voyage. Primarily, he maintains that he and his crew were never in any danger during the storm, and that they should not have been forced off the boat by the Coast Guard. In support of this, he cites his own long experience as a sailor, the extremely heavy construction of the boat, and the fact that the boat survived the storm intact and was eventually salvaged off the New Jersey coast. He says that "lying ahull"—that is, battening down the hatches and staying safely in the bunks—wasn't evidence of passivity on his part, but was rather an accepted heavy-weather strategy. In contradiction to crew member Karen Stimpson's recollection, Leonard insists that he took an active role in the handling of the boat, and that he did not take a drink of alcohol until after the Coast Guard arrived. He was ordered off the boat, he maintains, because his two crew members were inexperienced and terrified.

anywhere. It's hovering off the *Tamaroa*'s port quarter. He puts his flight helmet on and hears the *Tamaroa* talking to Hessel, telling him to stand by because their Avon crew still needs to be recovered. Oh, Jesus, he thinks. Moore pulls his gear back on and takes up his position at the jump door. Hessel has decided on another in-the-water rescue, and Moore watches the three Coast Guardsmen grab hands and reluctantly abandon ship. Even from a distance they look nervous. Hessel comes in low and puts them at his six o'clock again, barely able to find such a small target in his rearview mirror. Moore gets the nod and jumps for the third time; he's got the drill down now and the entire rescue takes ten minutes. Each Coast Guardsman that makes it into the aircraft gives Stimson a thumbs-up. Moore comes up last—"via bare hook," as the report reads—and Vriesman pulls him in through the door. The H-3 banks, drops her nose, and starts for home.

"When I got up into the helicopter I remember everyone looking in my and Sue's faces to make sure we were okay," says Stimson. "I remember the intensity, it really struck me. These guys were *so* pumped up, but they were also human — real humanity. They'd take us by the shoulders and look us in the eyes and say, 'I'm so glad you're alive, we were with you last night, we prayed for you. We were worried about you.' When you're on the rescuing side you're very aware of life and death, and when you're on the rescued side, you just have a sort of numb awareness. At some point I stopped seeing the risk clearly, and it just became an amalgam of experience and observation."

Stimson has been awake for 48 hours now, much of it above deck. She's starting to get delirious. She slumps into a web seat in the back of the helicopter and looks out at the ocean that almost swallowed her up. "I saw the most amazing things; I saw Egypt and I knew it was Egypt," she says. "And I saw these clay animals, they were over green pastures like the Garden of Eden. I could see these clay animals and also gorgeous live animals munching on grass. And I kept seeing cities that I recognized as being from the Middle East."

While Stimson drifts in and out of hallucinations, the H-3 pounds home through a seventy-knot headwind. It takes an hour and forty minutes to get back to base. Three miles off Martha's Vineyard the crew look down and see another Coast Guard helicopter settling onto a desolate scrap of land called Noman's Island. A Florida longliner named the *Michelle Lane* had run aground with a load of swordfish, and her crew had spent the night under an overturned life raft on the beach. An H-3 was dispatched from Air Station Cape Cod to take them off, and Hessel happens to fly by as they're landing.

Hessel touches down at 4:40 at Air Station Cape Cod, and the other H-3 comes in a few minutes later. (While landing at Noman's, as it turned out, the rotor wash flipped the raft over and knocked one of the fishermen unconscious. He was taken off in a Stokes litter.) It's almost dark; rain flashes down diagonally through the airfield floodlights and scrub pine stretches away darkly for miles in every direction. The six survivors are ushered past the television cameras and led into a changing rooms upstairs. Stimson and Bylander pull off their survival suits, and Bylander curls up on a couch while Stimson goes back downstairs. The simple fact of being alive has her so wired she can hardly sit still. The Coast Guardsmen are gathered with the reporters in a small television room, and Stimson wanders in and finds Leonard sitting miserably on the floor, back to the wall. He's not saying a word.

He didn't want to leave the boat, Stimson explains to a local reporter. It was his home, and everything he owned was on it.

Dave Coolidge, the Falcon pilot that flew the previous night, walks up to Stimson and shakes her hand. Camera bulbs flash. Boy, are we glad to see you two, he says. It was a long night, I was afraid you weren't going to make it. Stimson says graciously, When we heard you on the radio we said, Yes, we're going to make it. We're not just going to perish out here without anyone knowing.

The reporters gradually drift off, and Leonard retires to an upstairs room. Stimson stays and answers questions for the rescue crew, who are very interested in the relationship between Leonard and the two women. His reactions weren't quite what we expected, one of the Guardsmen admits. Stimson explains that she and Bylander don't know Leonard very well, they met him through their boss.

Sue and I had been working several months without a break, she says. This trip was going to be our vacation.

While they're talking, the phone rings. One of the Falcon pilots goes to answer it. What time was that? the pilot says, and everyone in the room stops talking. How many were they? What location?

Without a word the Coast Guardsmen get up and leave, and a minute later Stimson hears toilets flushing. When they come back, one of them asks the Falcon pilot where they went down.

South of Montauk, he says.

The Guardsmen zip up their flight suits and file out the door. A rescue helicopter has just ditched fifty miles offshore and now five National Guardsmen are in the water, swimming.

INTO THE ABYSS

The Lord bowed the heavens and came down,
thick darkness under his feet. The channels
of the sea were seen, and the foundations
of the world were laid bare.

—*Samuel* 22

"I didn't know there was a problem, I just knew the *Andrea Gail* was supposed to be in any day," says Chris Cotter, Bobby's Shatford's girlfriend. "I went to bed and just before dawn I had this dream. I'm on the boat and it's real grey and ugly out and it's rollin' and rockin' and I'm screaming, BOBBY! BOBBY! There's no answer so I walk around the boat and go down into the fishhole and start digging. There's all this slime and weeds and slimy shit and I'm hysterical and crazy and screaming for Bobby and finally I get down and there's one of his arms. I find that and grab him and I know he's gone. And then the wake-up comes."

It's the morning of October 30th; there's been no word from the *Andrea Gail* in over 36 hours. The storm is so tightly-packed that few people in Gloucester—only a few hundred miles from the storm's center—have any idea what's out there. Chris lies in bed for a while, trying to shake off the dream, and finally gets up and shuffles into the kitchen. Her apartment looks out across Annisquam Bay, and Christine can see the water, itself cold and grey as granite, piling up against the granite shores of Cape Ann. The air is warm but an ill wind is backing around the compass, and Chris sits down at her kitchen table to watch it come. No one has said anything about a storm, there was nothing about it on the news. Chris smokes one cigarette after another, watching the weather come in off the sea, and she's still there when Susan Brown knocks on the door.

Susan is Bob Brown's wife. She issues the paychecks for the Seagale Corporation, as Brown's company is called, and the week before she'd given Christine the wrong check by mistake. She'd given her Murph's check, which was larger than Bobby Shatford's, and now she's come back to rectify the mistake. Chris invites her in and immediately senses that something is wrong. Susan seems uncomfortable, glancing around and refusing to look Chris in the eye.

Listen, Chris, Susan says finally, I've got some bad news. I'm not sure how to say this. We don't seem to be able to raise the *Andrea Gail*.

Chris sits there, stunned. She's still in the dream—still in the dark slimy stink of the fishhole—and the news just confirms what she already knows: He's dead. Bobby Shatford is dead.

Susan tells her they're still trying to get through and that the boat probably just lost her antennas, but Chris knows better; in her gut she knows it's wrong. As soon as Susan leaves, Chris calls Mary Anne Shatford, Bobby's sister. Mary Anne tells her it's true, they can't raise Bobby's boat, and Chris drives down to the Nest and rushes in through the big heavy door. It's only ten in the morning but already people are standing around with beers in their hands, red-eyed and shocked. Ethel is there, and Bobby's other sister, Susan, and his brother, Brian, and Preston, and dozens of fishermen. Nothing's sure yet—the boat could still be afloat, or the crew could be in a life raft or drunk in some Newfoundland bar—but people are quietly assuming the worst.

Chris starts drinking immediately. "People didn't want to give me the details because I was totally out of my mind," she says. "Everybody was drunk cause that's what we do, but the crisis made it even worse, just drinkin' and drinkin' and cryin' and drinkin', we just couldn't conceive that they were gone. It was in the paper and on the television and this is my *love,* my *friend,* my *man,* my *drinking partner,* and it just couldn't be. I had pictures of what happened, images: Bobby and Sully and Murph just bug-eyed, knowing this is the final moment, looking at each other and this jug of booze goin' around real fast because they're tryin' to numb themselves out, and then Bobby goes flyin' and Sully goes under. But what was the final moment? What was the final, final thing?"

The only person not at the Crow's Nest is Bob Brown. As owner of the boat he may well not feel welcome there, but he's also got work to do—he's got a boat to find. There's a single sideband in his upstairs bedroom, and he's been calling on 2182 since early yesterday for both his boats. Neither Billy Tyne nor Linda Greenlaw will come in. Oh boy, he thinks. At nine-thirty, after trying a few more times, Brown drives twenty miles south along Route 128 through the grey rocky uplands of the North Shore. He parks at the King's Grant Inn in Danvers and walks into the conference room for the beginning of a two-day New England Fisheries Management Council meeting. The wind is moving heavily through the treetops now, piling dead leaves up against a chainlink fence and spitting rain down from a steel sky. It's not a storm yet, but it's getting there.

Brown takes a seat at the back of the room, notebook in hand, and endures a long and uninteresting meeting. Someone brings up the fact that the Soviet Union has disintegrated into different countries, and U.S. fishing laws need to be changed accordingly. Another person cites a *Boston Globe* article that says that cod, haddock, and flounder populations are so low that regulations are useless—the species are beyond saving. The National Marine Fisheries Service is not the sole institution with scientific knowedge on pelagic issues, a third person counters. The meeting finally adjourns after an hour of this, and Bob Brown gets up to talk with Gail Johnson, whose husband, Charlie, is out on the Banks at that moment. Charlie owns the *Seneca,* which had put into Bay Bulls, Newfoundland, a few weeks earlier with a broken crankshaft.

Did you hear anything from your husband? Brown asks.

Yeah, but I could hardly get him. He's east of the Banks, and they've got bad weather out there.

I know they do, Brown says. I know they do.

Brown asks her to call him if Charlie hears anything about either of his boats. Then he hurries home. As soon as he arrives he goes up to his bedroom and tries the single sideband again, and this time—thank God—Linda comes through. He can hear her only faintly though the static.

I haven't been able to reach Billy in a couple of days, Linda shouts. *I'm worried about them.*

Yeah, I'm worried too, says Brown. *Keep trying him. I'll check back.*

At six o'clock that night, the time he generally checks in with his boats, Brown tries one last time to raise the *Andrea Gail.* Not a sign. Linda Greenlaw hasn't been able to raise her, either, nor has anyone else in the fleet. At 6:15 on October 30th, two days to the hour after Billy Tyne was last heard from, Brown calls the Coast Guard in Boston and reports the vessel missing. I'm afraid my boat's in trouble and I fear the worst, he says. He adds that there have been no distress calls from her and no signals from her EPIRB. She has disappeared without a trace. In some senses that's good news because it may just mean she's lost her antennas; a distress call or EPIRB signal would be a different matter entirely. It would mean absolutely that something has gone wrong.

Meanwhile, the news media has picked up on the story. Rumors are flying around Gloucester that the *Allison* has gone down along with the *Andrea Gail,* and that even the *Hannah Boden* may be in trouble. A reporter from News

Channel Five calls Tommie Barrie's wife, Kimberly, and asks her about the *Allison.* Kimberly answers that she talked to her husband the night before by single sideband and that, although she could barely hear him, he seemed to be fine. Channel Five broadcasts that tidbit on the evening news, and suddenly every fisherman's wife on the East Coast is calling Kimberly Barrie to ask if she has any news about the fleet. She just repeats that she talked to her husband on the 29th, and that she could barely hear him. "As soon as the storms move offshore the weather service stops tracking them," she says. "The fishermen's wives are left hanging, and they panic. The wives always panic."

In fact the eastern fleet fared relatively well; they heave-to under heavy winds and a long-distance swell and just wait it out. Barrie even contemplates fishing that night but decides against it; no one knows where the storm is headed and he doesn't want to get caught with his gear in the water. Barrie keeps trying Billy every couple of hours throughout the night of the 28th and the following day, and by October 30th he thinks Billy may have drifted out of range. He radios Linda and tells her that something is definitely wrong, and Bob Brown should get a search going. Linda agrees. That night, after the boats have set their gear out, the captains get together on channel 16 to set up a drift model for the *Andrea Gail.* They have an extremely low opinion of the Coast Guard's ability to read ocean currents, and so they pool their information, as when tracking swordfish, to try to figure out where a dead boat or a life raft would have gone. "The water comes around the Tail and wants to go up north," Barrie says. "By talking to boats at different places and putting them together, you can get a pretty detailed map of what the Gulf Stream is doing."

Late on the night of the 30th, Bob Brown calls the Canadian Coast Guard in Halifax and says that the *Andrea Gail* is probably proceeding home along a route that cuts just south of Sable Island. He adds that Billy usually doesn't call in during his thirty-day trips. The Canadian cutter *Edward Cornwallis*—already at sea to help the *Eishin Maru*—starts calling for the *Andrea Gail* every quarter hour on channel 16. *"No joy on indicated frequency for contacting Andrea Gail,"* she reports later that morning. Halifax initiates a communications search as well, on every frequency in the VHF spectrum, but also meets with failure. The fishing vessel *Jennie and Doug* reports hearing a faint *"Andrea Gail"* at 8294 kilohertz, and for the next twelve hours Halifax tries that frequency but cannot raise her. Judith Reeves on the *Eishin Maru* thinks she hears someone with an English accent radioing the *Andrea Gail* that he's coming to their aid, but she can't make out the name of the vessel. She never hears the message again. A SpeedAir radar search picks up an object that might possibly be the *Andrea Gail,* and Halifax tries to establish radio contact, without success. At least half a dozen vessels around Sable Island—the *Edward Cornwallis,* the *Lady Hammond,* the *Sambro,* the *Degero,* the *Yankee Clipper,* the *Melvin H. Baker,* and the *Mary Hitchins*—are conducting communications searches, but no one can raise them. They've fallen off the edge of the world.

The Rescue Coordination Center in New York, meanwhile, is still trying to figure out exactly who is on the crew. Bob Brown doesn't know for sure—often owners don't even *want* to know—and even the various friends and family aren't one hundred percent certain. Finally the Coast Guard gets a call from a Florida fisherman named Douglas Kosco, who says he used to fish on the *Andrea Gail* and knows who the crew are. He runs down the list of crew as he knows it: Captain Billy Tyne, from Gloucester. Bugsy Moran, also from Gloucester but living in Florida. Dale Murphy from Cortez, Florida. Alfred Pierre, the only black guy on board, from the Virgin Islands but with family in Portland.

Kosco says that the fifth crew member was from the *Haddit*—Tyne's old boat—and that Merrit Seafoods in Pompano has his name. I was supposed to go on this trip, but

I got off at the last moment, he says. I don't know why, I just got a funny feeling and stepped off.

Kosco gives the Coast Guardsman a phone number in Florida where he gets messages. (He's offshore so much that he doesn't have his own phone.) I think they may have gone shorthanded—I hope they did, he says. I don't think Billy could've found anyone else so fast . . .

It's wishful thinking. The morning Kosco left, Billy called up Adam Randall and asked him if he wanted a job. Randall said yes, and Billy told him to get up to Gloucester as fast as possible. Randall showed up with his father-in-law, checked the boat over, and got spooked like Kosco had. He walked off. So Billy called David Sullivan and happened to catch him at home. Sully reluctantly agreed to go, and arrived at the State Fish Pier an hour later with his seabag over his shoulder. The *Andrea Gail* went to sea with six men, a full crew. Kosco doesn't know this, though; all he knows is that a last-minute decision five weeks ago probably saved his life.

At about the same time that Kosco confesses his good luck to the Coast Guard, Adam Randall settles onto the couch in his home in East Bridgewater, Massachusetts, to watch the evening news. It's a rain-lashed Halloween night, and Randall has just come back from taking his kids out trick-or-treating. His girlfriend, Christine Hansen, is with him. She's a pretty, highly put-together blonde who drives a sports car and works for AT&T. The local news comes on, and Channel Five reports a boat named the *Andrea Gail* missing somewhere east of Sable Island. Randall sits up in his seat. That was my boat, honey, he says.

What?

That's the boat I was supposed to go on. Remember when I went up to Gloucester? That's the boat. The *Andrea Gail.*

MEANWHILE, the worst crisis in the history of the Air National Guard has been unfolding offshore. At 2:45 that afternoon—in the midst of the *Satori* rescue—District One Command Center in Boston receives a distress call from a Japanese sailor named Mikado Tomizawa, who is in a sailboat 250 miles off the Jersey coast and starting to go down. The Coast Guard dispatches a C-130 and then alerts the Air National Guard, which operates a rescue group out of Suffolk Airbase in Westhampton Beach, Long Island. The Air Guard covers everything beyond maritime rescue, which is roughly defined by the fuel range of a Coast Guard H-3 helicopter. Beyond that—and Tomizawa was well beyond that—an Air Guard H-60 has to be used, which can be refueled in mid-flight. The H-60 flies in tandem with a C-130 tanker plane, and every few hours the pilot comes up behind the tanker and nudges a probe into one of the hoses trailing off each wing. It's a preposterously difficult maneuver in bad weather, but it allows an H-60 to stay airborn almost indefinitely.

The Air Guard dispatcher is on the intercom minutes after the mayday comes in, calling for a rescue crew to gather at "ODC," the Operations Dispatch Center. Dave Ruvola, the helicopter pilot, meets his copilot and the C-130 pilots in an adjacent room and spreads an aeronautical chart of the East Coast on the table. They study the weather forecasts and decide they will execute four midair refuelings—one immediately off the coast, one before the rescue attempt, and two on the way back. While the pilots are plotting their refueling points, a rescue swimmer named John Spillane and another swimmer named Rick Smith jog down the hallway to Life Support to pick up their survival gear. A crewcut supply clerk hands them Mustang immersion suits, wetsuits, inflatable life vests, and mesh combat vests. The combat vests are worn by American airmen all over the world and contain the minimum amount of gear—radio, flare kit, knife, strobe, matches, compass—needed to survive in any environment. They put their gear in duffel bags and leave the building by a side door, where they meet the two pilots in a waiting truck. They get in, slam the doors shut, and speed off across the base.

A maintenance crew has already towed a helicopter out of the hanger and fueled it up, and flight engineer Jim Mioli is busy checking the records and inspecting the engine and rotors. It is a warm, windy day, the scrub pine twisting and dancing along the edge of the tarmac and sea birds sawing their way back and forth against a heavy sky. The PJs load their gear in through the jump door and then take their seats in the rear of the aircraft, up against the fuel tanks. The pilots climb into their angled cockpit seats, go through the preflight checklist, and then fire the engines up. The rotors thud to life, losing the sag of their huge weight, and the helicopter shifts on its tires and is suddenly airborn, tilting nose-down across the scrub. Ruvola bears away to the southeast and within minutes has crossed over to open ocean. The crew, looking down out of their spotters' windows, can see the surf thundering against Long Island. Up and down the coast, as far as they can see, the shore is bordered in white.

In official terms the attempt to help Tomizawa was categorized as an "increased risk" mission, meaning the weather conditions were extreme and the survivor was in danger of perishing. The rescuers, therefore, were willing to accept a higher level of risk in order to save him. Among the actual crews these missions are referred to as "sporty," as in, "Boy, it sure was sporty out there last night." In general, sporty is good; it's what rescue is all about. An Air National Guard pararescue jumper—the military equivalent of Coast Guard rescue swimmers—might get half a dozen sporty rescues in a lifetime. These rescues are talked about, studied, and sometimes envied for years.

Wartime, of course, is about as sporty as it gets, but it's a rare and horrible circumstance that most pararescue jumpers don't experience. (The Air National Guard is considered a state militia—meaning it's state funded—but it's also a branch of the Air Force. As such, Guard jumpers are interchangeable with Air Force jumpers.) Between wars the Air National Guard occupies itself rescuing civilians on the "high seas," which means anything beyond the fuel range of a Coast Guard H-3 helicopter. That, depending on the weather, is around two hundred miles offshore. The wartime mission of the Air National Guard is "to save the life of an American fighting man," which generally means jumping behind enemy lines to extract downed pilots. When the pilots go down at sea, the PJs, as they're known, jump with scuba gear. When they go down on glaciers, they jump with crampons and ice axes. When they go down in the jungle, they jump with two hundred feet of tree-rappelling line. There is, literally, nowhere on earth a PJ can't go. "I could climb Everest with the equipment in my locker," one of them said.

All of the armed forces have some version of the pararescue jumper, but the Air National Guard jumpers—and their Air Force equivalents—are the only ones with an ongoing peacetime mission. Every time the space shuttle launches, an Air Guard C-130 from Westhampton Beach flies down to Florida to oversee the procedure. An Air Force rescue crew also flies to Africa to cover the rest of the shuttle's trajectory. Whenever a ship—of any nationality—finds itself in distress off North America, the Air National Guard can be called out. A Greek crewman, say, on a Liberian-flagged freighter, who has just fallen into a cargo hold, could have Guard jumpers parachute in to help him seven hundred miles out at sea. An Air Guard base in Alaska that recovers a lot of Air Force trainees is permanently on alert—"fully cocked and ready to go"—and the two other bases, in California and on Long Island, are on standby. If a crisis develops offshore, a crew is put together from the men on-base and whomever can be rounded up by telephone; typically, a helicopter crew can be airborne in under an hour.

It takes eighteen months of full-time training to become a PJ, after which you owe the government four years of active service, which you're strongly encouraged to extend. (There are about 350 PJs around the country, but developing them is such a lengthy and expensive process that the government is hard put to replace the ones who are lost every year.) During the first three months of training, candidates are weeded out through sheer, raw abuse. The dropout rate is often over ninety percent. In one drill, the team swims their normal 4,000-yard workout, and then the instructor tosses his whistle into the pool. Ten guys fight for it, and whoever manages to blow it at the surface gets to leave the pool. His workout is over for the day. The instructor throws the whistle in again, and the nine remaining guys fight for it. This goes on until there's only one man left, and he's kicked out of PJ school. In a variation called "water harassment," two swimmers share a snorkel while instructors basically try to drown them. If either man breaks the surface and takes a breath, he's out of school. "There were times we cried," admits one PJ. But "they've got to thin the ranks somehow."

After pretraining, as it's called, the survivors enter a period known as "the pipeline"—scuba school, jump school, freefall school, dunker-training school, survival school. The PJs learn how to parachute, climb mountains, survive in deserts, resist enemy interrogation, evade pursuit, navigate underwater at night. The schools are ruthless in their quest to weed people out; in dunker training, for example, the candidates are strapped into a simulated helicopter and plunged underwater. If they manage to escape, they're plunged in upside-down. If they still manage to escape, they're plunged in upside-down and blindfolded. The guys who escape *that* get to be PJs; the rest are rescued by divers waiting by the sides of the pool.

These schools are for all branches of the military, and PJ candidates might find themselves training alongside Navy SEALS and Green Berets who are simply trying to add, say, water survival to their repertoire of skills. If the Navy SEAL fails one of the courses, he just goes back to being a Navy SEAL; if a PJ fails, he's out of the entire program. For a period of three or four months, a PJ runs the risk, daily, of failing out of school. And if he manages to make it through the pipeline, he still has almost another full year ahead of him: paramedic training, hospital rotations, mountain climbing, desert survival, tree landings, more scuba school, tactical maneuvers, air operations. And because they have a wartime mission, the PJs also practice military maneuvers. They parachute into the ocean at night with inflatable speedboats. They parachute into the ocean at night with scuba gear and go straight into a dive. They deploy from a submarine by air-lock and swim to a deserted coast. They train with shotguns, grenade launchers, M-16s, and six-barreled "mini-guns." (Mini-guns fire 6,000 rounds a minute and can cut down trees.) And finally—once they've mastered every conceivable battle scenario—they learn something called HALO jumping.

HALO stands for High Altitude Low Opening; it's used to drop PJs into hot areas where a more leisurely deployment would get them all killed. In terms of violating the constraints of the physical world, HALO jumping is one of the more outlandish things human beings have ever done. The PJs jump from so high up—as high as 40,000 feet—that they need bottled oxygen to breathe. They leave the aircraft with two oxygen bottles strapped to their sides, a parachute on their back, a reserve 'chute on their chest, a full medical pack on their thighs, and an M-16 on their harness. They're at the top of the troposphere—the layer where weather happens—and all they can hear is the scream of their own velocity. They're so high up that they freefall for two or three minutes and pull their 'chutes at a thousand feet or less. That way, they're almost impossible to kill.

THE H-60 flies through relative calm for the first half-hour, and then Ruvola radios the tanker plane and says he's coming in for a refueling. A hundred and forty pounds of pressure are needed to trigger the coupling mechanism in the feeder hose—called the "drogue"—so the helicopter has to close on the tanker plane at a fairly good rate of speed. Ruvola hits the drogue on the first shot, takes on 700 pounds of fuel and continues on toward the southeast. Far below, the waves are getting smeared forward by the wind into an endless series of scalloped white crests. The crew is heading into the worst weather of their lives.

The rules governing H-60 deployments state that "intentional flight into known or forecast severe turbulence is prohibited." The weather report faxed by McGuire Air Force Base earlier that day called for *moderate* to severe turbulence, which was just enough semantic protection to allow Ruvola to launch. They were trained to save lives, and this is the kind of day that lives would need saving. An hour into the flight Dave Ruvola comes in for the second refueling and pegs the drogue after four attempts, taking on 900 pounds of fuel. The two aircraft break apart and continue hammering toward Tomizawa.

They are on-scene ten minutes later, in almost complete dark. Spillane has spent the flight slowly putting his wetsuit on, trying not to sweat too much, trying not to dehydrate himself. Now he sits by the spotter's window looking out at the storm. A Coast Guard C-130 circles at five hundred feet and the Air National Guard tanker circles several hundred feet above that. Their lights poke feebly into the swarming darkness. Ruvola establishes a low hover aft of the sailboat and flips on his floods, which throw down a cone of light from the belly of the aircraft. Spillane can't believe what he sees: massive foam-laced swells rising and falling in the circle of light, some barely missing the belly of the helicopter. Twice he has to shout for altitude to keep the helicopter from getting slapped out of the sky.

The wind is blowing so hard that the rotor wash, which normally falls directly below the helicopter, is forty feet behind it; it lags the way it normally does when the helicopter is flying ahead at eighty knots. Despite the conditions, Spillane still assumes he and Rick Smith are going to deploy by sliding down a three-inch-thick "fastrope" into the sea.

The question is, what will they do then? The boat looks like it's moving too fast for a swimmer to catch, which means Tomizawa will have to be extracted from the water, like the *Satori* crew was. But that would put him at a whole other level of risk; there's a point at which sporty rescues become more dangerous than sinking boats. While Spillane considers Tomizawa's chances, flight engineer Jim Mioli gets on the intercom and says he has doubts about retrieving anyone from the water. The waves are rising too fast for the hoist controls to keep up, so there'll be too much slack around the basket at the crests of the waves. If a man were caught in a loop of cable and the wave dropped out from under him, he'd be cut in half.

For the next twenty minutes Ruvola keeps the helicopter in a hover over the sailboat while the crew peers out the jump door, discussing what to do. They finally agree that the boat looks pretty good in the water—she's riding high, relatively stable—and that any kind of rescue attempt will put Tomizawa in more danger than he is already in. He should stay with his boat. *We're out of our league, boys,* Ruvola finally says over the intercom. *We're not going to do this.* Ruvola gets the C-130 pilot on the radio and tells him their decision, and the C-130 pilot relays it to the sailboat. Tomizawa, desperate, radios back that they don't have to deploy their swimmers at all—just swing the basket over and he'll rescue himself. *No, that's not the problem,* Buschor answers. *We don't mind going in the water; we just don't think a rescue is possible.*

Ruvola backs away and the tanker plane drops two life rafts connected by eight hundred feet of line, in case Tomizawa's boat starts to founder, and then the two aircraft head back to base. (Tomizawa was eventually picked up by a Romanian freighter.) Ten minutes into the return flight Ruvola lines up on the tanker for the third time, hits the drogue immediately and takes on 1,560 pounds of fuel. They'll need one more refueling in order to make shore. Spillane settles into the portside spotter's seat and stares down at the ocean a thousand feet below. If Mioli hadn't spoken up, he and Rick Smith might be swimming around down there, trying to get back into the rescue basket. They'd have died. In conditions like these, so much water gets loaded into the air that swimmers drown simply trying to breathe.

Months later, after the Air National Guard has put the pieces together, it will determine that gaps had developed in the web of resources designed to support an increased-risk mission over water. At any given moment *someone* had the necessary information for keeping Ruvola's helicopter airborne, but that information wasn't disseminated correctly during the last hour of Ruvola's flight. Several times a day, mission or no mission, McGuire Air Force Base in New Jersey faxes weather bulletins to Suffolk Air Base for their use in route planning. If Suffolk is planning a difficult mission, they might also call McGuire for a verbal update on flight routes, satellite information, etc. Once the mission is underway, one person—usually the tanker pilot—is responsible for obtaining and relaying weather information to all the pilots involved in the rescue. If he needs more information, he calls Suffolk and tells them to get it; without the call, Suffolk doesn't actively pursue weather information. They are, in the words of the accident investigators, "reactive" rather than "proactive" in carrying out their duties.

In Ruvola's case, McGuire Air Force Base has real-time satellite information showing a massive rain band developing off Long Island between 7:30 and 8:00 PM—just as he is starting back for Suffolk. Suffolk never calls McGuire for an update, though, because the tanker pilot never asks for one; and McGuire never volunteers the information because they don't know there is an Air Guard helicopter out there in the first place. Were Suffolk to call McGuire for an update, they'd learn that Ruvola's route is blocked by severe weather, but that he can avoid it by flying fifteen minutes to westward. As it is, the tanker pilot calls Suffolk for a weather update and gets a report of an 8,000-foot ceiling, fifteen-mile visibility, and low-level wind shear. He passes that information on to Ruvola, who—having left the worst of the storm behind him—reasonably assumes that conditions will only improve as he flies westward. All he has to do is refuel before hitting the wind shear that is being recorded around the air field. Ruvola—they all—are wrong.

The rain band is a swath of clouds fifty miles wide, eighty miles long, and 10,000 feet thick. It is getting dragged into the low across the northwest quadrant of the storm; winds are 75 knots and the visibility is zero. Satellite imagery shows the rain band swinging across Ruvola's flight path like a door slamming shut. At 7:55, Ruvola radios the tanker pilot to confirm a fourth refueling, and the pilot rogers it. The refueling is scheduled for five minutes later, at precisely eight o'clock. At 7:56, turbulence picks up a little, and at 7:58 it reaches moderate levels. *Let's get this thing done,* Ruvola radios the tanker pilot. At 7:59 he pulls the probe release, extends it forward, and moves into position for contact. And then it hits.

Headwinds along the leading edge of the rain band are so strong that it feels as if the helicopter has been blown to a stop. Ruvola has no idea what he's run into; all he knows is that he can barely control the aircraft. Flying has become as much a question of physical strength as of finesse; he grips the collective with one hand, the joystick with the other, and leans forward to peer through the rain rattling off the windscreen. Flight manuals bounce around the cockpit and his copilot starts throwing up in the seat next to him. Ruvola lines up on the tanker and tries to hit the drogue, but the aircraft are moving around so wildly that it's like throwing darts down a gun barrel; hitting the target is pure dumb luck. In technical terms, Ruvola's aircraft is doing things "without inputs from the controls"; in human terms, it's getting batted around the sky. Ruvola tries as low as three hundred feet—"along the ragged edges of the clouds," as he says—and as high as 4,500 feet, but he can't find clean air. The visibility is so bad that even with night-vision goggles on, he can barely make out the wing lights of the tanker plane in front of him. And they are right—*right*—on top of it; several times they overshoot the drogue and Spillane thinks they are going to take the plane's rudder off.

Ruvola has made twenty or thirty attempts on the drogue—a monstrous feat of concentration—when the tanker pilot radios that he has to shut down his number one engine. The oil pressure gauge is fluctuating wildly and they are risking a burn-out. The pilot starts in on the shut-down procedure, and suddenly the left-hand fuel hose retracts; shutting off the engine has disrupted the air flow around the wing, and the reel-in mechanism has mistaken that for too much slack. It performs what is known as an "uncommanded retraction." The pilot finishes shutting down the engine, brings Ruvola back in, and then reextends the hose. Ruvola lines up on it and immediately sees that something is wrong. The drogue is shaped like a small parachute, and ordinarily it fills with air and holds the hose steady; now it is just convulsing behind the tanker plane. It has been destroyed by forty-five minutes of desperate refueling attempts.

Ruvola tells the tanker pilot that the left-hand drogue is shot and that they have to switch over to the other side. In these conditions refueling from the right-hand drogue is a nightmarish, white-knuckle business because the helicopter probe also extends from the right-hand side of the cockpit, so the pilot has to come even tighter into the fuselage of the tanker to make contact. Ruvola makes a run at the right-hand drogue, misses, comes in again, and misses again. The usual technique is to watch the tanker's wing flaps and anticipate where the drogue's going to go, but the visibility is so low that Ruvola can't even see that far; he can barely see past the nose of his own helicopter. Ruvola makes a couple more runs at the drogue, and on his last attempt he comes in too fast, overshoots the wing, and by the time he's realigned himself the tanker has disappeared. They've lost an entire C-130 in the clouds. They are at 4,000 feet in zero visibility with roughly twenty minutes of fuel left; after that they will just fall out of the sky. Ruvola can either keep trying to hit the drogue, or he can try to make it down to sea level while they still have fuel.

We're going to set up for a planned ditching, he tells his crew. *We're going to ditch while we still can.* And then Dave Ruvola drops the nose of the helicopter and starts racing his fuel gauge down to the sea.

John Spillane, watching silently from the spotter's seat, is sure he's just heard his death sentence. "Throughout my career I've always managed—just barely—to keep things in control," says Spillane. "But now, suddenly, the risk is becoming totally uncontrollable. We can't get fuel, we're going to end up in that roaring ocean, and we're not gonna be in control anymore. And I know the chances of being rescued are practically zero. I've been on a lot of rescue missions, and I know they can hardly even *find* someone in these conditions, let alone recover them. We're some of the best in the business—best equipped, best trained. We couldn't do a rescue a little while earlier, and now we're in the same situation. It looks real bleak. It's not going to happen."

While Ruvola is flying blindly downward through the clouds, copilot Buschor issues a mayday on an Air National Guard emergency frequency and then contacts the *Tamaroa,* fifteen miles to the northeast. He tells them they are out of fuel and about to set up for a planned ditching. Captain Brudnicki orders the *Tam's* searchlights turned up into the sky so the helicopter can give them a bearing, but Buschor says he can't see a thing. *Okay, just start heading towards us,* the radio dispatcher on the *Tam* says. *We don't have time, we're going down right now,* Buschor replies. Jim McDougal, handling the radios at the ODC in Suffolk, receives—simultaneously—the ditching alert and a phone call from Spillane's wife, who wants to know where her husband is. She'd had no idea there was a problem and just happened to call at the wrong moment; McDougal is so panicked by the timing that he hangs up on her. At 9:08, a dispatcher at Coast Guard headquarters in Boston takes a call that an Air National Guard helicopter is going down and scrawls frantically in the incident log: *"Helo [helicopter] & 130 enroute Suffolk. Can't refuel helo due visibility. May have to ditch. Stay airborn how long? 20–25 min. LAUNCH!"* He then notifies Cape Cod Air Base, where Karen Stimson is chatting with one of her rescue crews. The five airmen get up without a word, file into the bathroom, and then report for duty out on the tarmac.

Ruvola finally breaks out of the clouds at 9:28, only two hundred feet above the ocean. He goes into a hover and immediately calls for the ditching checklist, which prepares the crew to abandon the aircraft. They have practiced this dozens of times in training, but things are happening so fast that the routines start to fall apart. Jim Mioli has trouble seeing in the dim cabin lighting used with night-vision gear, so he can't locate the handle of the nine-man life raft. By the time he finds it, he doesn't have time to put on his Mustang survival suit. Ruvola calls three times for Mioli to read him the ditching checklist, but Mioli is too busy to answer him, so Ruvola has to go through it by memory. One of the most important things on the list is for the pilot to reach down and eject his door, but Ruvola is working too hard to remove his hands from the controls. In military terminology he has become "task-saturated," and the door stays on.

While Ruvola is trying to hold the aircraft in a hover, the PJs scramble to put together the survival gear. Spillane slings a canteen over his shoulder and clips a one-man life raft to the strap. Jim Mioli, who finally manages to extract the nine-man raft, pushes it to the edge of the jump door and waits for the order to deploy. Rick Smith, draped in survival gear, squats at the edge of the other jump door and looks over the side. Below is an ocean so ravaged by wind that they can't even tell the difference between the waves and the troughs; for all they know they are jumping three hundred feet. As horrible as that is, though, the idea of staying where they are is even worse. The helicopter is going to drop into the ocean at any moment, and no one on the crew wants to be anywhere nearby when it does.

Only Dave Ruvola will stay on board; as pilot, it is his job to make sure the aircraft doesn't fall on the rest of his crew. The chances of his escaping with his door still in place are negligible, but that is beside the point. The ditching checklist calls for a certain procedure, a procedure that insures the survival of the greatest number of crew. That Mioli neglects to put on his survival suit is also, in some ways, suicidal, but he has no choice. His duty is to oversee a safe bail-out, and if he stops to put his survival suit on, the nine-man raft won't be ready for deployment. He jumps without his suit.

At 9:30, the number one engine flames out; Spillane can hear the turbine wind down. They've been in a low hover for less than a minute. Ruvola calls out on the intercom: *The number one's out! Bail out! Bail out!* The number two is running on fumes; in theory, they should flame out at the same time. This is it. They are going down.

Mioli shoves the life raft out the right-hand door and watches it fall, in his words, "into the abyss." They are so high up that he doesn't even see it hit the water, and he can't bring himself to jump in after it. Without telling anyone, he decides to take his chances in the helicopter. Ditching protocol calls for copilot Buschor to remain on board as well, but Ruvola orders him out because he decides Buschor's chances of survival will be higher if he jumps. Buschor pulls his door-release lever but the door doesn't pop off the fuselage, so he just holds it open with one hand and steps out onto the footboard. He looks back at the radar altimeter, which is fluctuating between ten feet and eighty, and realized that the timing of his jump will mean the difference between life and death. Ruvola repeats his order to bail out, and Buschor unplugs the intercom wires from his flight helmet and flips his night-vision goggles down. Now he can watch the waves roll underneath him in the dim green light of enhanced vision. He spots a huge crest, takes a breath and jumps.

Spillane, meanwhile, is grabbing some last-minute gear. "I wasn't terrified, I was scared," he says. "Forty minutes before I'd been more scared, thinking about the possibilities, but at the end I was totally committed. The pilot had made the decision to ditch, and it was a great decision. How many pilots might have just used up the last twenty minutes of fuel trying to hit the drogue? Then you'd fall out of the sky and everyone would die."

The helicopter is strangely quiet without the number one engine. The ocean below them, in the words of another pilot, looks like a lunar landscape, cratered and gouged and deformed by wind. Spillane spots Rick Smith at the starboard door, poised to jump, and moves towards him. "I'm convinced he was sizing up the waves," Spillane says. "I wanted desperately to stick together with him. I just had time to sit down, put my arm around his shoulders, and he went. We didn't have time to say anything—you want to say goodbye, you want to do a lot of things, but there's no time for that. Rick went, and a split-second later, I did."

According to people who have survived long falls, the acceleration of gravity is so heart-stoppingly fast that it's more like getting shot downward out of a cannon. A body accelerates roughly twenty miles an hour for every second it's in the air; after one second it's falling twenty miles an hour; after two seconds, forty miles an hour, and so on, up to a hundred and thirty. At that point the wind resistance is equal to the force of gravity, and the body is said to have reached terminal velocity. Spillane falls probably sixty or seventy feet, two and a half seconds of acceleration. He plunges through darkness without any idea where the water is or when he is going to hit. He has a dim memory of letting go of his one-man raft, and of his body losing position, and he thinks: My God, what a long way down. And then everything goes blank.

John Spillane has the sort of handsome, regular features that one might expect in a Hollywood actor playing a pararescueman—playing John Spillane, in fact. His eyes are stone-blue, without a trace of hardness or indifference, his hair is short and touched with grey. He comes across as friendly, unguarded, and completely sure of himself. He has a quick smile and an offhand way of talking that seems to progress from detail to detail, angle to angle, until there's nothing more to say on a topic. His humor is delivered casually, almost as an afterthought, and seems to surprise even himself. He's of average height, average build, and once ran forty miles for the hell of it. He seems to be a man who has long since lost the need to prove things to anyone.

Spillane grew up in New York City and joined the Air Force at seventeen. He trained as a combat diver—infiltrating positions, securing beaches, rescuing other combat divers—and then left at 21 to join the Air National Guard. He "guard-bummed" around the world for a year, returning to Rockaway Beach to lifeguard in the summer, and then signed up for PJ school. After several years of reserve duty he quit, went through the police academy, and became a scuba diver for the New York City Police Department. For three years he pulled bodies out of submerged cars and mucked guns out of the East River, and finally decided to go back to school before his G.I. Bill ran out. He started out majoring in geology—"I wanted to go stomp mountaintops for a while"—but he fell in love instead and ended up moving out to Suffolk to work full-time for the Guard. That was in 1989. He was 32, one of the most widely-experienced PJs in the country.

When John Spillane hits the Atlantic Ocean he is going about fifty miles an hour. Water is the only element that offers more resistance the harder you hit it, and at fifty miles an hour it might as well be concrete. Spillane fractures three bones in his right arm, one bone in his left leg, four ribs in his chest, ruptures a kidney, and bruises his pancreas. The flippers, the one-man raft, and the canteen all are torn off his body. Only the mask, which he wore backward with the strap in his mouth, stays on as it is supposed to. Spillane doesn't remember the moment of impact, and he doesn't remember the moment he first realized he was in the water. His memory goes from falling to swimming, with nothing in between. When he understands that he is swimming, that is *all* he understands—he doesn't know who he is, why he is there, or how he got there. He has no history and no future; he is just a consciousness at night in the middle of the sea.

When Spillane treats injured seamen offshore, one of the first things he evaluates is their degree of consciousness. The highest level, known as "alert and oriented times four," describes almost everyone in an everyday situation. They know who they are, where they are, what time it is, and what's just happened. If someone suffers a blow to the head, the first thing they lose is recent events—"alert and oriented times three"—and the last thing they lose is their identity. A person who has lost all four levels of consciousness, right down to their identity, is said to be "alert and oriented times zero." When John Spillane wakes up in the water, he is alert and oriented times zero. His understanding of the world is reduced to the fact that he exists, nothing more. Almost simultaneously, he understands that he is in excruciating pain. For a long time, that is all he knows. Until he sees the life raft.

Spillane may be alert and oriented times zero, but he knows to swim for a life raft when he sees one. It has been pushed out by Jim Mioli, the flight engineer, and has inflated automatically when it hits the water. Now it is scudding along on the wave crests, the sea anchors barely holding it down in the seventy-knot wind. "I lined up on it, intercepted it, and hung off the side," says Spillane. "I knew I was in the ocean, in a desperate situation, and I was hurt. I didn't know anything else. It was while I was hanging onto the raft that it all started coming back to me. We were on a mission.

We ran out of fuel. I bailed out. I'm not alone."

While Spillane is hanging off the raft, a gust of wind catches it and flips it over. One moment Spillane is in the water trying to figure out who he is, the next moment he is high and dry. Instantly he feels better. He is lying on the wobbly nylon floor, evaluating the stabbing pain in his chest—he thinks he's punctured his lungs—when he hears people shouting in the distance. He kneels and points his diver's light in their direction, and just as he is wondering how to help them—whoever they are—the storm gods flip the raft over again. Spillane is dumped back into the sea. He clings to the safety line, gasping and throwing up sea water, and almost immediately the wind flips the raft over a third time. He has now gone one-and-a-half revolutions. Spillane is back inside, lying spread-eagle on the floor, when the raft is flipped a fourth and final time. Spillane is tossed back into the water, this time clinging to a rubberized nylon bag that later turns out to contain half a dozen wool blankets. It floats, and Spillane hangs off it and watches the raft go cartwheeling off across the wave crests. He is left alone and dying on the sea.

"After I lost contact with the raft I was by myself and I realized my *only* chance of survival was to make it until the storm subsided," he says. "There was no way they could pick us up, I'd just ditched a perfectly good helicopter and I knew our guys would be the ones to come out and get us if they could, but they couldn't. They couldn't refuel. So I'm contemplating this and I know I cannot make it through the storm. They might have somebody on-scene when light breaks, but I'm not going to make it that long. I'm dying inside."

For the first time since the ordeal began, Spillane has the time to contemplate his own death. He isn't panicked so much as saddened by the idea. His wife is five months pregnant with their first child, and he's been home very little recently—he was in paramedic school, and in training for the New York City marathon. He wishes that he'd spent more time at home. He wishes—incredibly—that he'd cut the grass one more time before winter. He wishes there was someone who could tell his wife and family what happened in the end. It bothers him that Dave Ruvola probably died taking the helicopter in. It bothers him they're all going to die for lack of five hundred pounds of jet fuel. The shame of it all, he thinks; we have this eight-million-dollar helicopter, nothing's wrong with it, nobody's shooting at us, we're just out of fuel.

Spillane has regained his full senses by this point, and the circumstances he finds himself in are nightmarish beyond words. It is so dark that he can't see his hand in front of his face, the waves just rumble down on him out of nowhere and bury him for a minute at a time. The wind is so strong it doesn't blow the water so much as fling it; there is no way to keep it out of his stomach. Every few minutes he has to retch it back up. Spillane has lost his one-man life raft, his ribs are broken, and every breath feels like he is being run through with a hot fire poker. He is crying out in pain and dawn isn't for another eight hours.

After an hour of making his farewells and trying to keep the water out of his stomach, Spillane spots two strobes in the distance. The Mustang suits all have strobe lights on them, and it is the first real evidence he has that someone else has survived the ditching. Spillane's immediate reaction is to swim toward them, but he stops himself. There is no way he is going to live out the night, he knows, so he might as well just die on his own. That way he won't inflict his suffering on anyone else. "I didn't want them to see me go," he says. "I didn't want them to see me in pain. It's the same with marathons—don't talk to me, let me just suffer through this by myself. What finally drove me to them was survival training. It emphasizes strength in numbers, and I know that if I'm with them, I'll try harder not to die. But I couldn't let them see me in pain, I told myself. I couldn't let them down."

Believing that their chances will be slightly less negligible in a group, Spillane slowly makes his way toward the lights. He is buoyed up by his life vest and wetsuit and swimming with his broken arm stretched out in front of him, gripping the blanket bag. It takes a long time and the effort exhausts him, but he can see the lights slowly getting closer. They disappear in the wave troughs, appear on the crests, and then disappear again. Finally, after a couple of hours of swimming, he gets close enough to shout and then to make out their faces. It is Dave Ruvola and Jim Mioli, roped together with parachute cord. Ruvola seems fine, but Mioli is nearly incoherent with hypothermia. He only has his Nomex flight suit on, and the chances of him lasting until dawn are even lower than Spillane's.

Ruvola had escaped the helicopter unscathed, but barely. He knew that the rotors would tear him and the helicopter apart if they hit the water at full speed, so he moved the aircraft away from his men, waited for the number two engine to flame out, and then performed what is known as a hovering auto-rotation. As the helicopter fell, its dead rotors started to spin, and Ruvola used that energy to slow the aircraft down. Like downshifting a car on a hill, a hovering auto-rotation is a way of dissipating the force of gravity by feeding it back through the engine. By the time the helicopter hit the water it had slowed to a manageable speed, and all the torque had been bled out of the rotors; they just smacked the face of an oncoming wave and stopped.

Ruvola found himself in a classic training situation, only it was real life: He had to escape from a flooded helicopter upside down in complete darkness. He was a former PJ, though, and a marathon swimmer, so being underwater was something he was used to. The first thing he did was reach for his HEEDS bottle, a three-minute air supply strapped to his left leg, but it had been ripped loose during the ditching; all he had was the air in his lungs. He reached up, pulled the quick-release on his safety belt, and it was then that he realized he'd never kicked the exit door out. He was supposed to do that so it wouldn't get jammed shut on impact, trapping him inside. He found the door handle, turned it, and pushed.

To his amazement, the door fell open; Ruvola kicked his way out from under the fuselage, tripped the CO_2 cartridge on his life vest, and shot ten or fifteen feet to the surface. He popped up into a world of shrieking darkness and landsliding seas. At one point the crest of a wave drove him so far under the surface that the pressure change damaged his inner ear. Ruvola started yelling for the other crew members, and a few minutes later flight engineer Mioli—who'd also managed to escape the sinking helicopter—answered him in the darkness. They started swimming toward each other, and after five or ten minutes Ruvola got close enough to grab Mioli by his survival vest. He took the hood off his survival suit, put it on Mioli's head, and then tied their two bodies together with parachute cord.

They've been in the water for a couple of hours when Spillane finally struggles up, face locked up with pain. The first thing Ruvola sees is a glint of light on a face mask, and he thinks that maybe it's a Navy SEAL who has airlocked out of a U.S. submarine and is coming to save them. It isn't. Spillane swims up, grabs a strap on Ruvola's flotation vest, and clamps his other arm around the blanket bag. What's that? Ruvola screams. I don't know, I'll open it tomorrow! Spillane yells back. Open it now! Ruvola answers. Spillane is in too much pain to argue about it, so he opens the bag and watches several dark shapes—the blankets—go snapping off downwind.

He tosses the bag aside and settles down to face the next few hours as best he can.

One can tell by the very handwriting in the District One incident log that the dispatcher—in this case a Coast Guardsman named Gill—can't quite believe what he's writing down. The words are large and sloppy and salted with exclamation points. At one point he jots down, a propos of nothing: *"They're not alone out there,"* as if to reassure himself that things will turn out all right. That entry comes at 9:30, seconds after Buschor calls in the first engine loss. Five minutes later Gill writes down: *"39-51 North, 72-00 West, Ditching here, 5 POB [people on board]."* Seven minutes after that the tanker plane—which will circle the area until their fuel runs low—reports hearing an EPIRB signal for fifteen seconds, then nothing. From Gill's notes:

9:30—Tamaroa in area, launched H-65
9:48—Cape Cod 60!
9:53—CAA [Commander of Atlantic Area]/brfd—ANYTHING YOU WANT—NAVY SHIP WOULD BE GREAT—WILL LOOK.

Within minutes of the ditching, rescue assets from Florida to Massachusetts are being readied for deployment. The response is massive and nearly instantaneous. At 9:48, thirteen minutes into it, Air Station Cape Cod launches a Falcon jet and an H-3 helicopter. Half an hour later a Navy P-3 jet at Brunswick Naval Air Station is requested and readied. The P-3 is infrared-equipped to detect heat-emitting objects, like people. The *Tamaroa* has diverted before the helicopter has even gone down. At 10:23, Boston requests a second Coast Guard cutter, the *Spencer.* They even consider diverting an aircraft carrier.

The survivors are drifting fast in mountainous seas and the chances of spotting them are terrible. Helicopters will have minimal time on-scene because they can't refuel, it's unlikely conditions would permit a hoist rescue anyway, and there's no way to determine if the guardmen's radios are even working. That leaves the *Tamaroa* to do the job, but she wasn't even able to save the *Satori* crew, during less severe conditions. The storm is barreling westward, straight toward the ditch point, and wave heights are climbing past anything ever recorded in the area.

If things look bad for Ruvola's crew, they don't look much

better for the people trying to rescue them. It's not inconceivable that another helicopter will to have to ditch during the rescue effort, or that a Coast Guardsman will get washed off the *Tamaroa.* (For that matter the *Tamaroa* herself, at 205 feet, is not necessarily immune to disaster. One freak wave could roll her over and put eighty men in the water.) Half a dozen aircraft, two ships, and two hundred rescuers are heading for 39 north, 72 west; the more men out there, the higher the chances are of someone else getting into trouble. A succession of disasters could draw the rescue assets of the entire East Coast of the United States out to sea.

A Falcon jet out of Air Station Cape Cod is the first aircraft on-scene. It arrives ninety minutes after the ditching, and the pilot sets up what is known as an expanding-square search. He moves slightly downsea of the last known position—the "splash point"—and starts flying ever-increasing squares until he has covered an area ten miles across. He flies at two hundred feet, just below cloud cover, and estimates the probability of spotting the survivors to be one-in-three. He turns up nothing. Around 11:30 he expands his search to a twenty-mile square and starts all over again, slowly working his way southwest with the direction of drift. The infrared-equipped P-3 is getting ready to launch from Brunswick, and a Coast Guard helicopter is pounding its way southward from Cape Cod.

And then, ten minutes into the second square, he picks up something: a weak signal on 243 megahertz. That's a frequency coded into Air National Guard radios. It means at least one of the airmen is still alive.

The Falcon pilot homes in on the signal and tracks it to a position about twenty miles downsea of the splash point. Whoever it is, they're drifting fast. The pilot comes in low, scanning the sea with night-vision goggles, and finally spots a lone strobe flashing below them in the darkness. It's appearing and disappearing behind the huge swell. Moments later he spots three more strobes half a mile away. All but one of the crew are accounted for. The pilot circles, flashing his lights, and then radios his position in to District One. An H-3 helicopter, equipped with a hoist and rescue swimmer, is only twenty minutes away. The whole ordeal could be over in less than an hour.

The Falcon circles the strobes until the H-3 arrives, and then heads back to base with a rapidly-falling fuel gauge. The H-3 is a huge machine, similar to the combat helicopters used in Vietnam, and has spare fuel tanks installed inside the cabin. It can't refuel in midflight, but it can stay airborn for four or five hours. The pilot, Ed DeWitt, tries to establish a forty-foot hover, but wind shear keeps spiking him downward. The ocean is a ragged white expanse in his searchlights and there are no visual reference points to work off of. At one point he turns downwind and almost gets driven into the sea.

DeWitt edges his helicopter to within a hundred yards of the three men and tells his flight engineer to drop the rescue basket. There's no way he's putting his swimmer in the water, but these are experienced rescuemen, and they may be able to extract themselves. It's either that or wait for the storm to calm down. The flight engineer pays out the cable and watches in alarm as the basket is blown straight back toward the tail rotors. It finally reaches the water, swept backward at an angle of 45 degrees, and DeWitt tries to hold a steady hover long enough for the swimmers to reach the basket. He tries for almost an hour, but the waves are so huge that the basket doesn't spend more than a few seconds on each crest before dropping to the end of its cable. Even if the men could get themselves into the basket, a shear pin in the hoist mechanism is designed to fail with loads over 600 pounds, and three men in waterlogged clothing would definitely push that limit. The entire assembly—cable, basket, everything—would let go into the sea.

DeWitt finally gives up trying to save the airmen and goes back up to a hover at two hundred feet. In the distance he can see the *Tamaroa,* searchlights pointed straight up, plunging through the storm. He vectors her in toward the position of the lone strobe in the distance—Graham Buschor—and then drops a flare by the others and starts back for Suffolk. He's only minutes away from "bingo," the point at which an aircraft doesn't have enough fuel to make it back to shore.

Two hundred feet below, John Spillane watches his last hope clatter away toward the north. He hadn't expected to get rescued, but still, it's hard to watch. The only benefit he can see is that his family will know for sure that he died. That might spare them weeks of false hope. In the distance, Spillane can see lights rising and falling in the darkness. He assumes it's a Falcon jet looking for the other airmen, but its lights are moving strangely; it's not moving like an aircraft. It's moving like a ship.

THE *Tamaroa* has taken four hours to cover the fifteen miles to the splash point; her screws are turning for twelve knots and making three. Commander Brudnicki doesn't know how strong the wind is because it rips the anemometer off the mast, but pilot Ed DeWitt reports that his airspeed indicator hit 87 knots—a hundred miles an hour—while he was in a stationary hover. The *Tamaroa*'s course to the downed airmen puts them in a beam sea, which starts to roll the ship through an arc of 110 degrees; at that angle, bulkheads are easier to walk on than floors. In the wheelhouse, Commander Brudnicki is surprised to find himself looking *up* at the crest of the waves, and when he orders full rudder and full bell, it takes thirty or forty seconds to see any effect at all. Later, after stepping off the ship, he says, "I certainly hope that was the high point of my career."

The first airman they spot is Graham Buschor, swimming alone and relatively unencumbered a half mile from the other three. He's in a Mustang survival suit and has a pen-gun flare and the only functional radio beacon of the entire crew. Brudnicki orders the operations officer, Lieutenant Kristopher Furtney, to maneuver the *Tamaroa* upsea of Buschor and then drift down on him. Large objects drift faster than small ones, and if the ship is upwind of Buschor, the waves won't smash him against the hull. The gunner's mate starts firing flares off from cannons on the flying bridge, and a detail of seamen crouch in the bow with throwing ropes, waiting for their chance. They can hardly keep their feet in the wind.

The engines come to a full stop and the *Tamaroa* wallows beam-to in the huge seas. It's a dangerous position to be in; the *Tamaroa* loses her righting arm at 72 degrees, and she's already heeling to fifty-five. Drifting down on swimmers is standard rescue procedure, but the seas are so violent that Buschor keeps getting flung out of reach. There are times when he's thirty feet higher than the men trying to rescue him. The crew in the bow can't get a throwing rope anywhere near him, and Brudnicki won't order his rescue swimmer overboard because he's afraid he won't get him back. The men on deck finally realize that if the boat's not going to Buschor, Buschor's going to have to go to it. *SWIM!* they scream over the rail. *SWIM!* Buschor rips off his gloves and hood and starts swimming for his life.

He swims as hard as he can; he swims until his arms give out. He claws his way up to the ship, gets swept around the bow, struggles back within reach of it again, and finally catches hold of a cargo net that the crew have dropped over the side. The net looks like a huge rope ladder and is held by six or seven men at the rail. Buschor twists his hands into the mesh and slowly gets hauled up the hull. One good wave at the wrong moment could take them all out. The deck crewmen land Buschor like a big fish and carry him into the deckhouse. He's dry-heaving seawater and can barely stand; his core temperature has dropped to 94 degrees. He's been in the water four hours and twenty-five minutes. Another few hours and he may not have been able to cling to the net.

It's taken half an hour to get one man on board, and they have four more to go, one of whom hasn't even been sighted yet. It's not looking good. Brudnicki is also starting to have misgivings about putting his men on deck. The larger waves are sweeping the bow and completely burying the crew; they keep having to do head counts to make sure no one has been swept overboard. "It was the hardest decision I've ever had to make, to put my people out there and rescue that crew," Brudnicki says. "Because I knew there was a chance I could lose some of my men. If I'd decided not to do the rescue, no one back home would've said a thing—they knew it was almost impossible. But can you really make a conscious decision to say, 'I'm just going to watch those people in the water die?'"

Brudnicki decides to continue the rescue; twenty minutes later he has the *Tamaroa* in a beam sea a hundred yards upwind of the three Guardsmen. Crew members are lighting off flares and aiming searchlights, and the chief quartermaster is on the flying bridge radioing Furtney when to fire the ship's engine. Not only do they have to maneuver the drift, but they have to time the roll of the ship so the gunwale rides down toward the waterline while the men in the water grab for the net. As it is, the gunwales are riding from water-level to twenty feet in the air virtually every wave. Spillane is injured, Mioli is incoherent, and Ruvola is helping to support them both. There's no way they'll be able to swim like Buschor.

Spillane watches the ship heaving through the breaking seas and for the life of him can't imagine how they're going to do this. As far as he's concerned, a perfectly likely outcome is for all three of them to drown within sight of the ship because a pickup is impossible. "My muscles were getting rigid, I was in great pain," he says. "The *Tam* pulled up in front of us and turned broadsides to the waves and I couldn't believe they did that—they were putting themselves in terrible risk. We could hear them all screaming on the deck and we could see the chemical lights coming at us, tied to the ends of the ropes."

The ropes are difficult to catch, so the deck crew throw the cargo net over the side. Lieutenant Furtney again tries to ease his ship over to the swimmers, but the vessel is 1,600 tons and almost impossible to control. Finally, on the third attempt, they snag the net. Their muscles are cramping with cold and Jim Mioli is about to start a final slide into hypothermia. The men on deck give a terrific heave—they're pulling up 600 pounds deadweight—and at the same time a large wave drops out from underneath the swimmers. They're exhausted and desperate and the net is wrenched out of their hands.

The next thing Spillane knows, he's underwater. He fights his way to the surface just as the boat rolls inward toward them and he grabs the net again. This is it; if he can't do it now, he dies. The deck crew heaves again, and Spillane feels himself getting pulled up the steel hull. He climbs up a little higher, feels hands grabbing him, and the next thing he knows he's being pulled over the gunwale onto the deck. He's in such pain he cannot stand. The men pin him against the bulkhead, cut off his survival suit, and then carry him inside, staggering with the roll of the ship. Spillane can't see Ruvola and Mioli. They haven't managed to get back onto the net.

The waves wash the two men down the hull toward the ship's stern, where the twelve-foot screw is digging out a cauldron of boiling water. Furtney shuts the engines down and the two men get carried around the stern and then up the port side of the ship. Ruvola catches the net for the second time and gets one hand into the mesh. He clamps the other one around Mioli and screams into his face, You got to do this, Jim! There aren't too many second chances in life! This is gonna take everything you got!

Mioli nods and wraps his hands into the mesh. Ruvola gets a foothold as well as a handhold and grips with all the strength in his cramping muscles. The two men get dragged upward, penduluming in and out with the roll of the ship, until the deck crew at the rail can reach them. They grab Ruvola and Mioli by the hair, the Mustang suit, the combat vest, anything they can get their hands on, and pull them over the steel rail. Like Spillane they're retching seawater and can barely stand. Jim Mioli has been in sixty-degree water for over five hours and is severely hypothermic. His core temperature is 90.4, eight degrees below normal; another couple of hours and he'd be dead.

The two airmen are carried inside, their clothing is cut off, and they're laid in bunks. Spillane is taken to the executive officer's quarters and given an IV and catheter and examined by the ship's paramedic. His blood pressure is 140/90, his pulse is a hundred, and he's running a slight fever. *Eyes pearled, abdomen and chest tenderness, pain to quadricep,* the paramedic radios SAR OPS [Search-and-Rescue Operations] Boston. *Fractured wrist, possibly ribs, suspect internal injury. Taking Tylenol-3 and seasick patch.* Boston relays the information to an Air National Guard flight surgeon, who says he's worried about internal bleeding and tells them to watch the abdomen carefully. If it gets more and more tender to the touch, he's bleeding inside and has to be evacuated by helicopter. Spillane thinks about dangling in a rescue litter over the ocean and says he'd rather not. At daybreak the executive officer comes in to shave and change his clothes, and Spillane apologizes for bleeding and vomiting all over his bed. Hey, whatever it takes, the officer says. He opens the porthole hatch, and Spillane looks out at the howling grey sky and the ravaged ocean. Ah, could you close that? he says. I can't take it.

The crew, unshaven and exhausted after thirty-six hours on deck, are staggering around the ship like drunks. And the mission's far from over: Rick Smith is still out there. He's one of the most highly trained pararescue jumpers in the country, and there's no question in anyone's mind that he's alive. They just have to find him. *PJ wearing black ¼" wetsuit, went out door with one-man life-raft and spray sheet, two 12-oz. cans of water, mirror, flare kit, granola bar, and whistle,* the Coast Guard dispatcher in Boston records. *Man is in great shape—can last quite a while, five to seven days.*

A total of nine aircraft are slated for the search, including an E2 surveillance plane to coordinate the air traffic on-scene. Jim Dougherty, a PJ who went through training with Smith and Spillane, throws a tin of Skoal chewing tobacco in his gear to give Smith when they find him. This guy's so good, Guardsmen are saying, he's just gonna come through the front door at Suffolk Air Base wondering where the hell we all were.

THE DREAMS OF THE DEAD

All collapsed, and the great shroud
of the sea rolled on as it had
five thousand years ago.

—*Herman Melville,* Moby Dick

By the time word has spread throughout Gloucester that the fleet's in trouble, the storm has retrograded to within 350 miles of Cape Cod and developed such a steep pressure gradient that an eye starts to form. Satellite photos show a cyclonic swirl two thousand miles wide off the East Coast; the southern edge reaches Jamaica and the northern edge reaches the coast of Labrador. In all, three quarters of a million square miles of ocean are experiencing gale-force conditions, and an area three or four times that is indirectly involved in the storm. On the satellite photos, moist air flowing into the low looks like a swirl of cream in a cup of black coffee. Thick strands of white cloud-cover and dark Arctic air circle one-and-a-half times around the low before making it into the center. The low grinds steadily toward the coast, intensifying as it goes, and by the morning of October 31st it has stalled two hundred miles south of Montauk, Long Island. The worst

winds, in the northeast quadrant, are getting dragged straight across Gloucester Harbor and Massachusetts Bay.

So sudden and violent are the storm's first caresses of the coast that a tinge of hysteria creeps into the local weather bulletins: UNCONFIRMED REPORTS OF TWO HOUSES COLLAPSING HAVE BEEN RECEIVED FROM THE GLOUCESTER AREA . . . OTHER MASSACHUSETTS LOCATIONS UNDER THE GUN. . . SEAS OF 25 TO 45 FEET HAVE OCCURRED TODAY FROM GEORGES BANK EAST . . . THE DANGEROUS STORM ASSOCIATED WITH HIGH SEAS IS MOVING SOUTHEAST CLOSER TO NEW ENGLAND.

The first coastal flood warnings are issued at 3:15 AM on the 29th, based mainly on reports from Nantucket of sustained winds up to 45 knots. Predictions from the Weather Service's computers are systematically exceeding almost all atmospheric models for the area, and high tides are predicted to be two to three feet above normal. (These predictions, as it turns out, will be way too low.) The warnings go out via satellite uplink along something called the NOAA Weather Wire, which feeds into local media and emergency services. By dawn, radio and television announcers are informing the public about the oncoming storm, and the state Emergency Management Agency is contacting local authorities along the coast to make sure they take precautions. The EMA is based in Framingham, Massachusetts, outside of Boston, and has direct lines to Governor Weld's Office, the National Guard, the State Police barracks, and the National Weather Service. Any threat to the public health is routed through the EMA. If local communities don't have the resources to cope, state agencies step in; if state agencies can't handle it, the federal government gets called. The EMA is set up to handle everything from severe thunderstorms to nuclear war.

October 31st, on shore, is deceptively calm and mild; oak leaves skitter down the street and the midday sun has a thin warmth to it that people won't feel again until spring. The only sign that something is amiss is along the coast, where huge grey swells start to roll in that can be heard miles inland.

Swells are the outriders of sea weather, and if they keep getting bigger, the weather is approaching. The Gloucester Police Department blocks access to the shore but people go anyway, parking their cars half a mile away and walking through the rising wind and rain to hilltops where they can look out to sea. They are greeted by an ocean that has been wholly transformed. Swells march shoreward from the horizon in great, even bands, their white crests streaming sideways in the wind and their ranks breaking, reforming, and breaking again as they close in on Cape Ann. In the shallows they draw themselves up, hesitate, and then implode against the rocks with a force that seems to shake the entire peninsula. Air trapped inside their grey barrels gets blown out the back walls in geysers higher than the waves themselves. Thirty-foot seas are rolling in from the North Atlantic and attacking the town of Gloucester with a cold, heavy rage.

By midafternoon the wind is hitting hurricane force and people are having a hard time walking, standing up, being heard. Moans emanate from the electric lines that only offshore fishermen have ever heard before. Waves inundate Good Harbor Beach and the parking lot in front of the Stop-n-Shop. They rip up entire sections of Ocean Drive. They deposit a fifteen-foot-high tangle of lobster traps and sea muck at the end of Grapevine Lane. They fill the swimming pool of a Back Shore mansion with ocean-bottom rubble. They suck beach cobbles up their huge faces and sling them inland, smashing windows, peppering lawns. They overrun the sea wall at Brace Cove, spill into Niles Pond, and continue into the woods beyond. For a brief while it's possible to surf across people's lawns. So much salt water gets pumped into Niles Pond that it overflows and cuts Eastern Point in half. Eastern Point is where the rich live, and by nightfall the ocean is two feet deep in some of the nicest living rooms in the state.

In several places around the state, houses float off their foundations and out to sea. Waves break through a thirty-foot sand dune at Ballston Beach in Truro and flood the headwaters of the Pamet River. Six-thousand-pound boat moorings drag inside Chatham Harbor. The Pilgrim Nuclear Power Plant in New Hampshire shuts down because seaweed clogs the condenser intakes. A Delta Airlines pilot at Logan is surprised to see spray from breaking waves top the two-hundred-foot cranes on Deer Island; just sitting on the runway, his airspeed indicator clocks eighty miles an hour. Houses are washed out to sea in Gloucester, Swampscott, and on Cape Cod. Rising waters innundate half of the town of Nantucket. A man is swept off the rocks in Point Judith, Rhode Island, and is never seen again, and a surfer dies trying to ride twenty-foot shorebreak in Massachusetts. Plum Island is cut in half by the waves, as is Haugh's Neck and Squantum, in Quincy. Over one hundred houses are destroyed in the town of Situate, and the National Guard has to be called out to help the inhabitants evacuate. One elderly woman is taken from her house by a backhoe while surf breaks down her front door.

The winds have set so much water in motion that the ocean gets piled up against the continent and starts blocking the rivers. The Hudson backs up one hundred miles to Albany and causes flooding, and the Potomac does the same. Tides are five feet above normal in Boston Harbor, within one inch of an all-time Boston record. Had the storm occurred a week earlier, during the highest tides of the month, water levels would be a foot and a half higher, flooding downtown Boston. Storm surge and huge seas extinguish Isle of Shoals and Boone's Island lighthouses off the coast of Maine. Some Democrats are cheered to see waves obliterate the front of President Bush's summer mansion in Kennebunkport. Damage along the East Coast surpasses one and a half billion dollars, including millions of dollars in lobster pots and other fixed fishing gear.

"The only light I can shed on the severity of the storm is that until then, we had never—ever—had a lobster trap move offshore," says Bob Brown. "Some were moved thirteen miles to the west. It was the worst storm I have ever heard of, or experienced."

By nightfall on the 31st—with wave heights at their peak and the East Coast bearing the full brunt of the storm—the Coast Guard finds itself with two major search-and-rescue operations on its hands. In Boston, a Coast Guardsman starts telephoning every harbormaster in New England, asking if the *Andrea Gail* is in port. If the town is too small to have a harbormaster, they ask a town selectman to walk down to the waterfront and take a look. Coast Guard cutters also poke their way along the coast checking every harbor and cove they can find. In Maine's Jonesport area a cutter checks Sawyers Cove, Roque Harbor, Black Cove, Moose Peak Light, Chandler and Englishman Bay, Little Machias Bay, Machias Bay East Side, Machias Bay West Side, and Mistaken Harbor, all without success. The entire coast from Lubec, Maine, to eastern Long Island is scrutinized without turning up any sign of the *Andrea Gail.*

The search for Rick Smith is in some ways simpler than for the *Andrea Gail* because the pilots know exactly where he went down, but a single human being—even with a strobe light—is extremely hard to spot in such conditions. (One pilot missed a five-hundred-foot freighter because it was obscured by waves during one leg of his search.) As a result, the combined assets of half a dozen East Coast airbases are thrown into the search. Smith has a wife and three daughters at home and he knows, personally, a significant proportion of the people who are looking for him. He's one of the most highly trained survival swimmers in the world and if he hits the water alive, he'll probably stay that way. He might eventually die of thirst, but he's not going to drown.

The first thing the Coast Guard does is drop a radio marker buoy where the other Guardsmen were picked up; the buoy drifts the way a person would, and the search area shifts continuously southwestward. Planes fly thirty-mile trackline searches five hundred feet above the water, but in these conditions the chances of spotting a man are only one in three, so some areas get flown over and over again. There are so many planes in the air, and the search area is so limited, that it's a virtual certainty they'll find him. And indeed, they find almost everything. They find the nine-man life raft pushed out of the helicopter by Jim Mioli. A Guard diver is dropped from a helicopter to knife it so it won't throw off other searchers. They find the Avon raft abandoned by the *Tamaroa,* and rafts from other boats they didn't even know about. And then, just before dusk on the 31st, a Coast Guard plane spots a stain of Day-Glo green dye in the water.

PJs are known to carry dye for just such emergencies, and this undoubtably comes from Rick Smith. The pilot circles lower and sees a dark shape at the center—probably Rick Smith himself. The search plane crew drop a marker buoy, life raft, and flare kit, and the pilot radios the coordinates in to Boston. A helicopter is diverted to the scene and the cutter *Tamaroa,* two and a half hours away, changes course and starts heading for the spot. An H-60 launches from Elizabeth City, escorted by a tanker plane, and a Navy jet equipped with forward-looking infrared is readied for take-off. If the rescuers can't get Smith by helicopter, they'll get him by ship; if they can't get him by ship, they'll drop a life raft; if he's too weak to get into the life raft, they'll drop a rescue swimmer. Smith is one of their own, and they're going to get him one way or another.

It's full dark when the first helicopter, zeroed-in by the marker buoy, arrives on-scene. There's no sign of Smith. The Coast Guard pilot who spotted him, debriefed back on-base, says the dye was fresh and he was "awful sure" there was a man in the middle of it. The seas were too rough to tell whether he swam to the life raft that was dropped to him, though. Three hours later one of the helicopter pilots radios that they've spotted Smith near the radio marker buoy. Another H-60 and tanker plane prepare to launch from Suffolk, but no sooner are those orders given than the pilot on-scene corrects himself: He didn't spot a *person*, he spotted a *life raft*. It was probably dropped by the Coast Guard earlier that day. The Suffolk aircraft stand down.

Throughout that night the storm slides south along the coast and then doubles back on itself, heading toward Nova Scotia and dissipating by the hour. The convective engine of the storm that sucks warm moist air off the ocean is finally starting to break down in cold northern water. By the morning of November 1st the conditions are stable enough to evacuate John Spillane, and he's strapped into a rescue litter and carried out of his room and onto the aft deck of the *Tamaroa*. He's hoisted up into the belly of an H-3 and flown to Atlantic City, where he's rushed into intensive care and given two units of blood. A few hours later a Coast Guardsman tracks down a search pilot who says that he dropped green dye into the water to mark a line he'd seen. That explains the dye but not the person spotted at the center of it. A Coast Guard survival specialist named Mike Hyde says that Smith could stay warm virtually forever in a quarter-inch wetsuit, but that he might drown by inhaling water into his lungs. There aren't any charts or graphs for survival time in the conditions he was in, Hyde says.

If Smith made it through the storm, though, Hyde's personal guess is that he could survive another four days. Eventually, he'll die of dehydration. The sea is much calmer now, but the search has been going full-bore for seventy-two hours without turning up anything; chances are almost nonexistent that Smith is alive. On the morning of November 2nd—the storm now over Prince Edward Island and failing fast—the cutter *Tamaroa* makes port at Shinnecock Inlet, Long Island, and Ruvola, Buschor, and Mioli are taken off by motor launch. Rick Smith's wife, Marianne, is at Suffolk

Airbase for the event, and several people express concern over her watching the airmen reunited with their families.

What do they think, that I want those women to lose *their* husbands, too? she wonders. She takes John Brehm, the PJ supervisor, aside and says, Look, John, if they haven't found Rick by now, they're not going to. As far as I'm concerned, I'm a widow and I need to know what's going to happen.

Brehm expresses the hope that they might still find him, but Marianne just shakes her head. If he were alive, he'd signal, she says. He's not alive.

Marianne Smith, who's nursing a three-week-old baby, practically hasn't slept since the ditching. She found out about it late the first night, when someone from the airbase called and woke her up out of an exhausted sleep. It took her a minute to even understand what the person was saying, and when she did, he reassured her that it was a controlled ditching and everything would be fine. Things were not fine, though. First they wouldn't tell her which four crew members had been picked up by the *Tamaroa* (she understandably assumed one of them was her husband), and then they said they'd spotted him at the center of some green dye, and then they lost him again. Now she's between-worlds, treated as a widow by everyone on base but still reassured that her husband will be found alive. No one, it seems, can openly face the fact that Rick Smith is dead. The planes keep going out, the grids keep getting flown.

Finally, after nine days of round-the-clock flights, the Coast Guard suspends its search for Rick Smith. The consensus is that he must have hit the water so hard that he was knocked unconscious and drowned. Another possibility is that Spillane hit him when he landed, or that the life raft hit him, or that he jumped with his gunner's strap on. The gunner's strap is used to keep crewmen from falling out of helicopters, and if Smith jumped with it on, he'd have just dangled below the helicopter until Ruvola set it down.

John Spillane prefers to believe that Smith was knocked

out on impact. He was weighed down by a lot of gear, and he must have lost position during his fall and hit the water flat. Spillane's only memory of the fall is exactly that: starting to flail and thinking, "My God, what a long way down." Those words, or something very like them, are probably the last thoughts that went through Rick Smith's mind.

WHILE aircraft are crisscrossing the waters off the coast of Maryland, an even larger search continues for the *Andrea Gail.* Fifteen aircraft, including a Navy P-3 transferred from the Smith search, are flying grids southwest of Sable Island, where a life raft would most likely have drifted. A rumor ripples through Gloucester that Billy Tyne called someone on a satellite phone the night of the 29th, but Bob Brown chases the rumor down and tells the Coast Guard it's bogus. Half the boats in the sword fleet—the *Laurie Dawn 8, Mr. Simon, Mary T,* and *Eishin Maru*—sustain considerable damage and cut their trips short. The eastern half of the fleet misses the full fury of the storm ("Oh, we only had about seventy-knot winds," Linda Greenlaw recalls), but such extreme weather generally ruins the fishing for days, and most of the eastern boats head in as well.

Nothing is seen or heard of the *Andrea Gail* until November 1st when Albert Johnston, steaming for home, plows straight through a cluster of blue fuel barrels. They're a hundred miles southwest of Sable, and they all have *AG* stencilled on the side. "The barrels went down either side of the hull, I didn't even have to change course," says Johnston. "It was spooky. You know, just a few fuel barrels, that's all that was left."

An hour later Johnston passes another cluster, then a third, and calls their position in to the Coast Guard. The barrels don't, by themselves, mean the *Andrea Gail* went down—they could have just washed off the deck—but they're not a good sign. The Canadian and American Coast Guards keep widening the search area without finding anything; finally, on

November 4th, things start to turn up. A Coast Guardsman on a routine beach patrol around Sable Island finds a propane tank and radio beacon with *Andrea Gail* painted on them. The beacon is for locating fishing gear and has been switched on, which may have been a desperate attempt to surround the stricken boat with as many electronically active objects as possible. Normally they're stowed in the "off" position.

And then, on the afternoon of November 5th, an EPIRB washes up on Sable Island. It's an orange 406-megahertz model, built by an American company named Koden, and the ring switch has been turned off. That means that it can't signal even if it hits the water. The serial number is 986. It's from the *Andrea Gail*.

Like the bottled note thrown overboard from the schooner *Falcon* a century ago, the odds of something as small as an EPIRB winding up in human hands are absurdly small. And the odds of Billy Tyne disarming his EPIRB—there's no reason to, it wouldn't even save batteries—are even smaller. Bob Brown, Linda Greenlaw, Charlie Reed, no one who knows Billy can explain it. The fourteen-page incident log kept by the Canadian Coast Guard records the discovery of the propane tank and the radio beacon, but not of the EPIRB. The entire day, in fact, that the EPIRB is found—November 5th, 1991—is missing from the log. Rumors start creeping around Gloucester that the Coast Guard *did* pick up an EPIRB signal when the *Andrea Gail* was in trouble, but conditions were too severe to go out. And when, against all odds, the EPIRB washes up on Sable Island, the Coast Guard switchs it off to cover themselves.

Whether the rumors are fair or not, they're in some ways beside the point. Conditions severe enough to frighten the Coast Guard are severe enough to prevent a rescue, and by the time the EPIRB started signalling—if it ever did—the crew of the *Andrea Gail* were probably doomed anyway. Judging by the rescue attempts off Long Island, even a helicopter hovering directly over the *Andrea Gail* crew would have been powerless to help them. Regardless, the EPIRB is duly transported back to the United States for inspection by the Federal Communications Commission.

On November 6th, a Canadian pilot spots an uninflated life raft just off the Nova Scotia coast, but there's no one inside it, and he loses sight of it before it can be recovered. Two days later the *Hannah Boden,* steaming home after three weeks at sea, spots another cluster of fuel barrels marked *AG* on the side, but there's still no sign of the boat. Finally, a half hour before midnight on November 8th, the search for the *Andrea Gail* is permanently suspended. She's been missing for almost two weeks, and planes have searched 116,000 square miles of ocean without finding any survivors. All they turned up was a little deck gear.

"*I WENT* down to the fish pier a lot after the search ended," says Chris Cotter. "I went there a lot, I went there alone and I'd go through these things—you know, picturing what happened to their bodies, that kind of horror. I'd reject it from my mind and my soul as soon as it blew in, and then I'd remember the good things, he'd come back to me and it would be okay. I miss him immensely, though, I fight it all the time. Later, I tell myself. I'll see him later on."

The memorial service is held several days later at St. Ann's Church, just up the hill from the Crow's Nest Inn. It's the first service in thirteen years for Gloucestermen lost at sea, and it brings people out who don't even know the men who died. The sea was their domain, they knew it well, Reverend Casey says quietly to the thousand people packed into his church for the service. I urge you to mourn not just for these three men, but for all the other brave people who gave their lives for Gloucester and its fishing industry.

Mary Anne and Rusty Shatford read a poem about fishing, and Sully's brother speaks, and some of the Tyne family speak. Bob and Susan Brown are at the service, but they say very little and leave as soon as it's over. This is the third time men have died on one of Bob Brown's boats and, regardless of fault, people in town are not inclined to forget it. After the service the mourners drive and walk down the steep hill to Rogers Street and pile into the Crow's Nest Inn and the Irish Mariner, where a wake is held for the next couple of days. Food is brought and people go to Sully's brother's apartment, then back to the Crow's Nest, then over to the Tynes, and back to the Nest again, endlessly, all weekend long.

If the men on the *Andrea Gail* had simply died, and their bodies were lying in state somewhere, their loved ones could make their goodbyes and get on with their lives. But they didn't die, they disappeared off the face of the earth and, strictly speaking, it's just a matter of faith that these men will never return. Such faith takes work, it takes effort. The people of Gloucester must willfully extract these men from their lives and banish them to another world.

"The night before I found out about the boat, I had this dream," says Debra Murphy, Murph's ex-wife. "Murph was supposed to be home for my birthday, and in my dream—I don't know if he's standing there or if he's calling me—he says, 'I'm sorry, I'm not going to make it this time.' Then I wake up, and the phone call comes. It's from Billy's new girlfriend, who says there was a big storm out there and the *Andrea Gail* hasn't been heard from in a couple of days."

The first thing Debra does is drive over to Murph's parents' house to give them the bad news. They've never liked his fishing much—his father's in real estate, they live a quiet suburban life—and they sit there in shock while Debra tells them the boat is missing. She doesn't know much more than that one fact, and when she calls Bob Brown, all he can tell her is that the boat was last heard from on the 28th and that a search has been launched. Brown refuses to return her calls after that, so she starts talking to the Coast Guard every day asking how many flights went out, whether they see anything, what they plan to do next. Finally, after ten days of hell,

Debra sits her three-year-old son, Dale Jr., down and explains that his father's not coming back. Her son doesn't understand, and wants to know where he is.

He's fishing, honey, she answers. He's fishing in heaven.

Dale knows his father fishes lots of places—Hawaii, Puerto Rico, Massachusetts. Heaven must be just another place where his father fishes. Well, when's he coming back from fishing in heaven? he asks.

A couple of months later, as far as young Dale is concerned, his father *does* come back from fishing in heaven. Dale wakes up screaming in the middle of the night, and Debra rushes into his room, panicked. What's wrong, honey, what's wrong? she says.

Daddy's in the room, Dale answers. Daddy was just here.

What do you mean, Daddy was just here? Debra asks.

Daddy was here and told me what happened on the boat.

Three-year-old Dale, stumbling over the language, goes on to repeat what his father told him. The boat rolled over and caught his father on a "hook" (one of the gaff hooks for grabbing fish). The hook snagged his shirt and Murph wasn't able to free himself in time. He got dragged under, and that was it.

"My son has a lot of anger in him from losing his father," says Debra. "There'll be days where he'll just be really depressed and I'll say, 'What's the matter, Dale?' And he'll say, 'Nothin', Mom, I'm just thinking about my dad.' Oh, God, he'll look at me with these big brown eyes, the tears running down his cheeks and it kills me because there's nothing I can do. Not one thing."

Others, too, are visited. Murph's mother looks out the bedroom window one day and sees Murph ambling down their street in huge deck boots. Someone else spots him in traffic in downtown Bradenton. From time to time Debra dreams that she sees him and runs up and says, "Dale, where've you been?" And he won't answer, and she'll wake up in a cold sweat, remembering.

Back in Gloucester, Chris Cotter has a similar dream.

Bobby appears before her, all smiles, and she says to him, "Hey, Bobby, where you been?" He doesn't tell her, he just keeps smiling and says, "Remember, Christina, I'll always love you," and then he fades away. "He's always happy when he goes and so I know he's okay," says Chris. "He's absolutely okay."

Chris, however, is not okay. Some nights she finds herself down at the State Fish Pier, waiting for the *Andrea Gail* to come in; other times she tells her friends, "Bobby's coming home tonight, I know it." She dates other men, she continues with her life, but she cannot accept that he is gone. They never find a body, they never find a piece of the boat, and she holds onto these things as proof that maybe the whole crew is safe on an island somewhere, drinking margaritas and watching the sun go down. Once Chris dreams that Bobby is living below the sea with a beautiful blond woman. The woman is a mermaid, and Bobby's with her, now. Chris wakes up and heads back to the Crow's Nest Inn.

Within weeks of the tragedy, families of the dead men get a letter from Bob Brown asking them to exonerate him from responsibility. The letter is polite and to the point, saying that the *Andrea Gail* was "tight, strong, fully manned, equipped and supplied, and in all respects seaworthy and fit for the service in which she was engaged." Unfortunately, she was also overwhelmed by the sea. For several of the bereaved—Jodi Tyne, Debra Murphy—this is the only letter they get from Bob Brown. He doesn't write a sympathy card, he doesn't offer financial help; he just sends a letter protecting himself from future legalities. It's possible that he's too shy, or embarrassed, to deal intimately with the bereaved, but they don't see it that way. They see Bob "Suicide" Brown as a businessman who has made hundreds of thousands of dollars off men like their husbands. To a woman, they decide to sue.

The deaths of the six *Andrea Gail* crew fall under the

Death on the High Seas Act, a law passed by Congress in the early 1970s and then amended by the Supreme Court in 1990. A suit involving wrongful death on the high seas is limited to "pecuniary" loss, meaning the amount of money the deceased was earning for his dependents. Bobby Shatford, for example, was paying $325 a month in child support. Under the High Seas Act his ex-wife could—and does—sue Bob Brown for that money, but Ethel Shatford cannot sue. She has lost a son, not a legal provider, and has suffered no pecuniary loss.

The High Seas Act is a vestige of the hard-nosed English Common Law, which saw death at sea as an act of God that shipowners couldn't possibly be held liable for. Where would it end? How could they possibly do business? Had these men died in a logging accident, say, the family members could sue their employer for the loss of a loved one. But not on the high seas. On the high seas—defined as more than a marine league, or three miles, from shore—anything goes. The only way for Ethel Shatford to be compensated for the loss of her son would be to prove that Bobby's death had been exceptionally agonizing, or that Bob Brown had been negligent in his upkeep of the boat. Suffering, of course, is impossible to prove on a boat that disappears without a trace, but negligence is not. Negligence can be proven through repair records, expert witnesses, and the testimony of former crew.

Several weeks after the loss of the *Andrea Gail*, a Boston attorney named David Ansell agrees to represent the estates of Murphy, Moran, and Pierre in a wrongful death suit against Bob Brown. The other cases—including a wrongful death suit filed by Ethel Shatford—are handled by a Boston attorney who also specializes in maritime law. Brown's name is already known to Ansell: Ten years earlier, Ansell's law firm represented the widow of the man washed out of the *Sea Fever* on Georges Bank. Now Ansell has to prove Brown negligent once again. The fact that Brown acted like every other boat owner in the sword fleet—eyeballing structural changes, overloading the whaleback, failing to carry out stability tests—

isn't necessarily enough to clinch the case. Ansell packs his bags and heads to St. Augustine, Florida, where, five years earlier, Bob Brown altered the lines of the *Andrea Gail.*

The shipyard, St. Augustine Trawlers, has been closed and sold by the I.R.S., but Ansell tracks down a former manager named Don Capo and asks him to give a deposition. Capo agrees. In the presence of a notary public and Bob Brown's attorney, David Ansell questions Capo about the alterations to the *Andrea Gail:*

To your knowledge, sir, was there a marine architect on board the vessel in Mr. Brown's employ?

I don't recall any.

Were there any measurements or tests or evaluations done to determine the amount of weight being added to the vessel?

No, sir.

Were there stability tests performed, either hydraulic or reclining?

No, sir.

So far, Capo's testimony has been damning. Brown altered the vessel without consulting a marine architect and then launched her without a single stability test. To anyone but a swordfisherman or a marine welder this would seem unusual—negligent, in fact—but it's not. In the fishing industry, it's as common as drunks in bars.

How would you characterize the *Andrea Gail* compared to other vessels? Ansell finally asks, hoping to put the last nail in the coffin. Capo doesn't hesitate.

Oh, top of the line.

Ansell's line of attack has been blunted, but he has other avenues. For starters he can talk to Doug Kosco, who walked off the boat with six hours to go because he got a bad feeling. What did Kosco know? Had anything happened on the previous trip? Kosco works for the A.P. Bell Fish Company in Cortez, Florida, and when he's not at sea he's usually crashing at one friend's apartment or another. He's a hard man to find. "It's—how can I put it—a nomadic existence," says

Ansell. "These guys don't come home for dinner at five o'clock. They're gone three or four months at a time."

Ansell finally tracks Kosco down to his parents' house in Bradenton, but Kosco is uncooperative to the point of belligerence. He says that when he heard about the *Andrea Gail* he went into a three-month depression that cost him his job and nearly put him in the hospital. At one point Dale Murphy's parents invited him over to dinner but he couldn't deal with it; he never went. He'd known Murph as well as Bugsy and Billy, and all he could think was: That was supposed to have been me. Had Kosco gone on the trip, it's possible that he would've spent his last few moments pleading for his life—for this life, the one he's now leading. His wish was granted, in a sense, and it destroys him.

Ansell's case is fraying at the edges. He can't use Kosco's testimony because the man's too much of a mess; the Coast Guard says the EPIRB tested perfectly—although they won't release the report—and there's no hard evidence that the *Andrea Gail* was unstable. By the standards of the industry she was a seaworthy boat, fit for her task, and sank due to an act of God rather than any negligence on Bob Brown's part. The alterations to her hull may have helped her roll over, but they didn't cause it. She rolled over because she was in the middle of the Storm of the Century, and no judge is going to see it otherwise. Ansell's clients know that and decide to settle out-of-court. They probably won't get much—eighty or ninety thousand—but they won't run the risk of having Bob Brown completely exonerated.

Ansell starts negotiating a settlement, and the other suits are also settled in private. The relative stability of the *Andrea Gail* will never be debated in court.

ABOUT a year after the boat goes down, a man who looks exactly like Bobby Shatford walks into the Crow's Nest Inn and orders a beer. The entire line-up of regulars at the bartop turn and stare. One of the bartenders is too shocked to speak. Ethel, who's just gotten off her shift, has seen the man before, in town, and explains to him why everyone's staring. You look just like my son who died last year, she says. There's a photo of him on the wall.

The man goes over and studies it. The photo shows Bobby in a t-shirt, hat, and sunglasses down on Fisherman's Wharf. His arms are folded, he's leaning a little to one side and smiling at the camera. It was taken on a day that he was walking around town with Chris, and he looks very happy. Three months later he'd be dead.

Jesus, if I sent this photo home to my mother she'd think it was me, the man says. She'd never know the difference.

Luckily the man is a carpenter, not a fisherman. If he were a fisherman, he'd drain his beer and settle onto a barstool and think things over a bit. People who work on boats have a hard time resisting the idea that certain ones among them are marked, and that they will be reclaimed by the sea. The spitting image of a man who drowned is a good candidate for that; so are all his shipmates. Jonah, of course, was marked, and his shipmates knew it. Murph was marked and told his mother so. Adam Randall was marked but had no idea; as far as he was concerned, he just had a couple of close-calls. After the *Andrea Gail* went down he told his girlfriend, Chris Hansen, that while he was walking around onboard he felt a cold wind on his skin and realized that no one on the crew was coming back. He didn't say anything to them, though, because on the waterfront that isn't done—you don't just tell six men you think they're going to drown. Everyone takes their chances, and either you drown or you don't.

And then there are the nearly-dead. Kosco, Hazard, Reeves— these people are leading lives that, but for the merest of circumstances, should have already ended. Anyone who has been through a severe storm at sea has, to one degree or another, almost died, and that fact will continue to alter them long after the winds have stopped blowing and the waves have died down. Like a war or a great fire, the effects of a storm go rippling outward through webs of people for years, even generations. It breaches lives like coastlines and nothing is ever again the same.

"My boss took me to a hotel and the first thing I did was have three shots of vodka straight up," says Judith Reeves, after she got off the *Eishin Maru* 78 in Halifax on October 31st. (The engineer had rigged up some cables in the hold that, manually, turned the rudder. The captain shouted commands down to him from the bridge, he pulled the cables, and that was how they weathered the storm.) "I called my mom and then my roommate and I didn't sleep that whole first night because the hotel room wasn't rocking. Next morning I did 'Midday,' the CBS news show here, and then I went to the CBC studios for another interview, and that was the first time that I got scared. I started smoking and drinking and by the time I went to the third interview I was quite hammered. They wanted to do it live and I said, 'Are you sure about that?' I was in *such* demand by the media for two or three weeks, I mean the whole country was praying for me, it was kind of a high. But then I went home in December to see my mom and dad and as soon as I got back here I fell into a depression. I lost a lot of weight and started going on these long crying jags. You can only sustain that high level for so long before you break down; you finally become an ordinary person again."

Reeves keeps working as a fisheries observer and eventually meets, and marries, a Russian fisherman from one of her boats. Karen Stimson, who also spent several days at sea thinking she was going to die, breaks down more quickly than Reeves but not as badly. After the rescue she stays at a friend's apartment in Boston, avoiding reporters, and the next day she decides to go out and get a cappuccino. She walks into a cafe around the corner, orders, and then pulls a roll of bills out of her pocket to pay. The bills are wet with seawater.

The man at the cash register looks from her face to the wet bills to her face again and says, I know you! You're the woman they saved off that boat!

Stimson is horrified; she pushes the money at him, but he just waves her away. No, no, it's on us. Just thank God you're alive.

Thank God you're alive . . . She'd hadn't thought about it like that but, yes, she could well be swirling around in the freezing black depths off Georges right now. She grabs her coffee and runs out the door, sobbing.

TWO weeks after the search for Rick Smith has been called off, Marianne gets a telephone call from a man named John Monte of Westhampton Beach, Long Island, who says that he's a psychic and that Rick Smith is still alive. He tells her that he talked to Suffolk Airbase and that they want to resume searching for him.

Marianne's heart sinks. It's taken her two weeks to accept the fact that her husband is dead, and now she's supposed to start hoping all over again. There's no way Rick could still be alive, but she's afraid of what people might think if she discourages a search, so she gives her okay. The PJs at the base are worried about the same thing—what Marianne will think—so they give their okay as well. Monte gets a local lawyer named John Jiras interested in the case, and Jiras drafts a letter to New York State Representative George Hochbrueckner demanding that the search be resumed. Hochbrueckner passes the letter along to Admiral Bill Kime, Commandant of the U.S. Coast Guard, and the case filters through the command structure back to D1 Comcen in Boston. A response is drawn up explaining how thorough the search was and how unlikely it would be that a man could survive twenty-six days at sea, and that is sent back up the ladder to Kime. Meanwhile, Monte gives Marianne a list of press contacts to call to publicize the case—and himself. "It's the only time in my life I thought I was going crazy," she says. "I finally told him to get lost. I couldn't take it anymore."

After almost a month, Marianne Smith is able to start absorbing the loss of her husband. As long as the planes are going out she holds onto some shred of hope, and that keeps her in a ghastly kind of limbo. Several weeks after Rick's death, she dreams that he comes up to her with a sad look on his face and says, I'm sorry, and then gives her a hug. It's the only dream she ever has of him, and it constitutes a goodbye of sorts. Marianne takes her children to a memorial service in Rick's hometown in Pennsylvania, but not to the one on Long Island, because she knows there are going to be a lot of television cameras there. ("Children don't grieve in front of crowds—they grieve in bed saying, 'I want Daddy to read me a book,'" she says.) George Bush sends her a letter of sympathy, as does Governor Mario Cuomo. Marianne discovers that, as a widow, she makes people extremely uncomfortable; either they avoid her or treat her like a cripple. Marianne Smith, who started out as an avionics technician for an F-16 squadron, decides to face her widowhood by going to law school and becoming a lawyer.

John Spillane gets a job as a New York City fireman, in addition to his PJ status. One night he's half awakened by the station alarm, and for some reason the room lights don't go on. He's terrified. He finds himself by the exit pole thinking, "It's okay, you've been through this before, just keep your head." All he knows is that it's dark, there's not much time and he's got to go downward—exactly the same situation as in the helicopter. By the time he finally understands where he is, he's put on all his fire-fighting clothes. He's fully-cocked and ready to go.

The storm hasn't yet finished with people, though; hasn't stopped reverberating through people's lives. Eighteen months after the ditchings, a nor'easter roars up the coast that, even before it's fully formed, meteorologists are referring to as the "Mother of All Storms." It has a distinct eye, just like a hurricane, and a desperately low central barometric pressure. One ship in its path watches wave heights jump from three feet to twenty feet *in less than two hours.* The storm drops fifty inches of snow on the mountains of North Carolina and and sets all-time barometric records from Delaware to Boston. Winds hit 110 miles an hour in the Gulf of Mexico, and the Coast Guard rescues 235 people off boats during the first two days alone. Wave heights surpass sixty feet off much of the East Coast and creep up toward one hundred feet off Nova Scotia. Data buoys record significant wave heights—the average of the top third—only a few feet lower than in the storm that sank the *Andrea Gail.* By the narrowest of margins the "Halloween Gale," as that storm has come to be known, retains the record for most powerful nor'easter of the century.

Caught in the worst of this is the 584-foot *Gold Bond Conveyor,* the freighter that, two years earlier, had relayed the *Satori's* mayday to Boston. The *Gold Bond Conveyor* has a regular run between Halifax and Tampa carrying gypsum ore, and on March 14th, about a hundred miles southeast of where Billy Tyne went down, she runs into the Mother of All Storms. She's the only vessel of any kind to encounter both storms at their height, and they happen to be two of the most powerful nor'easters of the century. One could say the vessel was marked. That evening the captain radios Halifax that waves are breaking over their upper decks, and shortly after midnight he calls again to say that they're abandoning ship. The seas are a hundred feet and the snow is driving down sideways in the dark. Thirty-three men go over the side and are never seen again.

But it's still not over; the Halloween Gale has one last shoulder to tap. Adam Randall has been working steadily on the *Mary T,* but in February, Albert Johnston hauls her out for repairs and Randall has to find another job. He finds one on the *Terri Lei,* a tuna longliner out of Georgetown, South Carolina. The *Terri Lei* is a big, heavily-built boat with a highly experienced crew, and she's due to go out at the end of March. Chris Hansen, Randall's girlfriend, drives him to Logan Airport for the flight south, but all the planes are grounded because of the blizzard—the Mother of All Storms. He gets a flight out the next day, but when he talks with Chris Hansen on the phone from South Carolina, she tells him she's worried about him. Are you okay? There's a funny sound in your voice, she says.

Yeah, I'm fine, he says. I don't really want to go on this trip. It'll be good, though—maybe I'll make some money.

The night before leaving, the crew of the *Terri Lei* go to a local bar and get into a fight with the crew of another boat. Several men wind up in the hospital, but the next day, bruised and sore, the crew of the *Terri Lei* cut their lines and head out to sea. They're going to work the deep waters just off the continental shelf, due east of Charleston. It's spring, the fish are working their way up the Gulf Stream, and with a little luck they'll make their trip in ten or twelve sets. On the night of April sixth they finish setting their gear and then Randall calls Chris Hansen on the ship-to-shore radio. They talk for over half an hour—ship to shore isn't cheap, Randall's phone bill is regularly five hundred dollars—and he tells Chris that they'd had some bad weather but it's passed and all their gear is in the water. He says he'll call her soon.

Randall's a tough one to categorize. He's an expert fisherman and marine welder but has also, at various times, considered hairdressing or nursing as careers. He has a tattoo of a clipper ship on one arm, an anchor on the other, and a scar on his hand where he once stitched himself up with a needle and thread. He has the sort of long blond hair that one associates with English rock stars, but he also has the muscled build of a man who works hard. ("You can hit him with a hammer and he won't bruise," Chris Hansen says.) Randall says that at times he can feel ghosts swirling around the boat, the ghosts of men who died at sea. They're not at peace. They want back in.

The next morning the crew of the *Terri Lei* start hauling their gear in choppy seas and gusty winds. They're 135 miles offshore and there are a lot of boats in the area, including a freighter en route from South America to Delaware. At 8:45 AM the Charleston Coast Guard pick up an EPIRB distress signal, and they immediately send out two aircraft and a cutter to investigate. It might be a false alarm—the weather is moderate and no ships have reported trouble—but they have to respond anyway. They home in on the radio signal and immediately spot the EPIRB amidst a scattering of deck gear. A short distance away floats a life raft with the canopy up and *Terri Lei* stencilled on one side.

The boat herself has vanished and no one signals from the raft, so a swimmer drops into the water to investigate. He strokes over and hauls himself up on one of the grab lines. The raft is empty. No one got off the *Terri Lei* alive.

AFTERWORD

"*I'M SORRY* the way I was when I first met you," Ricky Shatford told me in a Gloucester bar not long ago. The book had been out for about three months, and the Shatford family—and Gloucester—had been rocked by a wave of publicity. Summer people were visiting Cape Pond Ice, tourists were booking rooms at the Crow's Nest, the Shatfords were being stopped in the street. "You were writing about my baby brother and I couldn't deal with it," Ricky went on. "I told people I was going to kill you."

The first time I'd ever gone into the Crow's Nest, it had taken me half an hour to work up the nerve. It wasn't the bar—I'd been in rough bars before—it was what I was going in there for. I was going in there to ask a woman about the death of her son. I wasn't a fisherman, I wasn't from Gloucester, and I wasn't a journalist, at least by my own definition of the word. I was just a guy with a pen and paper and an idea for a book. I slid a steno pad under my belt against the small of my back, where it was hidden by my jacket. I put a tape recorder and a smaller notebook in my jeans pocket in case I needed them. Then I took a long breath and I got out of the car and walked across the street.

The front door was heavier than I expected, the room was darker, and there were a dozen men clutching beers in the indoor gloom. Every single one turned and looked at me when I walked in. I ignored their looks and walked across the room and sat down at the bar. Ethel came over, and after ordering a beer I told her that I was writing about dangerous jobs, particularly fishing, and that I wanted to talk to her. "I know you lost your son a couple of years ago," I said. "I was living in Gloucester at the time, and I remember the storm. It must have been very hard for you. I can't imagine how hard that must have been."

What I didn't know was that there was a court case going on, and that Ethel's first thought was that I was working undercover for Bob Brown's insurance company. She wasn't suing him, but whenever a boat goes down, there are always people asking questions, looking for an angle. Within weeks of the sinking, in fact, a couple of lawyers had slid into the Nest, trying to interest her in a lawsuit. They were so insistent that some of the boys at the bar felt compelled to help them leave.

Ethel was friendly with me, but guarded. She talked about watching the local news, waiting for word of the *Andrea Gail*. She talked about the memorial service, and how people had stuck by her after the tragedy. She bought me a beer, and gave me the names of other fishermen who might be able help out. And then I walked back out of the bar. It was a warm day in early spring, snow lingering in the northern exposures and a rich, loamy smell that mixed with salt air off the ocean. Reefer rigs crawled down Main Street and pick-up trucks pulled in and out of Rose's parking lot, tires spraying gravel. The men in the trucks didn't smile as they drove. *This isn't exactly a town that begs to be written about*, I remember thinking. *These aren't men who really want to be asked about their lives.*

And to an extent, I was right. The guys in those pick-up trucks—and on barstools at the Crow's Nest, and walking down Main Street in their deck boots and fishing gear—had no particular reason to talk to me. Men in working towns can nurture a harsh kind of pragmatism that weeds out sentimental acts, such as talking to writers, and it's generally hard to coax them out of that. If I were a Gloucester native, or had worked as a fishermen, perhaps it would have been different. But I wasn't, and the only thing I had going in my favor—other than the fact that Ethel seemed to like me, which counted for more than I realized—was that I worked as a freelance climber for tree companies. I was living on Cape Cod, but did occasional jobs in Boston, and often I'd combine trips into the city with research jaunts up to Gloucester. I'd walk into the Crow's Nest at the end of the day, tired and dirty from a day of climbing, and settle onto a stool at the bar. "Look, I don't know a thing about fishing," I'd say. "So if you don't tell me about it, I'm going to get it all wrong."

That seemed to work; gradually, the fishermen started to talk. They told me about their grandfathers dory-fishing for cod on the Grand Banks. They told me about winter gales on Georges. They told me about getting thrown out of their house by their girl-friend for one reason or another, usually good ones. And they told me about the sea. "She's a beautiful lady," one guy said, jerking his thumb oceanward out the bar door, "but she'll kill ya without a second thought."

Usually the only thing I had in front of me during these conversations was a beer, though occasionally, if the conversation looked promising enough, and I'd established a good rapport with the guy, I'd pull the steno pad out from behind my jacket. Otherwise, I'd periodically excuse myself to go to the men's room, which—given the evening's activities—was usually necessary anyway. There I'd scribble down a few stories and then I'd go back out into the bar. When I'd really become friendly with someone, such as Chris Cotter, I'd ask if I could interview them with a tape recorder, out of the bar, some place where we could talk without being interrupted. Usually they said yes. One guy said yes, but tried to give me the slip while I was following him in my car through town. I finally tracked him down at the Green Tavern, and we ended up talking for three hours. And a few people—like Ricky Shatford—would have nothing to do with me at all.

Ricky was angry about his brother's death, he told me later, and I was something to focus all that on. He didn't like me writing about his family, and he didn't like me writing about something I couldn't know for sure. The *Andrea Gail* had been lost without a trace. Why not just let it lie there?

Unfortunately, Ricky was articulating exactly my own insecurities about the project. Every time I ventured into the Crow's Nest, I felt like an intruder, and I'd had several excruciating dreams about the loss of the *Andrea Gail.* In one, I dreamed I'd drilled tiny holes in her hull before her last trip to see if she'd still float; and in another I dreamed I was in the wheel-house with Billy Tyne as she went down. I didn't have to die, though, because I was a journalist, and I just looked guiltily on as we plunged into the trough of another enormous wave. *My God, you never really stopped to think how terrifying this must have been for those guys*, I remember thinking. *Those were six real men out there, not just names out of a newspaper. Don't ever forget that.*

The one encouraging dream I had was in 1994, when I wrote a magazine article about the *Andrea Gail.* Most people in Gloucester liked the article, but there were the inevitable dissenting voices, and they traumatized me for months. The idea that you could do as good and thorough a job as possible and still leave people angry at you, shook some long-held illusion about journalism. In the dream I was walking along a deserted beach, and a figure strode towards me down the dunes. It was Bobby Shatford, and he walked up to me and stuck his hand out. "So, *you're* Sebastian Junger," he said. "I've been wanting to meet you. I liked your article."

"Thanks, Bobby," I said. "That means a lot, coming from you."

We'd never loosened our grip, and we just stood there, holding hands. Down the beach, the rest of the Shatford family was having a cook-out. I was headed there, but Bobby couldn't come. He had to stay away.

When I finally talked to Ricky, it seemed as close as I was going to get to shaking Bobby Shatford's hand. Ricky was a fisherman, he was Bobby's older brother, and he'd wanted to kill me. Those are tough hurdles to clear. One summer night in a Gloucester bar, though, we got to talking, and he told me what it was like to lose his younger brother. To me, Ricky had always been the scary older brother who careened around town looking for trouble; now here he was, telling me about the most painful thing in his life. It wasn't an easy thing to listen to.

"When we were kids we were a real close family," says Ricky. "Me and Bobby and Rusty slept in the same bed together. Bobby worked down at the wharf, Bob Brown built the *Miss Penny* and Looper was running it and I remember one time we were down at Rosie's doing the last-minute preparations and on the way out I yelled to Bobby on the State Fish Pier, *HEY BRO*! That trip we hit one of the first storms I ever encountered in my life, it was '83 and we were crazy, it was December on the southeast part of Georges and the water was still warm, the *Rush* was right next to us and they lost every window they had. We gave them our Loran to get back home."

A few years later Ricky went down to Florida to run a shark-fishing boat—"I was a highliner back then," he says, "I was pretty damn good with shark." When Bobby and his wife split up, Ricky invited him down to Florida to fish and got him a job on another boat. At one point the captain didn't show up for a trip, so the owner handed the boat over to Bobby. Ricky and Bobby fished side by side for a while, making a lot of money, and then Bobby ran into his own trouble and wound up back in Gloucester. "I always thought it was safer to go fishing on the Grand Banks for thirty days than stay on land for thirty days," says Ricky. "Bobby and I had some brawls down in Florida, just me against him. We had a club and Bobby and I just destroyed the place—tables, chairs, people."

From Florida Ricky went on to Hawaii. There was a lot of swordfishing in the Pacific, and Ricky was given a state-of-the-art ninety-foot boat and two salaried Filipino crew. In September, 1991, he called up the Crow's Nest and asked to speak to Bobby. Bro, he said, I got this big beautiful boat, why don't you come out and fish with me?

The owner had even offered to pay Bobby's plane ticket. Bobby declined. "He said he was really in love with this chick," says Ricky. "So I said, 'Alright, I love you, bro,' and he said, 'I love you too.' And that was the last thing we said to each other."

A month later Ricky got the news. He was two days out of Hawaii with all his gear in the water, and he called up the High Seas operator to make contact by satellite phone with the boat's owner, who was fishing off Samoa. The operator told Ricky there was "stand-by traffic" for him—a call waiting to be patched through—and then she connected Ricky to his boss. The boss said that Bob Brown had been leaving messages on his assistant's answering machine in California. Uh-oh, Ricky thought, stand-by traffic, a message from Bob Brown . . . something's happened to Bobby.

Sure enough, the stand-by call was from his sister, Mary Ann. Ricky, I love you, she started off, and then she said that Bobby's boat was missing. "I just figured they were gone," says Ricky. "So I went outside and told my crew, I said, 'My brother's boat is missing and I think we're just gonna haul the line and go in.' I hauled with tears in my eyes, I was bullshit with God for something like that happening. We got in and got drunk and then I just flew home."

At the memorial service Ricky saw people he hadn't seen

in twenty years—friends from grade school, old fishing buddies, mothers from the neighborhood. He stayed in Gloucester a couple of weeks and then went right back out to Hawaii, knocking two windows out of the wheelhouse during a storm on the first trip out. All he could think about was how his mother would feel if she lost two sons instead of just one, and he decided to cut down on his risks. He would go to the Grand Banks no later than October, and even October would be subject to Ethel's approval. "You'll have a choice in the matter," he told her. Still, risk was a difficult thing to avoid, and he even found himself seeking it from time to time. After a few more years in Hawaii he moved back to Gloucester with his wife and started fishing with a man whose father had been lost at sea. The two of them, he said, did crazy things on the boat, fishing late in the season through really severe weather.

"We felt untouchable," was how he explained it. "We felt like there was no way that God could do that to the same families twice."

By the time I talked with Ricky, the book had—against all expectations—become a bestseller, and I was spending a lot of time in Gloucester, staying at the Crow's Nest, showing media people around town. It was an odd feeling: I remembered Gloucester as a gray, rocky town where I supported myself doing treework and wondering, at age thirty, exactly where my life was going. Now here I was, giving television interviews from the Nest while the regulars tried to ignore the lights and keep drinking their beer. When people said I'd put Gloucester on the map, I replied that it was more like Gloucester had put me on the map. There were any number of people—Chris, Ethel, local fishermen—without whom I could not have written this book. Had they not lived the lives they did, and agreed to talk with me about them, the book would not exist. In that sense, I'm indebted to them; in that sense, the book is as much their work as mine. Writers often don't know much about the world they're trying to describe, but they don't necessarily need to. They just need to ask a lot of questions. And then they need to step back and let the story speak for itself.

New York City
January 11, 1998

ACKNOWLEDGMENTS

ONE of the most difficult tasks in writing this book was to get to know—to whatever extent this is possible—the men who died at sea in the Halloween Gale. That required contacting their friends and family and reopening wounds that had only begun to heal. With that in mind, I would like to thank the Shatford family, Chris Cotter, Tammy Cabral, Debra Murphy, Mildred Murphy, Jodi Tyne, Chris Hansen, and Marianne Smith for their willingness to talk about such a painful episode in their lives.

The survivors of the storm also had difficult stories to tell, and I am indebted to Judith Reeves, Karen Stimson, John Spillane, and Dave Ruvola for talking about their experiences so openly. I would also like to thank all the people who answered my questions about fishing, bought me beers at the Crow's Nest, got me onto fishing boats, and generally taught me about the sea. They are—in no particular order—Linda Greenlaw, Albert Johnston, Charlie Reed, Tommy Barrie, Alex Bueno, John Davis, Chris Rooney, "Hard" Millard, Mike Seccareccia, Sasquatch, Tony Jackett, and Charlie Johnson. In addition, Bob Brown was kind enough to talk to me despite the obviously delicate issues surrounding the loss of his boat.

This material first appeared as an article in *Outside* magazine, and I must thank the editors there for their help. Also, Howie Sanders and Richard Green in Los Angeles.

Finally, I must thank my friends and family for reading draft after draft of this manuscript, as well as my editor, Starling Lawrence, his assistant, Patricia Chui, and my agent, Stuart Krichevsky.

P.S.

Ideas, interviews & features …

About the book

About the author

Read on

The Perfect Storm on Screen

by Tom Conway

WRITERS GENERALLY HAVE an ambivalent relationship with Hollywood. Movies are seldom cited as a measure of literary success and Hollywood adaptations have a reputation for dumbing down, plot alteration and general bastardisation. And, of course, there's the notion of 'selling out'.

Junger, however, was different. He made the trip to Hollywood early on, before the book was even published. Despite its apparently unlikely subject – the story of six commercial fishermen – the manuscript generated substantial interest. After three days of meetings, the rights were bought by Spring Creek (who had a production agreement with Warner Brothers) for what Junger says was 'more money than I'd earned over the course of my whole life'.

He heard little about the project until 1997 when *The Perfect Storm* went into the *New York Times* bestseller list. Suddenly there was a flurry of activity, and Wolfgang Petersen, director of submarine drama *Das Boot*, was picked to direct. Junger met Petersen and liked him immediately, and from that point on the movie was out of his hands: 'I don't know anything about making movies, and there is nothing I could say that a Gloucester fisherman couldn't say better.'

The movie was shot on location in Gloucester, Massachusetts. The families and friends of the men who were lost at sea aboard the *Andrea Gail* still lived and worked in the town, and although the film honoured the lives of those men, it meant that the community would effectively have to relive the terrible tragedy. The filmmakers built vessels in the exact likeness of the *Andrea Gail* and the *Hannah Boden*, and painful memories were stirred when 'the ghost ship' *Hannah Boden* sailed out of the harbour for a second time.

During the first week of filming it seemed a chilling possibility that life would imitate art as news came that Florida was bracing itself for the biggest emergency evacuation in its history. As Hurricane Floyd gathered force in the Caribbean, the people of Gloucester were making preparations to secure buildings and boats. The impending irony of the situation was palpable, but thankfully the storm died down and changed course, allowing Gloucester and the film crew to breathe a collective sigh of relief.

The film starred George Clooney as Billy Tyne and Mark Wahlberg as Bobby Shatford, and the presence of these Hollywood stars in a small fishing village caused quite a stir – they were often to be spotted having a few drinks and 'getting into character' at the Crow's Nest. It wasn't all plain sailing though as Petersen put them through their paces as swordfishermen to prepare for the role, and according to Clooney there were more than a few instances of seasickness during filming.

The real star, however, was the storm. ►

‘The movie was shot on location in Gloucester, Massachusetts. The families and friends of the men who were lost at sea aboard the *Andrea Gail* still lived and worked in the town, and although the film honoured the lives of those men, it meant that the community would effectively have to relive the terrible tragedy.’

The Perfect Storm on Screen *(continued)*

◀ Petersen's vision was to recreate the terror of the fisherman's real-life experience on screen, a feat that would require special things from his special effects team. The digital simulation of water is notoriously difficult to pull off, so the researchers teamed up with Industrial Light and Magic to make a cinematic breakthrough, bringing to life the meteorological beast at the heart of the story. Many scenes in the film feature entirely computer-generated water, but boundaries were pushed when it came to the real stuff too; the filmmakers created the largest soundstage tank in the world at 22 feet deep. Extraordinarily for a story about fishermen, no fish were hurt during the making of the movie. Walt Conti at Edge Innovations created approximately four animatronic swordfish and a hundred models for the production, so none of the fish seen on screen are real.

The film was released in June 2000 to a mixed critical response, but it went on to gross $328,718,434 worldwide. ■

> ‘We forget that nature can crush any one of us very easily and unexpectedly and it doesn't matter to nature at all.’

Watching the Storm

Interview by Lucy Miller

LOOKING BACK, WITNESSING the storm was a pivotal moment in my life. I knew I was watching something that didn't happen very often, but I had no idea it would change my life. It was October 1991. I was 29 and I was living with my girlfriend in Gloucester, on the coast of New England, where I was working as a climber for tree companies. I was at home working when the ocean rose up and covered the street to our house and the wind was incredibly strong. My girlfriend and I got up and ran outside as fast as we could to a sheltered back shore that faces the open ocean. Standing there watching, I was tremendously excited. The waves were enormous, exploding against these huge summer houses and tearing them to pieces. They were certainly over 35 feet high. The wind was screaming. I felt I was watching the equivalent of what a religious person would call 'the hand of God'. My life changed in those hours, even though I didn't know it. I was at that point in my life where I felt I had no direction. I was dawdling as a writer, spending most of my time working for tree companies. I don't see it as a moment of truth, though. The moment came a few months later when I hit my leg with a chainsaw and was injured quite badly. It forced me to take stock of myself. It jolted me. I realised my life wasn't going as planned. I kept thinking: 'You're about to turn 30, what are you doing? Where are you going?'

After hurting my leg I thought I might write a book on dangerous jobs and when ▶

Author photo © Fourth Estate 1998, by Dan Deitch

LIFE *at a Glance*

BORN:

17 January 1962, Belmont, Massachusetts.

EDUCATED:

Graduated from Concord Academy in 1980, and received a BA in Cultural Anthropology from Wesleyan University in 1984.

CAREER:

After college Junger began writing for *The City Paper* in Washington DC. Not sure about a career in journalism, he left to take a job climbing trees for a lumber company. When he injured his leg with a chainsaw he turned back to journalism and set about researching what would become *The Perfect Storm*. It became a worldwide bestseller and rode the *New York Times* bestseller list for over three years.

He subsequently published *Fire*, a ►

Watching the Storm *(continued)*

◄ I learnt that a Gloucester fishing boat had been lost in the storm, taking six fishermen, I thought that might make an interesting focus. At the time, watching the storm, I hadn't thought about what was happening 500 miles out into the Atlantic. I hadn't thought that there, in the heart of the storm, the winds were 104 miles an hour and the waves were over 70 feet high, but the more I learnt, the more fascinated I became. I wrote *The Perfect Storm* – perfect in meteorological terms in that it couldn't have been any worse – over four years. The first half I wrote living in a pretty remote house in the woods near Cape Cod. The second half I wrote in New York, but I didn't think people would want to read it. The strangest thing was having my book come out and seeing people reading it. I look at storms differently now. We forget that nature can crush any one of us very easily and unexpectedly and it doesn't matter to nature at all. I believe in something the philosopher John Stuart Mill said, that the only immoral act is the one which increases the amount of suffering in the world. Over the last few years I have covered a lot of wars, been sent on magazine assignments, and at the back of my mind there have been the eternal questions: Is this voyeuristic? Is this bad? And I answer those questions by asking: 'Well, am I causing harm? No. Then it's okay.' I am an atheist – I don't believe that a God or any kind of afterlife exists. At the most, maybe there is some kind of soul that accompanies the body. Certainly there are things about existence and metaphysics that we don't understand. After my book was published, I bought a small second-hand sail boat. My father had a little boat and he'd take me out sailing when I was a kid. The storm didn't put me off, but I am always aware – more now than ever – of how exposed you are.

I love what I do. I love writing. For the moment I am completely fulfilled. I just know that I will want to have a family. I don't want to find that I am so absorbed with my work that suddenly I'll realise I am 55 and have never had a family. ■

Reprinted by permission from the *Express*, 24 July 2000

LIFE *at a Glance* *(continued)*

◂ collection of his writings uncovering the extremes of nature and of human nature. He continues to write independent, entrepreneurial journalism.

He received a National Magazine Award in 2000 for 'The Forensics of War', published in *Vanity Fair* in 1999.

He is a keen surfer and marathon runner, and owns a bar with friends in Manhattan called the Half King.

Have You Read?

Other titles by Sebastian Junger

A Death in Belmont
Sebastian Junger's latest book is a haunting portrait of 1960s America that revolves around a brutal and notorious murder.

'Reads like a classic whodunit, but it is a hundred times more satisfying'
Daily Telegraph

Fire
A collection of journalism exploring dangerous situations. Junger takes you to places you wouldn't dream of going yourself, from the wildfires of the western United States, to war zones in Kosovo and Afghanistan.

'This is frontline reporting of the highest order from the dangerous, blade-sharp edge of things' *The Times*

Find Out More

WATCH . . .

The Perfect Storm
The Hollywood adaptation starring George Clooney and some very big waves.

SURF . . .

www.perfectstorm.org
Writing *The Perfect Storm* inspired Sebastian Junger to establish the Perfect Storm Foundation in order to help provide educational and cultural opportunities for young people whose parents make their living in the commercial fishing industry. The Foundation is a scholarship fund, but also aims to expand young people's experience beyond the fishing community by supporting the spirit of discovery and adventure.

www.weather.com/newscenter/specialreports/sotc/
Learn more about storms; the weather channel presents the top 10 Storms of the Century.

http://www.nationalgeographic.com/afterthestorm
A fascinating interview with the author following his extraordinary success.

www.swordfishingcentral.com
Intrigued by the adrenaline rush and danger of swordfishing? This online sport-fishing community will tell you all you need to know about how to get involved yourself.

en.wikipedia.org/wiki/Swordfish
Facts, links and all you need to know about these unusual creatures.

If You Liked This, Why Not Try More from the *Stranger Than* series . . .

The Naked Civil Servant
Quentin Crisp
'You first have to find who you are. Then, you have to be it like mad.'

In a world where flamboyance and fleeting fame have become everyday, one figure is still unsurpassed in the profession of being – Quentin Crisp, the original celebrity and self-proclaimed 'stately homo of Britain'.

From an unhappy childhood in Surrey to his notorious life in London, *The Naked Civil Servant* chronicles Crisp's exuberant exploits, his daring lifestyle and his genius for self-invention. This is a remarkable memoir, a comic masterpiece and a testament to the resilience of the human spirit, and an account which propelled him to international fame.

'Quentin Crisp is a tonic and a delight'
Guardian

Wild Swans
Jung Chang
Breathtaking in its scope, unforgettable in its descriptions, this is a masterpiece which is extraordinary in every way.

Through the story of three generations of women in her own family – the grandmother given to the warlord as a concubine, the Communist elite mother, the disgraced daughter – Jung Chang reveals the epic history of China's twentieth century.

Few books have had such an impact as *Wild Swans*: a popular bestseller which has sold more than 10 million copies and a critically acclaimed history; a tragic tale of nightmarish cruelty and an uplifting story of bravery and survival.

'Riveting, an extraordinary epic'
Mail on Sunday

Angela's Ashes
Frank McCourt
Before the film, before the Pulitzer Prize, before the international acclaim, there was a book. The memoir of a New York schoolteacher's poverty-stricken childhood in Limerick, the energy, wit, passion and sheer power of the story caught the imagination and captured the hearts of those who read it – and they then told everyone they knew to read it too.

A story that has moved millions; a classic of modern autobiography; a tale too human, too captivating not to be read.

'[It] sings with irreverent wit' *The Times*

Longitude
Dava Sobel
The dramatic human story of an epic scientific quest, *Longitude* is a phenomenon, an international bestseller so successful that it launched a whole new wave of writing. ▶

If You Liked This . . . *(continued)*

◀ The 'longitude problem' was the thorniest dilemma of the eighteenth century: without the ability to measure it sailors throughout the ages had been literally lost at sea. With £20,000 at stake, it became a web of political intrigue and intellectual brilliance, of personal ambition and foul play. And at its very heart stood John Harrison, a self-taught Yorkshire clockmaker, who battled the establishment in his quest to make the perfect timekeeper and scoop the spoils.

'A true-life thriller, jam-packed with political intrigue, international warfare, personal feuds and financial skullduggery'

FRANCIS WHEEN, *Daily Mail*

The Diving-Bell and the Butterfly
Jean-Dominique Bauby
When a book is 'written' by a paralysed man flickering one eyelid, it might seem that the fact of writing is more remarkable than the book itself. Not when that book is *The Diving-Bell and the Butterfly*.

On December 9, 1995, Jean-Dominique Bauby suffered a massive stroke, locking his mind in the prison of his body. He then produced a work so unusual, moving and beautiful that it was published, read and admired around the world. With grace and economy, it describes his life before and after the stroke, his continuing imaginative freedom, and how he comes to terms with what has happened. It is a book that illuminates the very business of being alive.

'[He] goes to the core of what it means to be human' *Observer*

Fermat's Last Theorem
Simon Singh
When a book about a fiendish mathematical conundrum tops the bestseller lists there is clearly something remarkable about it. Particularly when – unlike some scientific bestsellers – it is so enthusiastically read and recommended.

This brilliantly lucid account of three centuries of attempts to solve Pierre de Fermat's notorious mathematical theorem – and its eventual solution by an English mathematician who toiled in secret for years – opens the door on a hidden world of beauty and obsessive passion. It is a superb model of the readable but informative popular science book. And you *really* don't have to be a mathematician to enjoy it.

'Like the chronicle of an obsessive love affair. It has the classic ingredients that Hollywood would recognise' *Daily Mail*

The Lighthouse Stevensons
Bella Bathurst
This is the biography of an extraordinary family; a story of high endeavour and remarkable ingenuity, and of men pushed to the limit and beyond.

Robert Louis Stevenson may have been the most famous of the Stevensons but he was by no means the most productive. The Lighthouse Stevensons, all four generations ▶

If You Liked This . . . *(continued)*

◀ of them, built every lighthouse around Scotland. Undaunted by formidable conditions, they achieved astonishing and innovative feats of engineering. The same formidable energy that Robert Louis put into his writing, his ancestors put into this visionary and inspiring quest to illuminate the seas.

'A splendid book which preserves the memory of great deeds performed in a heroic era' *Sunday Times*

In the Heart of the Sea
Nathaniel Philbrick
One of the greatest sea yarns ever spun, *In the Heart of the Sea* is the true story of the extraordinary events which inspired Herman Melville's masterpiece *Moby-Dick*.

When the whaleship *Essex* set sail from Nantucket in 1819 the unthinkable happened. In the very furthest reaches of the South Pacific, she was rammed and sunk by an enraged sperm whale and her twenty crewmen forced to take to the open sea in three small boats. Ninety days later one surviving boat was rescued off the coast of South America – and a terrifying story of desperation, cannibalism and courage revealed.

'As gripping as it is grisly, with a cracking narrative and a terrible moral dilemma at its heart' *Daily Mail*

Bad Blood
Lorna Sage
Hailed as one of most extraordinary memoirs

of recent years, *Bad Blood* is a moving and devastatingly funny portrait of a family and a young girl's place in it.

Told with both passion and compassion, Lorna Sage here brings to life her girlhood in post-war provincial Britain. From the restrictions of the 40s to the freedoms of the 60s, this is an account of a life and times inextricably mixed. An international bestseller and prizewinner, *Bad Blood* is a brilliant exploration of family life and childhood memories – and of breaking the rules and breaking out.

'She lifts your spirits even as she hurts your heart' ALLISON PEARSON

Seabiscuit
Laura Hillenbrand
In 1938 one figure received more press coverage than Hitler, Mussolini and Roosevelt. He was a cultural icon and a world-class athlete – and an undersized, crooked-legged racehorse by the name of Seabiscuit.

Misunderstood and mishandled, Seabiscuit had spent seasons floundering in the lowest ranks of racing until a chance meeting of three men. Together, they created a champion. This is a story which topped the bestseller charts for over two years; a riveting tale of grit, grace, luck and an underdog's stubborn determination to win against all odds.

'A moving, emotion-charged rollercoaster'
Mail on Sunday ▶

If You Liked This . . . *(continued)*

◀ ***Toast***
Nigel Slater
This is a coming of age with a difference – a culinary pilgrimage through the extra-ordinary childhood of award-winning food writer Nigel Slater. Moving and humorous in turn, it captures the tastes, treats and torments of daily life in 60s suburban England.

From Fray Bentos steak-and-kidney pie and cheese on toast to tapioca and Angel Delight, this is a remarkable, evocative portrait of childhood, adolescence and sexual awakening; a bitter-sweet bestseller served up with seasoning and flair.

'*Toast* connects emotions, memory and taste buds. Genius' LYNNE TRUSS

Reading Lolita in Tehran
Azar Nafisi
In Iran in the late 90s, Azar Nafisi and seven young women, her former students, met every Thursday to discuss forbidden works of Western literature. Shy and uncomfortable at first, they began to open up – not only about the novels they were reading but also about their own dreams and disappointments. Their personal stories intertwine with those they are reading – *Pride and Prejudice, The Great Gatsby* and *Lolita* – in this rare glimpse of women's lives in revolutionary Iran. A work of great passion and beauty, it is an uplifting account of quiet resistance in the face of repression.

'All readers should read it . . . engrossing, fascinating, stunning' MARGARET ATWOOD

The Motorcycle Diaries
Ernesto 'Che' Guevara
Che Guevara. Most of us know him now as a face on a T-shirt. These frank, irreverent diaries reveal the complex and appealing human being behind the iconic revolutionary image.

In 1952, eight years before the Cuban revolution, two young men from Buenos Aires set out to explore South America on the back of a motorcycle. It was the journey of a lifetime, full of breathtaking scenery, hilarious escapades, and eye-opening encounters with poverty and exploitation. A journey on which Che discovered adventure, America and his own radical future.

'A revolutionary bestseller' *Guardian*

Stuart
Alexander Masters
This is the story of Stuart Shorter: thief, hostage taker, psycho and street raconteur. It is also one of the most remarkable, moving and funny biographies ever written.

It is a story told backwards, as Stuart wanted, from the man he was when Alexander Masters met him, to a 'happy-go-lucky little boy' of twelve. Brilliant, humane and original, it is a prize-winning bestseller which is as extraordinary and unexpected as the life it describes.

'Bollocks brilliant. Possibly the best biography I have ever read' MARK HADDON ■